STRANGER THAN FICTION

VIJAYABHASKAR NATARAJAN

Know yourself! Know it well!

Copyright © 2012 Vijayabhaskar Natarajan

All rights reserved.

ISBN: 9798343665659

DEDICATION

I dedicate this book to my loving wife Nithya and fabulous daughters Shreya and Sanskriti

CONTENTS

Acknowledgments   Pg i

PART A - INTRODUCTION

1. ABOUT MY QUEST   Pg iv
2. USING THE CORRECT TERMS WHILE PURSUING SPRITUALITY   Pg vii
3. DRIVERS OF MY RUMINATIONS   Pg ix
4. ABOUT MY LEARNING SYSTEM   Pg xii
5. HOW KNOWLEDGE ABOUT SYSTEMS DESIGN ASPECTS HELPED ME   Pg xv

PART B - SPIRITUALITY

1. BEFORE EVERYTHING ELSE   1
2. ABOUT THIS INTELLIGENT ENERGY   3
3. OF GOOD AND EVIL   5
4. THE GREAT MERGE   8
5. ON EQUALITY   11
6. ABOUT THE VALUE SYSTEMS   15

7	THE CONSTRUCT OF THE UNIVERSE – PART 1	19
8	AN INVERTED THOUGHT	23
9	THE CONSTRUCT OF THE UNIVERSE – PART 2	26
10	THE CONSTRUCT OF A HUMAN	32
11	THE DOMINATION OF ASTRAL BODY OVER GROSS BODY	36
12	MY VIEW ON AFFLUENCY	39
13	FORMATIVE YEARS OF A HUMAN	41
14	THE EXPERIENCES THROUGHPUT	44
15	VARNASHRAMADHARMA – IN MY POINT OF VIEW	47
16	KALACHAKARAM OR WHEEL OF TIME	50
17	THE 3 – IMPERFECTIONS	54
18	FORMATIVE YEARS OF A GROUP	57
19	THE LAW OF KARMA	59
20	THE FIELD OF KARMA	64
21	LIVING AN ORGANIC LIFE	67
22	THE TRIGUNAS	69
23	SOME SYSTEMS OF KNOWLEDGE	72
24	THE PANCHAKOSHANAS OR 5 SHEATHS	76
25	ABOUT THE NEXT PROTAGONIST	81

26	COMMUNICATIONS FLOW BETWEEN ASTRAL & PHYSICAL BODIES	84
27	ABOUT THE CHAKRAS	87
28	TRI-DOSHAS OR 3 – MALAISES	90
29	THE VAK SYSTEM OR THE SYTEM OF SPEECH IN HUMANS	96
30	POSSIBLE MODES OF OPERATIONS OF THE GREAT DIVINE ENERGY	99
31	NETI-NETI (NEITHER THIS …NOR THAT…)	102
32	NETI-NETI – PART 2- MORE ON THE CONCEPT OF ADHRSTA	104
33	THE EXPERIENCES THROUGHPUT – PART 2	107
34	WORKS OF MAYA ON OUR INNER FACULTIES	109
35	CHITTAM OR THE IMPRESSIONS OF THE SOUL	111
36	WORKINGS OF THE CONSCIOUSNESS-MIND-BODY COMPLEX – PART 1	113
37	WORKINGS OF THE CONSCIOUSNESS-MIND-BODY COMPLEX – PART 2	117
38	WORKINGS OF THE CONSCIOUSNESS-MIND-BODY COMPLEX – PART 3	120
39	THE 3-TYPES OF DEATHS	123
40	ABOUT THE LAYERS OF THE DIVINE ENERGY	128
41	ABOUT THE LAYERS OF THE DIVINE ENERGY – PART 2	131

42	THE ESSENTIAL DIVINE BLESSING	133
43	FOOD AS A SATTVIC CONSTITUENT	136

PART C – SOME ECONOMICS FOR SPIRITUALISTS

1	AN ALTERNATE VIEW ON ECONOMICS	143
2	IDENTIFYING THE SKEW IN THE COST OF LIVING	146
3	OBSERVING THE DIFFERENT NODES AND LAYERS IN THE ECONOMY	152
4	TRANSFORMATIONS OF MONEY	156
5	ADMINISTRING THE ECONOMY IN NOVEL WAYS – PART 1	158
6	ADMINISTRING THE ECONOMY IN NOVEL WAYS – PART 2	163
7	ADMINISTRING THE ECONOMY IN NOVEL WAYS – PART 3	168
8	SOME SUGGESTED FINANCIAL REFORMS	172
9	SOME LABOUR MARKET OBSERVATIONS AND IDEAS	177
10	EVALUATION OF A NATIONAL ECONOMIC MODEL – AN ABSTRACT CONCEPT AND DESIGN	187
11	MY POINT OF VIEW ON GNH (GROSS NATIONAL HAPPINESS) INDEX	192

PART D – SOME POLITICS FOR SPIRITUALISTS

1	A CLASSIC CLASSIFICATION PROBLEM	196
2	DYNAMIC POLITICAL SYSTEMS	201
3	SOME STRATEGIES FOR A PRO-PEOPLE GOVERNMENT	204
4	SOME MORE ON THE FICTIONAL IRON CLAD CONSTITUTION	213

PART E – SOME SOCIAL ASPECTS FOR SPIRITUALISTS

1	WHY TEACHING AS A PROFESSION IS VITALLY IMPORTANT	219
2	TOP 10 EVILS OF TODAY's WORLD	221
3	VALUE EDUCATION AT SCHOOLS AND UNIVERSITIES	226
4	THE 3-DEGRESS OF ATTRACTIONS	228
5	IMPORTANCE OF GOTRA AND KULA SYSTEMS	231
6	SOME ESG THOUGHTS VALID IN CURRENT TIMES	234

PART F – END NOTES	237
ABOUT THE AUTHOR	227

ACKNOWLEDGMENTS

I acknowledge the influence of countless great masters who chanced upon this earth in the past and I also acknowledge the guidance and influence of my dad and mom.

PART A

INTRODUCTION

1 ABOUT MY QUEST

I am an avid seeker of truth and constantly in the endeavor to gather spiritual knowledge and intelligence. Given the current state of chaos and confusion existing in the world, I convinced myself that the best way forward to get clarity and purpose in life is to be in the knowledge seeking endeavor myself. I believe that religion is inspired by culture and spirituality is inspired by the universal truths or 'Ways of Working of the Universe'. I consider myself to be more of a spiritualist and omnist than a religionist.

I have been writing about these possible truths on my website – mayoan.com under the topic – 'Spirituality'.

This book is an honest attempt by a simple everyday average person (like me) to resolve the mystery around the purpose of life and the 'hidden' truths of the universe and its ways of workings. This average person is affected by the current chaos and confusion, reigning with the world with little or no guidance being received from established schools of thought surrounding one's religion and Godmen and the state of imbalance and incoherence affecting them. This book deeply looks at the relevance of spiritual guidance as it exists now in the world in a multitude of forms. I am not claiming to be a guru or some authority. I am just interested in writing about my quest and the related experiences to know the truth as I see it. Hence, I even named this book as 'Stranger Than Fiction'.

I chose my knowledge sources randomly but with utmost care since I believe that whatever time you spend on the source of knowledge (books, podcasts, videos etc.,) in the quest should be worthy of the quest with little or no time wasted on frivolity. These sources are a range of spiritual texts from India like the Upanishads, commentaries. Puranas etc.,

I have also referred to some websites for additional information to avoid 're-inventing the wheel' and which are promptly acknowledged in the references section of each chapter.

This book targets the average human on earth, who is having complications about understanding the purpose of life and how his religion can help him and who is interested in knowing the truths that can possibly make his life fulsome. I am assuming that an average person is more religionist than a spiritualist. But I am trying to find answers, as a spiritualist, to some of the basic questions that crosses an average person's mind in his lifetime.

1. Why do we even exist?
2. What are the basic functions of a human?
3. What is a ghost?
4. What is a soul?
5. Does 'Law of Karma' work?
6. Will science and religion ever converge?
7. Why should I be a good human?
8. Why does evil exist if God exists?
9. Why is there a feeling that justice is delayed?
10. Why do I 'feel' at 'heart' but 'think' at my 'brain'?
And so forth.

I am hopeful that an average human, be a Christian, a Hindu, a

Buddhist etc., or anybody is trying to find the purpose of life at least in some part of his life's journey. He is afraid of death and what comes after that. Hence the topic I cover is evolving from these basic concerns and I sincerely try to remove any religious affiliations as we are one mankind on earth though we follow different religions. Hope, my experiences (with the backdrop of me being a Information Technology professional and not an established guru) will inspire other common men from other professions to go independent and explore.

My self-driven quest is based on the angst – Do I always need somebody to guide me to God? What if I am the only person on Earth? Then, how shall I receive the guidance? How do I trust my Guru? What if I spent decades with a Guru and then later, I find him to be lacking? If some deep-thinking common man, asks to himself – 'What do other people think about the purpose of life? then I want to be able to tell them about my ruminations. This is an attempt to make a common man think about spirituality on his own.

2 USING THE CORRECT TERMS WHILE PURSUING SPRITUALITY

A seeker, when he is treading the path of spirituality, may come across several texts of various types – some religious, some medical, some philosophical, some etymological and so on.

He must be careful before accepting any spiritual term as final. I have a personal simple rule – trust the words and its purported meanings of the 2 ancient languages – Tamil and Sanskrit. I am fully aware that there are other ancient languages like Latin, that others may choose as the basic ones for consolidating terms.

Though I may not be an expert in Sanskrit, I chose these 2 languages – Tamil and Sanskrit as my basis – for the below reasons:

1. Foremost – I am comfortable with these languages. With Tamil, I am an expert user too.
2. I think, a large set of religious/spiritual texts originating from India are based on these 2 languages. My earlier introduction to spirituality happened through Tamil primarily.
3. I feel that the words, grammar etc., are very systematic and the meanings are consistent and is suitable for sweet and poetic expressions.
4. The richness of the languages is seen expressed in the various styles of poems written in these 2 languages since ancient times.

5. With Sanskrit, the hymns I have so far listened to with music sounds divine with rich meanings. Most of the temples in India use Sanskrit for divine oblations/chants.

6. Both these languages host advanced medicinal knowledgebase including that of the astral body and a full-fledged system of medicine called as Ayurveda (Sanskrit) and Siddha (Tamil). And the terms used with respect to the human bodies – gross and astral are remarkably same in both the languages. In my opinion, without the knowledge pertaining to the astral body neither the spiritual quest nor the medicinal quest will be complete.

So, for the serious spiritual seekers, the below are my notes on the 'terms' to be accepted:

1. Use the terms from ancient languages like Sanskrit and Tamil that recognizes the astral body and its functions and preferably that has an ancient system of medicine attached to it.

2. Know that the recent linguists might have mapped one or more profound ancient terms to new terms without thinking deeply. So, what was before, a profound concept might have been mapped to a mundane thing that is in vogue now. Try to know the profound meaning of the term and stick to it.

3. When you are accepting new terms into your language, directly use the term, as-it-is, with the profound meaning and be cautious about its synonym/antonym mappings.

4. It helps greatly if you know at least one language like Tamil or Sanskrit that has a treasure trove of rich spiritual literature. If not, it is still ok to follow the spiritual path but be aware of the construct of the human species and the universe in all the dimensions possible. I hope your deep meditating sessions will reveal the eternal truths of the universe along with the divine blessings.

3 DRIVERS OF MY RUMINATIONS

In this chapter I am writing about the driving reasons for my ruminations – especially on spirituality.

Since my younger days, I have considered myself to be having a strong scientific bent of mind. I fully understood and appreciated the scientific methods of exploration. At the same time, I could not ignore the details of the spiritual body of knowledge as seen when I was growing up in India and which still influences me. I also strongly think that there may be many versions of the same truth that need exploration and detailing and hence I consider myself an omnist
and I am quite comfortable that way!

Some of the details that influenced my ruminations are as follows:

1. India is a country that has more than 600 official languages, several prominent cultures – both serving as linguistic and cultural boundaries of the states. Even though the differences are stark, the knowledge body arising out of the Sanatana dharma principles are almost the same in the various parts of the country. Great saints and seers have risen time and again in India espousing these Sanatana principles and reinforcing the faith amongst the population. This long-drawn presence and the detailing associated with it cannot be ignored by any serious-minded thinkers.

2. The knowledge bodies consist primarily of Vedas, Upanishads and Puranas. There are other esoteric texts written by experts of various times. The systems of knowledge surrounding it are very deep in its perceptions. We can see literatures around Vedas, Bhasyams surrounding Vedas in almost all the various cultures of India that too sometimes in native language. There are about 200+ Upanishads which are deep treatises of various naturally occurring

phenomena. The literal meaning of the word purana is "Ancient". Though it is described as collection of mythology and folklore in recent times, since it transcends so many cultures and carries history-like descriptions, I think there is more to this than that meets the eyes.

> *The word Purana literally means "ancient, old", and it is a vast genre of Indian literature about a wide range of topics, particularly legends and other traditional lore. The Puranas are known for the intricate layers of symbolism depicted within their stories (from brainly.in).*

I must admit that I have not read any of the primary texts in their entirety or all its significant parts due to my academic and professional commitments which has taken a significant slice on my available time.

3. In various literatures like Puranas, there are too many detailing which makes me believe that these may require more soul searching.
These details exist as

- Sathees (100 names), Tri-sathees (300 names) & Sahasranamas (1000 names) that are being attributed to some deities that are sometimes seen carrying too many astounding concepts in its meanings. These are written as the attributes of a supreme deity but these attributes, to me, look also like a data dictionary that contains/describes terminologies about what can be expected in the spiritual realm consisting of the 2 dimensions, MAHAT and the divine manifestation. For me, this supreme manifestation/deity, Prakruti and the soul(s) of the universe (undifferentiated as male or a female) represent the holy trinity! Various interpretations of this holy trinity is encapsulated in the Vedanta concepts of Advaita, Vishishtadvaita and Dwaitha.
- Names of gods, demons, asuras, kings, places, events (event times) etc., are same in several different literatures that are supposed to be written (or were spoken) in different times by different authors. For instance, there are 18 major puranas that have overlapping contents, but which perhaps originated in different places and times from different personalities.
- Ancient temples carry the same events as stone-inscriptions, sculptures and paintings. These temples were commissioned by different kings and their men in different times.

As I understand Sanatana dharma, inquiry is a state of mind that is basic to human existence. I firmly believe that such an inquiring state of mind has heavily influenced the Indian culture for thousands of years and hence the detailing is to be treated with a lot of intellectual respect than seen in current times. It is too naive to think that all the representations are a figment of imagination. I believe that our forefathers are great intellectuals who understands how to draw a line between imagination and reality quite well.

They know how mal-information, misinformation and hiding the truths will impact common men and hence their works are too be treated with high-respect that it demands.

4. The subject content surrounding the human astral or ghost body was too detailed, consisting of chakras and major & minor Nadis holding the Panchapranas. The names and functions described are also very detailed and aligning with 2 major system of medicine – Ayurveda and Siddha.

5. While the allopathic way of medicine is based on scientific inquest, the stark ignoring of certain para normal events like presence of ghosts, and the incompleteness of the knowledge about birth, death and possible after-lives and inability to explain all the congenital defects, auto-immune diseases, functions of involuntary muscles etc., were searing into my consciousness and not allowing me to accept it as default.

6. A scientist who is exploring deep into quantum space and astronomical arrangements and anything in-between is seen lacking when it comes to the question of what happens when a person dies – absolutely nothing. This is despite the fact that everyone – including the scientist will die one day! This is a fundamental reason why I am trying to look for knowledge sources outside of scientific bodies of knowledge.

7. The way holy faith is seen integral in several cultures of India as seen in the traditions, sacraments and rituals with its deep meaning and manifesting in its arts, crafts, literatures, music & dance and even in its various cuisine styles and that too in a scale that is humongous, – is too profound for me to trust only science as the source of knowledge to trust. I tend to think that there is "an invisible hand of God" that make all this possible. I am fully aware that there are other cultures around the globe that too have similar manifestations.

4 ABOUT MY LEARNING SYSTEM

Have you ever wondered about a situation where, say the planet earth disappears completely and all the references of the great things that happened here/were ideated here/recorded here is gone completely! What a colossal loss would it be for the universe to lose sight of all the pursuits of human excellence that happened here! Can we even assume that the divine (and intelligent) energy
is callous enough to lose such vital information?

Suppose this entire creation and the activities are to support the primordial question - 'Who am I?', and if the planet earth disappears with all of 'pursuit of human excellence' knowledge (remember - we have the zillion other species too), isn't that a serious flaw in the knowing-self process of this divine energy?

So, could it be possible that all such knowledge/visions is not lost but stored in a retrievable format somewhere in some place of this universe? Maybe it is waiting for a spiritually awakened person to unlock them as visions! Maybe it is waiting for a scientist to unlock the portals and dimensions that reveal the past! Who knows!

But for an ordinary person, who is acquiring knowledge through schools, universities, self-experiences, experiences from others, media etc., perhaps this hidden knowledge is revealed as an intuition deriving from all his memory stores of knowledge which connects/co-relates and presents itself in an epiphanic moment blessed in addition profoundly by the divine energy itself!

I devised a learning system for myself when exploring the subject of knowing the ways of working of the universe.

STRANGER THAN FICTION

The tenets of this value system are:

1. Don't ignore any sources. But it does not mean wasting one's time on frivolity.
2. Initially all the bits of knowledge are to be considered as plain statements.
3. You have to be careful and do your due diligence when asserting a statement as true or false.
4. Build your repository of truths and Falsehoods and make sure to use them as steppingstones.
5. Do not lose your assertions. If you are editing your assertions, then it is a step backward.
6. Wait for the epiphanic moment that reveals additional knowledge about the ways of working of the universe. Are you able to discern this revelation as something blessed and not your own?
7. Repeat from 1

It is far easier to gain any subject knowledge by using the guidance of a subject matter expert like a professor or from troves of books on that subject or from other media. But when you are on a conquest to acquire spiritual knowledge, I firmly believe that you are mostly on your own, especially in the present times.

This is because, in the current situation, education, spirituality, travel or anything that imparts you additional knowledge is run as a business with profit as motive. Seems you really need to have a divine blessing to chance upon a guru who imparts you true knowledge! Think of the horror, when you select your guru early in life, religiously follow him for knowledge only to discover after several decades that he is a charlatan! That is why I keep emphasizing that in the quest for spiritual knowledge you should mostly be on your own but keep your eyes and ears open as knowledge acquiring channels.

I also believe that spirituality is religion-agnostic and is purely focusing on the ways of working of the universe. Religion on the other hand is influenced by local/regional culture and historic/current figures/events and will generally point you towards the path of spirituality. Due to local /regional/temporal flavors sometimes it can be strict and sometimes it can be liberal. You are a blessed person if you can transcend the religious steppingstones and reach the spiritual plane. Maybe you will be surprised to find others on this common spiritual plane who arrived from other paths built with other steppingstones!

STRANGER THAN FICTION

Unlike gaining expertise in the field of spirituality, it is relatively simple to gain proficiency in earthly subjects if we are persistent and determined. I follow the below four steps to learn on earthly subjects. The 2nd one was added after the new era of the internet and super connectivity coupled with information glut.

1. Create a one-line definition of what you want to learn and use the right choice of words.
2. Search for the above string in the images section of common search engines like google. If you are lucky, you may find several image depictions of what you want to learn. The idea is to be a visual learner first - try to see what you want to learn and then imagine the scene when learning even an abstract learning target like concepts.
3. Be resourceful and try to gain some lightweight articles that touch upon the subject to root you firmly.
4. Go after other sources like books from various authors, vlogs, podcasts, white papers to gain depth in the subject matter.

I feel like a nomad in this universe jotting down in my diary. I am not a profound expert in science or an SME (Subject Matter Expert) but a keen observer who looks at everything in an expanded context and who is able to co-relate things fast.

5. HOW KNOWLEDGE ABOUT SYSTEMS DESIGN ASPECTS HELPED ME

I am fortunate to have played several roles in the software sector including that of architecting. Though I studied Mechanical Engineering, I started my career as a Software Engineer.
Early on, I was interested in the below knowledge areas:
- Design for purpose (quality)
- Design for use/handling (ergonomy)
- Design for appeal (aesthetics)
- Design for manufacturing (focusing on JIT/lean, reuse, re-purpose etc.,)

The above knowledge areas helped me focus on my job better - especially in software systems design. What is systems design?

As per the definition from geeksforgeeks.org –

> *System design is the process of defining the architecture, components, modules, interfaces, and data for a system to satisfy specified requirements. It involves translating user requirements into a detailed blueprint that guides the implementation phase. The goal is to create a well-organized and efficient structure that meets the intended purpose while considering factors like scalability, maintainability, and performance.*

For me, the concepts of systems design for any problem domain, translated into the below thoughts -

STRANGER THAN FICTION

Whenever you think of any problem area, be it in software design/architecture or any everyday problems that you see all around you, such as in politics/economics etc., if you have ingrained systems design approach inside you, then the following happens:

- The elements, stage, inputs, outputs, process etc., of the problem space, unravels/dismantles itself and becomes visible in your mind
- You understand the communications flow around and in the problem space
- You understand the different actors (need not be human, always), influencers and patrons in the problem space
- You tend to mentally visualize the working model and hence suddenly become aware of inefficiencies, bottlenecks, waste, chaos/turbulence etc.,

This should be adequately supported by some knowledge in the area that you are focussing on. You can try to have a general interest in fields or areas such as art, economy, politics etc., as time permits and be a polymath.

Hence, I suggest you invest your time carefully - since we do not have unlimited time in our productive part of life. Be mindful about quality in even in areas such as -

- Movies/videos that you watch (presently I understand that it may take much over an average person's lifespan to watch all of YouTube!)
- Music that you listen to
- Books that you read
- Other knowledge gaining experiences as such

Quality matters in all aspects of inputs to you as a person/system!!

While designing solutions for problems you address, being a polymath, be aware that a simple or complex design is always not the right solution. Look for solutions that not only excels in itself (fit for purpose) but also enable/enhance other integrating systems/aspects in a better way.

To provide an example from the software industry, while taking up a component/product design, I take into consideration the following aspects:

- Vision of the product, its expected life span, roadmaps etc.,
- The setting environment (What else in this can be reused/re-purposed)
- MVP or minimum viability of the product of the current delivery
- Time allowed for current delivery
- Budget allowed for current delivery

- Impacts expected (on reach, use by head count, productivity benefits etc.,)
- Choice of technology, standards and frameworks
- Compliance, conformance, performance, NFR related concerns
- Ability to expand/scale/extend easily
- Ability to integrate with excellent data ingestion and egestion qualities
- Other fitment for purpose aspects...

Above everything, if you are a strong visual learner, it helps!!

STRANGER THAN FICTION

PART B

SPRITUALITY

STRANGER THAN FICTION

1 BEFORE EVERYTHING ELSE

Before anything else there was two things or rather one – void and the until then 'blissful' energy.

Void need not be explained – nothing exists. Strangely, the term 'blissful energy' is not sufficient either to describe the 'blissful' energy.

Consider a spectrum of emotions like a spectrum of colours or a spectrum of frequencies. Now why would the 'blissful energy' be termed as that when we know that the spectrum of emotions contains an infinite range of emotions. Why use the term – 'blissful'?

Hence for time being let us term this 'blissful' energy as just as an energy with infinite power and infinite intelligence – the latter two qualifiers will be taken up for analysis later. I am just trying to differentiate this infinite energy from the definition of energy as seen in the scientific field using these two qualifiers. Let us not even try to classify it as a divine or evil energy or using any attributes at this point.

Borrowing on the thermodynamical terms – this energy is perhaps an infinite source and an infinite sink.

Perhaps, what happens between this source and sink is pure excitement/magic. Assuming it has been energy for a long long time, and is not self-aware, (remember we talked about this 'intelligent' energy unlike the term energy as used in science) what can be its purpose of being 'present' in an even bigger 'void'? This line of thinking about being present and not self-aware and being embedded in void does not lead to any reasonable outcomes.

STRANGER THAN FICTION

What can trigger or alter its state and for what reason? At this time, we are seriously considering its another attribute – 'intelligence' of this energy. The primary being 'infinite'. Since this energy is all by itself, what purpose can it serve? Will its 'intelligence' allow it to remain 'idle'- so to speak? (Isn't idle energy an oxymoron?).

Thus, it is an assumption that at some phase, this energy comes out of its current status quo state and becomes self-aware. It understands that it has infinite potential and what it lacks is the answer to the question – 'Who am I'? On an alternate thought, surprisingly this is the same thought that occurs in the mind of intelligent humans when they are deep in their pursuit of human excellence.

Thus, the state of this infinite energy is suddenly altered, and this humongous energy ball is finally 'buzzing' between the source and the sink capabilities.
After the 'buzz' is settled there is again a long pause and just the two – rather one exists – 'blissful' energy. No one knows how long the pause will be or how many such buzzes happened earlier and to add to this – there was no concept of space and time.

What we can infer is that this buzz can perhaps be termed as 'Genesis' and between two geneses we understand that the whole thing reverts to what is called out in the beginning of this chapter.

2 ABOUT THIS INTELLIGENT ENERGY

This infinite and intelligent energy is called a 'blissful' energy for a reason. Perhaps, It is the most preferred state for a highly evolved human who is in pursuit of excellence as a purpose in his/her life.

We cannot stop but think about the infinite emotions or states or experiences other than 'bliss' itself that exist in our vocabulary. Some of the other qualifiers that we use for this infinite energy, in place of the word blissful are – merciful, healing, divine, benevolent, pure, white, soothing, peaceful etc.,

We also cannot ignore that there are diabolical states of this energy too if we recall the other end of the experiences-spectrum. At one end you have all the goodness and then on the other end of this spectrum you have all the undesirable states. Who or what will decide the state to be assumed of this infinite energy? Remember time and space or the universe still does not exist at this point. This self-aware infinite energy has an intelligence that can be deployed to find and assume the most stable/preferred state.

Assuming all the states of these good and bad has to be experienced by this very 'intelligent' infinite energy to find the quietest (read as 'blissful'/'peaceful') state, there has to be one or more experiments that the 'buzz' (refer to chapter 1) enables. This buzz is what we refer to as the 'Genesis'. So, this whole thing gives us the notion that the intelligent energy has thrashed about in seas of experiences ranging from bliss to diabolical.

Just in a hypothetical sense, at that state, if a human swims in this intelligent energy, he may experience a range of states from divine to diabolical. Which means, it can present him with states of being in-delirious, in-love, in-lust, in-rage, in-being-merciful or of any other actions that match to their corresponding states from the spectrum of emotions of this infinite energy.

Thus, the experiences can be in the range of being godly to devilish! Thus the idea of good versus evil emerges.

If all these cycles of self-analysis by the intelligent energy is not conclusive or if this energy assumes that it needs some more different experiments to identify the true nature of itself, it may use the buzz to create the new type of 'Genesis'.

In this new Genesis, as part of a new type of experiment, the intelligent energy acts like an explosion– and low and behold the mass or the mass system with all its underlying paraphernalia gets emitted (big bang?) by the intelligent energy which expands with God speed and results in the creation of this universe. It can also be like a jelly of co-existing mix of the energy and the mass system causing the formation of this universe. Thus, primordial energy is more like the dark energy since we, as humans, are capable of seeing only the universe and not the parent energy form.

Thus, by creating this universe, infinite energy creates a new type of experiment to experience the different states, independent of itself. The newly created universe is supposed to supply it with all its experiences independently to identify the most stable or preferred state. This infinite energy then plugs its 'monitoring wires' and 'controlling processes' into the newly created universe to track the experiences. Thus, we say that this infinite energy is omnipotent, omniscient and omnipresent and is a guiding light in the newly created universe. There is another name for the holder of these properties – God!

3 OF GOOD AND EVIL

For a long time, every time the 'buzz' happened within the intelligent energy, the self-aware portion of it tries to identify itself with either of the good or evil states. Perhaps after several such validations, the intelligent energy has selected 'good' (a.k.a. 'blissful') as a preferred state. Even when the universe manifested out of this intelligent energy as part of new experiments to find about itself, in the earlier big bangs (geneses), it is possible to think that there were spectacular clashes between good and evil. I am thinking about not just kings vs kings but in terms of angels vs demons or devas vs asuras. But what comforts us is that most civilizations since a very long time, through its written or unspoken constitutions, have upheld the need to support good behaviours over evil. There is always a sense of delivering justice, preserving the rights and freedom of individuals, upholding the law, establishing order and maintaining peace etc. There were wars of epic proportions to fight for freedom, justice and to establish order. All of these clearly point out that, after the horrendous wars between good and evil in the past, we are at the cusp of a universal timeline, where the good is prevailing over evil decisively and is still managing to keep control!

The fact that the good has not completely won this war is evident when we see the decadent state of existence in several parts of this world (Since I am not able to see this effect on a universal scale, I am just zooming-in on an observable context) where brutal regimes or corrupt governments or conniving individuals and groups exist alongside the hopeless and stressed-out people.

Since the universe has a bias for good over evil now, I am taking liberty to term this intelligent energy as 'divine' energy henceforth. So, to reach a further desirable stable state (that is being in good or blissful state) the divine energy has to work towards establishing a majorly 'blissful' state and in the process, it should expel all diabolical states or purge evil or to contain it in some way that it is extremely difficult for evil to manifest again and disturb the universal equilibrium.

When we zoom out of this idea, then perhaps it is possible to think that during one of the experiments where it manifested this universe, this divine energy might have created the protagonist defending the good and an antagonist whose raison-d'etre is to manifest evil. Now, this seems more like an epic battle between God and Satan in that manifested universe! When the experiments of the divine energy involving several big bangs consistently resulted in the win of good over evil, a point of inflexion happened where the divine energy decisively concluded that the preferred state is being in good or blissful state, and it may decide not to allow evil to manifest.

But we are taking about an infinite range of experiences in the experience spectrum where one end is good and the other end is evil and hence, we need, not just one or several of such good vs evil universal wars but innumerable wars of different intensities between good and evil and whose results consistently pointing to 'good' being the most desirable state of existence.

Now in the context of the protagonist (God) and the antagonist (Satan), since they are self-aware, neither of them is going to accept the others mandate quite easily and they may deploy all assets and powers under them to establish their reign. Going by the signs, we are fortunate that so far good prevailed over evil at least in this earth realm (hence of the universe itself, by extrapolation) since we see the above earthly factors supporting freedom, justice, order etc., clearly pointing to the preference for a 'good' stable state of existence.

The weapons that the protagonist might pick for the fight may align with his values and they may be called out to be valour, intelligence, righteousness, fearlessness etc. Similarly the weapons that the antagonist may pick for the fight may align with his values and they may be called out to be avarice, cruelty, power (corrupt), deceit etc.,

What is the role of fate and freewill in this?

Though the karmic powers set the stage and skin for any soul and also the general indicative direction of fate of that soul (for example, say at birth the soul is a horse and not an elephant), we cannot underestimate the power of freewill. If there is enough goodwill and determination, the soul can definitely chart a different course than that predicted by fate. If a large number of souls in a group have that goodwill and determination, then they can set a new direction out of their collective freewill for their group. If we keenly observe history, we can see many such transformations in the history - say for instance the emergence of the ultra-modern Japan after the 2nd world war. Knowing these kind of transformations - group or individual- inspire many a soul that are at the verge of losing hope.

Hence such historical events, where the good prevails over evil, should be a standard part of school textbooks to reinforce faith on good over evil!

There are 2 fundamental aspects in the universe -
1. There is a time for everything to happen
2. Everything happens due to one or more reasons (collective effect)

A good soul, using his positive karmic load, can leverage the effect of 2 over 1 using his/her freewill. As an example, he/she may provide additional persuasive reasons to make things happen early (for example a saintly person blesses a devotee to remove his bad health sooner) or to make things happen late (for example genuine group worship by some good followers seeking long peaceful period for the earth; during which time, the group negative karma is slowly dispelled and thus any leftover bad effects happen late in reduced magnitude , assuming no accumulation of negative karma by the same group in the said period).

4 THE GREAT MERGE

Assuming that one of the primary reasons for the universe to be created is to answer the primordial question that occurred in the divine energy - a question that reverberates in the sub-consciousness of all the living beings - 'Who am I'?

In one of the self-knowing experiments, during one of the geneses, it manifested part of itself as the universe as a stage and all the souls as the actors. These souls took the skin of different life forms and went about in pursuit of excellence hoping that at one revealing moment of their life - they will know the answer to their existence and the related question - 'Why something exists and not nothing?'. This great divine energy in infinite form is deeply absorbed into the independent life of all souls and the stage itself.

When each one of the souls, while in pursuit of excellence, realize their ultimate potential and see themselves as part of the divine energy, understand its blissful nature and accept with profound humility that they are not what their 'skins' tell but they are part of the formless, blissful and divine energy itself - a moment of grand awakening happens to them- that they are God himself/herself and their ultimate purpose of live is to know this.

This profound concept of self-realization (this for me is the real enlightenment) is encapsulated in the 4 grand statements or mahavakyias of the Upanishads.

They are given below:

      1. Prajnanam Brahma – Consciousness is Brahman.
      2. Aham Brahmasmi – I am Brahman.
      3. Tat Tvam Asi – That Thou Are/Art.

4. Ayam Atma Brahma – This Self is Brahman.

The word Brahman has a liberal meaning - God'.

If we accept that the divine energy has created the universe as stage and created body-sheaths over the soul for supporting the pursuit of excellence, the reverse must also be true. That is, if we mentally peel off our body-sheaths and other subtle layers and peek inside we should feel the soul itself and when we further pass our glance beyond the soul , we identify that we are part of the divine energy. When this realization happens - suddenly it is no longer 'Me' or 'I' - it is 'all of US' as part of the divine energy. At this realization, we have dropped 'Ahankara' or the concept of 'I - ness'. 'Ahankara' is the feeling that gives you the feeling of 'you'.

The 'inside travel' or the involution is said to be accomplished by meditative practices. The reverse process of dropping the body-sheath in the mind and gradually identifying with the divine energy is what I call as the GREAT MERGE.

If the above is the ultimate realization that the souls should achieve independently, is it possible that the divine energy has set reminders or clues for us to know this true knowledge about self?
I think the answer to this question is a big 'Yes'. We have at least 4 big clues left by this divine energy. At least 3 out of 4 aspects are the fundamental aspects of all the living beings.

1. EAT - when the food merges with the body and provides energy for all your activities
2. SLEEP - when you lose the idea of 'you' or 'I-ness' and be in a merged state till you wake up
3. SEX - when a merge feeling (bliss?) is reached in climax
4. MEDITATE - This probably is a privilege of the humans only till now. In this process you drop the body-sheath and deep dive into your core and realize that you are not this body or mind. This is more like a self-aware guided (perhaps with the help of an able guru) process that leads us to realize our merged state with the divine energy.

So it is like the infinite divine energy, created strands of itself as soul (consider soul as an IDENTITY for that spun off strand of energy) and applied body-sheath over it and gave it a stage (some part of the universe to pursue their excellence). It created not one strand but billions and zillions from its infinite capacity and put them in their place in this universe with appropriate body-sheaths. And these souls with the new body-sheaths and the 'I-ness' interact with other similar souls in a manner, best fit with their free-will and go on about living their lives , perhaps unknowing till the moment of awakening or self-realization that - they have to merge at some time in their soulful journey. With the knowing above, we should be able to deduce that when all or most of the souls have reached their maximum potential through evolution into higher species and involution in the mind, and when the awakening moment happens and they reach their supreme state , the universe will dissolve with the divine energy knowing the answer to its primordial question - 'Who am I?'. And thus, the current cycle ends and after a pause a new genesis may start again.

The merging of the awakened/enlightened soul into the divine energy is perhaps called as 'Mukthi' in Upanishads.

5 ON EQUALITY

On the one hand it seems the universe is pointing to the fact that once the soul is released to achieve its purpose, it can take any of the skins in any given part of the stage to execute its free will and work towards its maximum potential.

Soul is not only an identity for the underlying burst of energy bundle released by the divine energy into this visible universe to discover the purpose. In my opinion, the divine energy has a highly significant controlling function on the soul - that is to promulgate the law of karma. So the divine energy has to track the thoughts and deeds of these individual souls (in different forms) with its infinite intelligence and decide whether they exercised their free will in the right way. Based on the activities and thoughts, each soul carries a repository of karma - a sum total reflection of karma from all good deeds and bad deeds - arising out of its free will. This load of karma on the soul has the capacity to affect the current life or if it is found to be significant at the time of death, can decide the next skin and stage that this soul is expected to take. For this reason it is reasonably safe to assume that once a soul is created, it is indestructible till the great merge.

Before somebody starts pointing to me that there are extraordinary senses present in animals and birds (like the pigeon's homing sense or dolphin's echo-locating sense), I would like to state that in a general perspective, of a given body of a species, there are 6 base senses that we can identify. Not all base 6 senses are present in all the species. The 6 base senses are as given below with
samples of species:

1. Sense of Touch - Samples include some trees, plants, creepers, grass etc., (One sensed organisms)

2. Sense of Touch and Taste - Samples include some species of fish and sea organisms (Two sensed organisms)
3. Sense of Touch, Taste and Smell - Samples include some species of ants, termites and leeches (Three sensed organisms)
4. Sense of Touch, Taste, Smell and See - Samples include some Insects (four sensed organisms)
5. Sense of Touch, Taste, Smell, See and Hear - Samples include some animals and birds (Five sensed organisms)
6. Sense of Touch, Taste, Smell, See, Hear and Think - Humans (Six sensed organism)

Let us consider the case of humans since this species is supposed to be special with its sixth sense - ability to think and become self-aware.

Up to the point of the soul and to some extent of the astral body(In a simple sense, all forms have this physical form, astral form and the Karana Shariram form that houses the soul) which includes - the basic burst of divine energy plus the soul as identity and the astral body cover for the form taken - there is perhaps no difference between a male and a female. If you try to think from the point of the divine energy, given its infinite intelligence, perhaps, it always encapsulates multiple reasons to engineer a design. That too when considering a sophisticated design like the human, for each aspect of the design, it might have considered several reasonings.

Hence when the final physical form of the human species was completed by grand design, it might have considered a way to effect reproduction so that this species can continue to multiply and excel. Perhaps this is the most important and fundamental reason for creating the male and female forms. At some point in time, primarily due to the need to hunt for food and the fact that the females were weak while and after undergoing the process of giving birth, males were considered strong and 'superior'. In current context, considering we are not in such pre-historic settings, it is absurd to continue with this belief and believe in male superiority and continue the culture of dominating the females. Besides the need for reproduction, perhaps the other significant reason for the divine energy to construct male and female forms are to make the species experience sex as an aspect to remind 'the great merge'. Other reasons like motherly nourishment, love, security and similar other experiences may also have played a role in creating the female form. Thus, the divine energy by diversifying into 2 different forms, is multiplying the experiences of the soul.

In the current setting, it is not the physical strength that decides who is calling shots in a setting like family, but perhaps it is the financial strength that defines the leadership position. If a woman is capable of asserting herself as an independent soul, and not dependent on a man for living, getting herself into financially independent state by using her intelligence and subsequently a stable job, then she too should be able to consider the higher purposes of life and not just worry about food, shelter and clothing. This does not mean she has to always consider her male partner as a competitor. She being independent should in no way affect her ability to love her family.

Also, we all seem to know how karma works. Hypothetically speaking, at some point in time and in a place, if a dominant male population starts and persists the culture of male domination and sets them as societal rules, it may be sensed by the divine energy as not the right thing (since male domination is not one of the many reasons it considered for creating the male and female forms !) and hence it will set the karmic actions rolling where the dominant-males are set to be born as females in the same male dominant society and experience the 'being-dominated' woes. The divine energy will do this relentlessly till the wrongful soul learns that male-domination is not the right thing, assuming that it is the only 'sin', that it sensed in the wrongful soul. It - "Male Domination" works against the fundamental principle of the individual soul as a traveller in the universe collecting experiences under several skins and stages and working towards the ultimate realization on the purpose of life.

In my opinion, in the current setting of this world, there is gross injustice meted out to our female counterparts by not recognizing them as equals. For example, we do not see God-woman but only god-men mostly in any part of the world. Hugely responsible jobs like being business leaders, world leaders and community leaders are all men! We have to take conscious effort to remove this prejudice and probably the best place to start is to design an iron-clad constitution where the rights of the women are protected. Perhaps, one step towards this would be to reserve 50+-5 % percentage of all the important jobs (as mentioned above) to females thus ensuring equality.

We, as humans, have this special capability as the 6th sense - the ability to think. Before we attempt to think about higher purposes of life, we should use it to ensure basic hygiene in our society - one of which is to ensure equal treatment of women in all aspects of life.

This equality principle applies also to people who identifies with other genders too. We cannot be judgemental about their disposition since the purpose of life is to collect experiences in the journey of life and excel as human. Perhaps nature has blessed them to experience life a bit different from the rest of us.

STRANGER THAN FICTION

In the current state of affairs, we seem to be getting an impression that only males are destined to take on higher purposes in life including establishing mastery on spiritual aspects. It seems, to a lot of women, that she has to play a subordinated role in the family/society. And if she decides to accomplish higher purposes of life including mastery of spiritual science, then the current situation is such that she is being subconsciously guided to accept that she has to be born as a male (in her next birth) to achieve this. This perception created by long-established societal norms is as cruel as it sounds! It is high time that -we humans- use our sixth sense to dispel this unacceptable belief before we attempt to elevate ourselves spiritually.

6 ABOUT THE VALUE SYSTEMS

Initially we talked about possible wars between good and evil on a universal scale. It is interesting to observe how good and evil permeates in this universe.

Inside a single average human, we can understand that he is good mostly and when no one is waiting to observe and pass on judgement, sometimes he has the 'bad' side too. The intensity of good or bad is decided by the intensity with which he aligns himself with divinity or evil. This can be understood by the concept of what I call as the 'Value System'.

A simple example of a value system is the 10 commandments, and the complex example of a value system is the principles of Bhagavad Gita. These value systems reflect the notion of good and evil that existed in that time period when they originated. Sometimes, they may hold references to eternal knowledge that is beneficial to the entire mankind that stands the test of time.

We have to accept that value systems can be present in different groupings too. As long as it is rational and harmless to anyone, we can accept it. Some of the samples of such groupings are given below:

- Country as a grouping with constitution as the value system
- Scientists as a grouping with the principles of science (integrity of knowledge, collegiality, honesty, objectivity, openness etc.,) as the value system
- Students as a grouping with the value system imposed by the learning institution
- Local Community as a grouping with the value system imposed by the local culture

We start to see that for a single person several value systems successively from big to small can apply as he may be living in a country of his choice, working as a scientist, teaching students and living in a local neighbourhood. To add more to this, the defense in depth principle used in cybersecurity applies here too. For example, the value system expected of a human (generic) in Earth subsumes the value system adopted by a country in its constitution for its citizen (specific) and it is fair enough to expect sometimes that both may be identical to a large extent. The value system imposed by the constitution on the citizens (generic) of a country subsumes the value system imposed by local community(specific) or local group (specific) or even the family of that person or his self-guided concept of being a fine individual. The defense in depth implementation in cyber security protects data. Similarly, the defense in depth concept applied as a series of value systems, generic to specific, protects the ethos expected of a genuine human who is in pursuit of excellence.

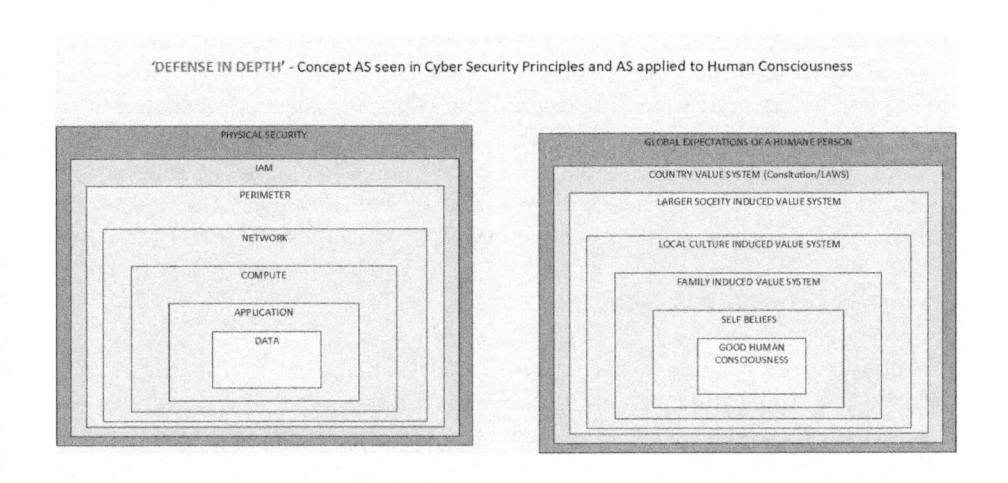

'DEFENSE IN DEPTH' - Concept AS seen in Cyber Security Principles and AS applied to Human Consciousness

PHYSICAL SECURITY	GLOBAL EXPECTATIONS OF A HUMANE PERSON
IAM	COUNTRY VALUE SYSTEM (Constitution/LAWS)
PERIMETER	LARGER SOCIETY INDUCED VALUE SYSTEM
NETWORK	LOCAL CULTURE INDUCED VALUE SYSTEM
COMPUTE	FAMILY INDUCED VALUE SYSTEM
APPLICATION	SELF BELIEFS
DATA	GOOD HUMAN CONSCIOUSNESS

One thing that piques me is that, while a value system like the constitution is playing a significant role in guaranteeing the fundamental rights of a citizen, one or more of such a citizen(s) sometimes can, in the name of exercising his rights, hurt the feelings and sentiments of a larger group. (for example, a cult leader with undesirable ways, is living among a good community and the community is not able to do anything about it). So the constitution should also take part in defining the rules around acceptable groupings in the country and help protect the group values by framing suitable generic grouping laws as long as the groups under question do not violate the constitution or any of the

STRANGER THAN FICTION

higher
accepted principles of groupings.

But the most important value system is the one he assumes for himself, that can turn him into an angel or a monster or anywhere in-between, irrespective of the larger value systems that he is subscribing to. Sometimes the value system of a group can also influence his significant behaviour - for example of a person
belonging to a crime syndicate.

For an individual, his parents, family, friends, other elders of the family or community can help build his individual value system in his childhood and possibly in later stages too (since when does learning stop?).

He absorbs from his local/country laws and community and expands his/her value system. If his individual value system fails for any reason (like crime of passion), at least one of the higher context value systems should advise him on acceptable or avoidable acts. A kleptomaniac can consider himself to be flawless by his own value system, but the country's laws will dictate that what he does as kleptomaniac is against law and will carry consequences like imprisonment/fines etc. Sometimes, one's individual value system can be so diabolical and fully aligned with evil that he will disregard any and all other value systems present in his living context. One such example of such a flaw is the
emergence of a psychopath.

Another large hidden factor is the impact of his karmic load in the current birth that will influence his decision to adopt one or many suitable value systems. Sometimes, we may be able to see strange things like a seasoned thief emerging from a highly respectable family! Sometimes a remarkable guru emerges from a very poor family! How strange can fate be?

Good or evil can manifest inside a single person or in any of the groupings. We, in fact, can detect a range of goodness and evil in the individuals or/and in the groupings. Any judicial setting should be careful enough to check where the majority of the evil prevailed - inside a grouping or inside an individual. Thus, we must understand that the law of karma not only affects individuals but also the groupings. Sometimes the groupings are implicit and not externally manifested. But as long as that sense of grouping prevailed as beliefs and actions happened out of that belief-system, karma will never miss!

STRANGER THAN FICTION

A species is supposed to act according to the value systems it subscribes to. Let us consider the case of a human. As stated above there are several value systems that humans subscribe to. If all these value systems is fulling aligned to the consciousness of safeguarding of dharma or righteousness, (In Hinduism it is called the 'Krishna Consciousness'), and then, if the individual is aligning his actions by all of these value systems (including the faith based value system), then he is said to be living a principled life.

A person living a principled life is said to be guided by the goodness of the universe and all his thoughts and actions are properly justified as per the value systems that he adopts. If a person is mis-aligned or living by some rouge value system, he is just being obstinate and is liable to be punished by the law of karma.

7 THE CONSTRUCT OF THE UNIVERSE – PART 1

When the time for the new experiment is on, the divine energy rolls out a spatial canvas for creating the universe. I use a term from the Samkhya Philosophy to refer to this dark matter/energy - MAHAT!

The below picture is my visualisation of how the construct of the universe has been blessed upon by the divine energy.

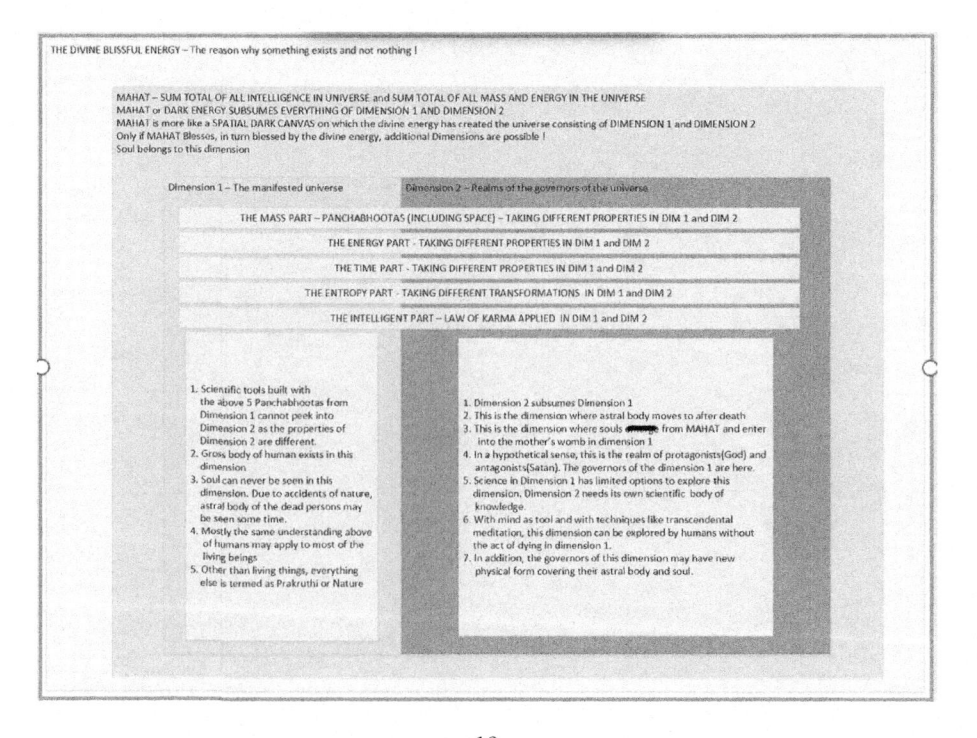

THE DIVINE BLISSFUL ENERGY – The reason why something exists and not nothing !

MAHAT – SUM TOTAL OF ALL INTELLIGENCE IN UNIVERSE and SUM TOTAL OF ALL MASS AND ENERGY IN THE UNIVERSE
MAHAT or DARK ENERGY SUBSUMES EVERYTHING OF DIMENSION 1 AND DIMENSION 2
MAHAT is more like a SPATIAL DARK CANVAS on which the divine energy has created the universe consisting of DIMENSION 1 and DIMENSION 2
Only if MAHAT Blesses, in turn blessed by the divine energy, additional Dimensions are possible !
Soul belongs to this dimension

Dimension 1 – The manifested universe	Dimension 2 – Realms of the governors of the universe
THE MASS PART – PANCHABHOOTAS (INCLUDING SPACE) – TAKING DIFFERENT PROPERTIES IN DIM 1 and DIM 2	
THE ENERGY PART - TAKING DIFFERENT PROPERTIES IN DIM 1 and DIM 2	
THE TIME PART - TAKING DIFFERENT PROPERTIES IN DIM 1 and DIM 2	
THE ENTROPY PART - TAKING DIFFERENT TRANSFORMATIONS IN DIM 1 and DIM 2	
THE INTELLIGENT PART – LAW OF KARMA APPLIED IN DIM 1 and DIM 2	
1. Scientific tools built with the above 5 Panchabhootas from Dimension 1 cannot peek into Dimension 2 as the properties of Dimension 2 are different. 2. Gross body of human exists in this dimension 3. Soul can never be seen in this dimension. Due to accidents of nature, astral body of the dead persons may be seen some time. 4. Mostly the same understanding above of humans may apply to most of the living beings 5. Other than living things, everything else is termed as Prakruthi or Nature	1. Dimension 2 subsumes Dimension 1 2. This is the dimension where astral body moves to after death 3. This is the dimension where souls emerge from MAHAT and enter into the mother's womb in dimension 1 4. In a hypothetical sense, this is the realm of protagonists(God) and antagonists(Satan). The governors of the dimension 1 are here. 5. Science in Dimension 1 has limited options to explore this dimension. Dimension 2 needs its own scientific body of knowledge. 6. With mind as tool and with techniques like transcendental meditation, this dimension can be explored by humans without the act of dying in dimension 1. 7. In addition, the governors of this dimension may have new physical form covering their astral body and soul.

STRANGER THAN FICTION

Some of the possible observations on the construct of the universe are as below:

1. MAHAT

Mahat serves as an infinite sink and source. It can be considered as the sum total of all intelligence, mass and energy in the universe. Consider a facility manager in a factory floor. When all work is finished and we are ready to call it a day, the facility manager will turn off the master switch and then all the lights will be out. Similarly, I think the divine energy will absorb the MAHAT when it is time and with that the whole universe will be gone in a flash!

This is akin to a scientist pressing the emergency button to shut down an experiment gone wrong. Why would it consider that the experiment has gone wrong? Say, the antagonist is winning and therefore disorder (bloody wars, mayhem, gore, adharma etc.,) is going beyond unacceptable levels, this may happen!

Not to be seen as simplistic and to add on to this line of thought, if any protagonist who has mandate to establish order over dis-order in the universe, is present in a given cycle, the switching-off part may be delegated to him/her. In a hypothetical sense, protagonist may shepherd all the souls to experience the great merge and expect them to use their intelligence to merge themselves into divine energy which is the true state of all souls. On contrary, the antagonist, may try to lure all the souls away from the divine energy and force them to assume different skins in different stages (thus assuming mass and perhaps in diabolical forms promoting dis-order) . When the war between good and evil is over in favour of good, then it is no longer a worry whether to be in mass form or energy form as each soul can take its own time to revert to its true state.

Assuming the divine energy is continuously monitoring the state of the universe and comparing it to its own state (default to blissful state) , when there comes a moment when the blissful state of the divine energy matches with the state of the universe, then the divine energy can dissolve the universe. If the divine energy is not blissful and hence is not content with itself, it will allow the universe to exist and it will learn from the outcomes of activities in the universe to move itself to the contented blissful state. At some point, if the experiment related to the manifestation of this universe reaches a contented blissful state, the dissolution can occur at this point.

2. UNIVERSE AS THE STAGE

Stage or the setting or the manifested Universe - In my opinion, the manifested universe has at least 2 dimensions. Dimension 1 is the visible universe that we all see. Dimension 2 is the place where at least the astral bodies (of humans and other species) are located. It helps if we think that a single human has existence in both the dimensions and in MAHAT (the soul part). In dimension 1 - his physical form (called as 'sthula') with all the systems of body exists. The astral-body or ghost-body (called as 'Sukshma') with all the Nadi systems and chakras is present in the dimension-2 and the soul (called as 'Karana Shariram') is embedded in MAHAT and can move freely in the MAHAT. A human is set on his activities by his free will and is constrained by his karmic load.

Sometimes, I tend to think that there are indeed 3 dimensions with MAHAT itself as the root dimension. And soul is in fact embedded inside MAHAT.

Imagine this:

You are walking on a neighbourhood street

Picture this in the context of the above:

1. Your human form is walking on a neighbourhood street- Dimension 1
2. Your astral form is walking on a hazy path - Dimension 2
3. You soul as a burst of energy is vibrating/moving in a infinite black jelly (like lattice vibrations) called MAHAT - Dimension 3

On a lighter note, since it is depressing for some to think of us as some form of lattice vibrations, I can restrict the discussion to only the 2 dimensions that matter for life to blossom. But that kind of thinking (feeling depressed) may be considered as a slight on the grand design by the divine force. Also, it is akin to you insulting self since we are all part of the divine state after the great merge. I would suggest strongly not to insult this divine energy either intentionally or unintentionally, however light it is, because that may become one of the many reasons why it would not select you as the protagonist for the next cycle!!

As an additional thought, I have 2 more interesting observations as given below.

- The state of soul itself as seen embedded in MAHAT: There are these advanced souls and the less fortunate souls. The advanced souls might have escaped the cycle of life and death, and the less fortunate souls are caught by forces of the law of karma and pushed to a different stage and re-birth.

- Some scripts talk about the state of the human embryo (not fully developed human form) in the mother's foetus where it is supposed to be in a uncomfortable state (because of rebirthing/current suffering) and promising itself that it will do well and follow the divine directives post birth. Since the central nervous system is not fully developed, It is safe to assume that the assumed uncomfortable state of a human embryo might have come from the impressions originating in the soul itself and enforced by law of karma or akin.

Because of the above 2 reasons, I tend to think that some form of law of karma is active in the MAHAT too guiding and directing the souls in its pure-soul state.

8 AN INVERTED THOUGHT

We initially considered the possibility of the existence of diabolical states within the intelligent energy, while discussing why it is being called as 'divine' energy. Why would it even consider this diabolical state? In a simplistic rendition of this energy, it can be depicted as a humongous ball of intelligent energy surrounded by a even bigger void.

The more I think about it, and try to co-relate to an analogy, I can picture the image of an intelligent sleeping/dreaming human inside a dark box with no exit.

Look around us - and try to see the positive things that the divine energy has provided us to experience in our life - the blues, the greens, sun, family, friends, love, food and what not?! But certain states/events like wars, lies, deceits, glum, stress, abandoned old people, raising substance abuse, ignoring of education, callousness, corrupt governments, raising crime rates, homelessness, unemployment etc., are all man-made creations that help spread dis-order. Humans do not need any help from any other co-habitant species of this planet to promote this undesirable state!

Remember that the divine energy is providing us with great blessing and peace on one hand and we are providing very undesirable feedback that we excel in dis-order! We expect divine intervention to sort out our life's problems and comfort us. Is it wrong for the divine energy to expect good feedback that will comfort it and allow it to be in a blissful stable state and not experience the disturbing diabolical state? What if all the souls of the universe in different realms/planets is doing the same thing - i.e promote disorder? And what if the divine energy, then considers that the diabolical state is the most desired state?

Probably, with respect to this earth planet, the divine energy is getting the right kind of feedback not from humans but from the other species who are inclined to nature to a great extent. Then, the human goes on about environmental abuse triggering climate change and laying out the groundwork for the next mass extinction! Multiply this experience in all other parts of the universe and consider the feedback that the divine energy is receiving!! It is terrifying to me and directly points to me about the possible diabolical state it is experiencing while receiving the feedback!!

So, what can we do to be a responsible citizen of this universe?

Firstly, be thankful for what it has provided! Says the right words in the deeply felt daily prayers before any form of deity that you believe in.

Pray for guidance and to keep your thoughts and deeds pure. As humans, consciously act with honesty and integrity. Try to gain intelligence every counting day by being a learner till death. I consider that the final lesson I may take is when I am experiencing the process of death myself!

Conduct community events to celebrate festivals especially those that espouse the virtues of good winning over the evil. Come together and protect the environment. Be respectful of other lives. Conduct mass prayers to promote good will and peace and believe in it with deepest faith. And the list expands.

As a responsible democratic government, adopt an iron-clad constitution that guarantees at least the bare minimum guarantees around the below aspects:

1. Building an effective governance system that consciously avoids administrative power concentration anywhere in the democratic institutions. e.g. Imagine a ring of hands clasping each other's wrist!
2. Ensuring wealth distribution (I sincerely do not believe that the divine energy has created wealth as part of this universe only for a few to experience its benefits! If this is happening - what a shame it is on humanity!)
3. Built-in fail-safe mechanisms to avoid corruption
4. Guaranteeing not just the rights of individuals but also of the respectable groups.
5. Directives to ensure basic minimum wages for the adult population which I think can reduce crimes like human -trafficking, modern slavery, crimes related to exploitation etc., It can also cushion the sudden impact of job-loss of the primary member of the family and thus protect a very important composition of the society - that is the family itself!

6. Free education
7. Effective and efficient tax system
8. Free housing for the low-income population when the government has the capability eventually, as we practice good governance
9. Free basic level food distribution at least thrice a day from easily accessible community centres when the government has the capability eventually, as we practice good governance
10. Free centrally managed health care system
11. Ensuring equality of females and other oppressed sects/genders
12. A measuring and monitoring system that tracks the health of the nation including the mental state of its population and a very effective daring response mechanism
13. A measuring and monitoring system that tracks the performance and growth of the nation and a dynamic adjustment system the continually course corrects.
14. Respect for environment and careful use of rare resources and practicing sustainability
15. Acknowledging the right of other species as the co-habitants of this planet.

Probably, I would think that standards institutions like ISO/BSI should step-in and create a constitutional framework for nations to enable them to develop and implement an iron-clad constitution and this should be enforceable (within a given time period) by the UN. This probably should be done after engineering some UN reforms.

When all the right things happen and it is sustainable, this will reflect in the happy state of minds in the population. With this in mind, we should include in our daily prayer that - all is well and all is good and when this is the feedback coming from all the lives of the universe to the divine energy, then why should not we believe that it will be in a blissful state?

When this happens, the image of an intelligent human sleeping inside a dark box will no longer hold good and we can replace it with the movie where continuously all happy faces and events surrounding them plays out in the mind of the intelligent human floating in a blissful light or anything that is even more joyful to imagine!

9 THE CONSTRUCT OF THE UNIVERSE – PART 2

I considered the universe to be consisting of 3 dimensions - Dimension 1 is the visible universe; Dimension 2 is the dimension where the astral bodies exist, and Dimension 3 is MAHAT in which souls are embedded. (As a crude example, when a criminal is hanged by a state, his astral body will still exist in an intact manner and when the karmic forces tear upon the astral body too, the soul will still remain in MAHAT. Thus, we can say that in this 3D universe, the human body-astral body-soul complex exist as 3 super-imposed 3D layers.)

We have to perhaps consider the probability density functions of the colours of this creation process (mass, time, entropy, space and energy) , the universal constants , an intuitive idea to consider an empirical system encapsulating all the above elements, the four fundamental forces of nature and finally a cosmic mathematical model (function) involving all of the above to find a universal law that works in Dimension 1.The constants may differ in different zones of the universe and between dimensions.

How to integrate the 2 dimensions and MAHAT is anybody's challenge!

As per some contents of puranas I have come across, the dissolution of the universe during the pralaya (deluge) time happens as follows:

First the deluge (water) appears and breaks the earth - Earth is gone
Next fire vaporises water - Water is gone
Then air removes fire and ashes - Fire is gone
Then the space sucks in the air - Air is gone
MAHAT removes the space - Space is gone
Finally, MAHAT itself is gone (assuming most of the souls has experienced the great merge)

In the creation, (say at the big bang), the reverse is expected to happen during the creation of the Prakruti.
First MAHAT is formed
Next Space is drawn
Air/Prana/Gases fills in the space adequately
Fire follows Air
Water follows Fire
Earth forms over water
I am not able to imagine the exact time sequence or the overlap of events, now. I am also not sure at what point the souls (energy bursts or the zillions of 'Karana Shariram' or causal bodies) are embedded in the MAHAT matrix as part of creation. This remains ADHRSTA to me, at this time!

About **TANMATRAS**:

These are more like properties of the universe (subtle elements) which can be directly sensed in the MAHAT from the soul/Prakruti to provide feedback to the divine energy. Sensing of these properties by different living beings are done by their respective sensory organs. Not all tanmatras are sensed by any one particular species.

I think the below may be true:

- The external sensory organs (eyes, ears, nose, tongue, skin) - senses
- The internal sensory organ - mind – holds thoughts
- Another internal sensory organ - brain – thinks (act of thinking)
- The cittam - experience the tanmatras (what can be the related verb word?) - experience consciousness
- The soul – stores the various impressions

Living beings have sensory perceptions to understand the manifestation of at least some of the tanmatras. Some tanmatras can be sensed and some can be felt through lateral effects. Some universal laws may be tied to the tanmatras as part of the grand design.

Let us look at some of the tanmatras and their states. Though popular literatures only talk about tanmatras as related to the sensory organs, of especially human, I think we have to seek and look out for other tanmatras as I consider them to be a bedrock in the construction of the universe.

STRANGER THAN FICTION

S.No	Name of Tanmatra	Sense organ of living beings	Any related applicable laws of the universe (this list may not be complete)	Any indicative associated physical characteristics /attributes (this list may not be complete)
1	Sound	Ear	laws related to sound	Frequency, Vibration
2	Touch	Skin	laws related to force and energy	Frequency, Vibration
3	Vision	Eyes	laws related to light	Frequency
4	Taste	Tongue	<Still unknown>	<Still unknown>
5	Smell	Nose	<Still unknown>	<Still unknown>
6	Pain	Central Nervous System	<Still unknown>	<Still unknown>
7	Mass	Whole Body	All laws related to mass and energy	Mass, Inertia, Entropy
8	Energy	Whole Body	All laws related to mass and energy	Momentum, Velocity, Angular Velocity, Torque, Force, Acceleration, Vibration, Frequency, Entropy
9	Time	Brain	<Still unknown>	Entropy, Frequency
10	Space	Brain	Laws related to four fundamental forces	Frequency, Entropy
11	Magnetic Force	Brain (In some birds as ESP)	All laws related to electro-magnetic forces	Frequency, Entropy
12. So on and so forth				

STRANGER THAN FICTION

Disclaimer: I am not able to list all the tanmatras and the related laws and properties. We need to deploy the SMEs (starting with the scientists) to complete the table above.

One interesting factor I sensed is the role of frequency as a fundamental attribute of all tanmatras. If sound and vision can be represented in frequencies, can we also represent taste, smell and pain in terms of frequencies?

It will be arrogant on our part to think that we are the only species given special capabilities to think and therefore to dominate as a primary predator in this planet. There may be other species that are having extra-sensory perception capabilities (ESPs) that may correspond to their abilities to sense tanmatras that are beyond the grasp of human sensory perceptions.

Consider the case of a bird. They are able to sense the tanmatra that enables them to fly. A young bird while growing the wings may not be aware of that tanmatra, but when it grows wings and is physically ready, they may sense this tanmatra (feeling of flying) and their primordial urges will push it into flying. This tanmatra is sensed by a bird naturally and therefore the evolution has supported growing wings while humans indirectly understood this tanmatra and mastered aerodynamics and related physical laws and developed airplanes that enables them to fly.

Tanmatras - point to something very rudimentary - something that can be sensed. Some tanmatras have been mastered by humans and we have been able to build the scientific body of knowledge around it. Some tanmatras are understood but not tamed by science(humans) yet (like feeling of lust, phobias etc.,). Some are still unknown to humans but understood by other species; Some are still unknown to any species; Not all tanmatras are measurable.

If you could describe the sensing of anything and describe it in words, there could be the possibility of finding a new tanmatra. Open a dictionary (we are talking about the dictionary maintained by human species!) and look for the words describing the 'sensing' part like (bliss, euphoria, pain etc.,). and you will know how complex the creation is. Probably it is more artistic than scientific! The point is - we should establish mastery over those tanmatras whose understanding makes our lives better.

Let us consider the sixth sense of a human. We know definitely that this is not a tanmatra of the universe. It is a capability embedded in each human to understand the divine ways of working. It will be arrogant on our part to think that only we possess the 'capability to think' to connect with divine! We don't know what other species have achieved because we always depend on our language to describe them and not able to exclude our capability to dominate them while trying to understand them. (I cannot remove the picture of a scientist working under a dictatorship - where obviously the dictator need not have the same brain potential as the scientist!) They may have sense organs that can sense other tanmatras that we do not even know exists! Also, what we describe as the 'ability to think' may exist in them in some other capacity. This have to viewed in the context of how the divine energy may approach the design of any species (not just human) and not necessarily the other way around (species developing capabilities by evolution that helps them connect with divine!) - which is also a possibility.

As an existentialist, you may deploy 4 different methods - any one or all four - to experience the divine and the divine ways of working:

Bhakthi Yoga or Worshipping the God - You can pick any God as your favourite and as long as it aligns with goodness, the divine energy will bless you. This is critical to building a faith-based value system. Of course, the atheist can ignore this and settle on the other 3 ways.

Jnana Yoga or Path of the Intelligence - This is the path of a scientist. He/she deploys his/her intelligence in pursuit of human excellence and try to figure out the ultimate knowledge.

Karma Yoga or Path of believing in 'Work is Worship' - For those who are not blessed with the scientist's mind, they can settle on this. What you do makes you. So, whatever is that you are doing (as your job) do it with full care and attention while pursuing human-excellence. Even a sports person knows that his physical/mental capabilities is what is powering him in his pursuit of excellence.

Kriya Yoga - Do not start this without an accomplished Guru. It is also called under several other names such as 'Raja Yoga', 'Kundalini Yoga' or 'Transcendental Meditation'.
Points 2 & 3 - above expects you to fully deploy your mental/physical capabilities in pursuit of excellence as human and I hope that, as long as you are sincere, you will be divinely guided to the ultimate answer at some time/space as blessed by divine.

STRANGER THAN FICTION

An accomplished soul, through transcendental meditation techniques can understand the divine nature of this universe and get a special status in the society! But, at least until now, we are not made to understand the all-pervasive nature of this divine energy that extends into our every second of every minute of our life!

Picture this -
You are trying to connect with this divine energy after years of penance. Once the connection is made, you zoom out and try to see who else is connected - It strikes you like a bolt - all the trillions and trillions of species in all the realms of the universe are connected just like you - you just became aware of this now! Then you think about the thousands of experiences (as described as a sense in your dictionary) that you are made to sense. Think about the sum total of all experiences of all the living beings of all species in their different characters! Finally, you may lose your breadth if you deduce that - all the massive universal-scale sensing is being done by this divine energy and not only that, but it has also devised an intelligent system (Karmic engine) that stores the karma (+ or -) of each action of each living being. It uses this stored information to adjust the stage (universe) for a soul in the current journey or in its next life. Be mindful that all other living things that this soul comes into contact with has also been considered similarly by this divine energy! It has assembled all of these living things in a stage whose construction is seen as an unfathomable infinite intelligence. It is such a bewildering universe scale of wizardry that I
consciously/subconsciously bow down before its potential, intelligence, power, might and benevolence and what not!

We are probably a tiny spot somewhere in the universe and the divine energy has not yet prioritized our feedback-based processes. But if it knows how we are endangering other billions of lives in this tiny planet in the name of economic activities and spoiling their in-pursuit-of-excellence activities, all it needs to do was to release an enraged hard breadth - 'Hrmmmm', and we humans will be removed to oblivion!

10 THE CONSTRUCT OF A HUMAN

We discussed about the construct of the universe which we often state as the 'STAGE'. Now we have to discuss the construct of the ACTORS. Since the human species is the most complex of all the organisms in this planet earth, let us take this as a sample to explore the construct of species. This is not any way related to the anatomy of the human body in dimension 1 explaining the different body systems or the explanation of astral body with the chakras and the Nadi systems in dimension 2.

Similar to the stage, the actor is also seen spanning the dimension 1, dimension 2 and the MAHAT.

I am presenting a picture of the construct of a human spanning the 3 dimensions:

STRANGER THAN FICTION

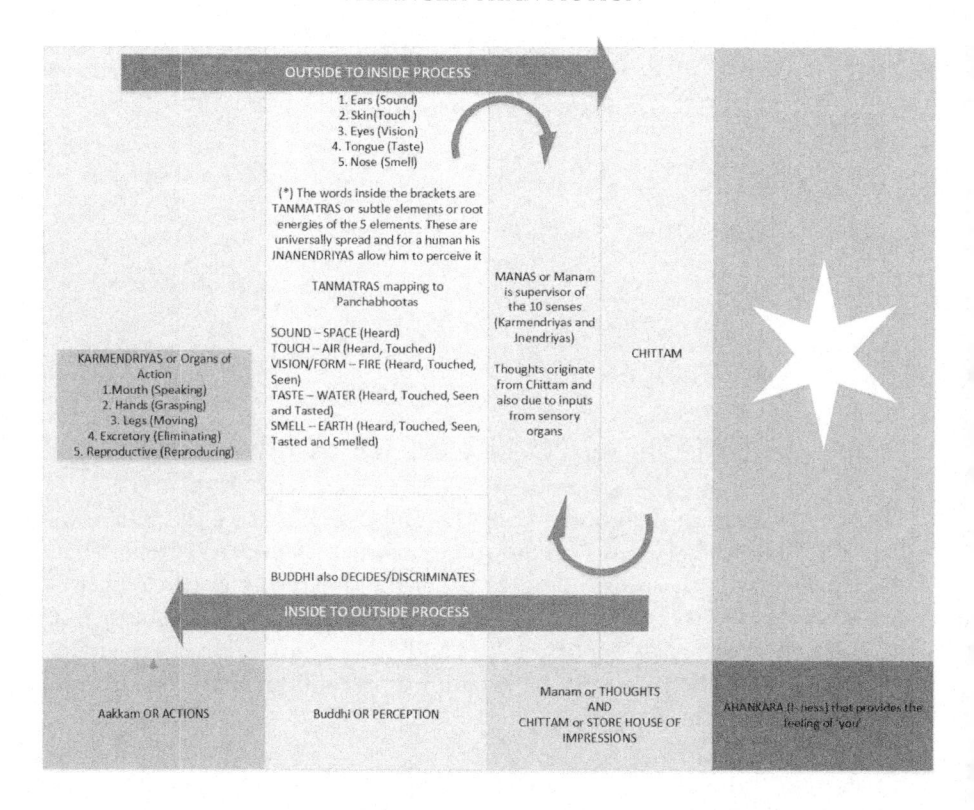

OUTSIDE TO INSIDE PROCESS

1. Ears (Sound)
2. Skin (Touch)
3. Eyes (Vision)
4. Tongue (Taste)
5. Nose (Smell)

(*) The words inside the brackets are TANMATRAS or subtle elements or root energies of the 5 elements. These are universally spread and for a human his JNANENDRIYAS allow him to perceive it

TANMATRAS mapping to Panchabhootas

SOUND – SPACE (Heard)
TOUCH – AIR (Heard, Touched)
VISION/FORM – FIRE (Heard, Touched, Seen)
TASTE – WATER (Heard, Touched, Seen and Tasted)
SMELL – EARTH (Heard, Touched, Seen, Tasted and Smelled)

KARMENDRIYAS or Organs of Action
1. Mouth (Speaking)
2. Hands (Grasping)
3. Legs (Moving)
4. Excretory (Eliminating)
5. Reproductive (Reproducing)

MANAS or Manam is supervisor of the 10 senses (Karmendriyas and Jnendriyas)

CHITTAM
Thoughts originate from Chittam and also due to inputs from sensory organs

BUDDHI also DECIDES/DISCRIMINATES

INSIDE TO OUTSIDE PROCESS

Aakkam OR ACTIONS | Buddhi OR PERCEPTION | Manam or THOUGHTS AND CHITTAM or STORE HOUSE OF IMPRESSIONS | AHANKARA (I-ness) that provides the feeling of 'you'

The above construct is an inside out perspective and also and outside in perspective that is valid in both dimensions - 1 & 2.

The organs of action carry out the karmic activities as guided by the manas and rooted by the 'I'-ness factor called AHANKARA. The five organs of actions are Mouth, Hands, Legs, Excretory organ and Reproductive organ. The sensory organs under the guidance of buddhi or perception are Hearing, Touching, Seeing, Tasting and Smelling.

Together these Karmendriyas (action organs) and Gnanendriyas (sensory organs) along with the tanmatras (Universal properties - Sound, Touch, See, Taste and Smell) form an very effective and efficient input systems to the human. Again, manas is where the thoughts accumulate and the buddhi selects or discerns the thoughts to be selected for consideration and execution as actions.

The physical body of a human will have the buddhi, manas, Karmendriyas and Gnanendriyas. For a powerful soul, like a sage or a rishi or someone who is practicing transcendental meditation, these can also be present in the astral body in the almost same strength.

This advanced soul can also build a new dimension-2 body over their astral body (similar to the governors in dimension 2). For ordinary souls, based on their level of intelligence/knowledge/practices the same four can be present in lesser intensity. Thus, in the death of a average person, his ghost represented by the astral body may have only a limited intensity of the actions/perceptions and thus it will be unlike how it was in the living form. It may not be surprising to see it being startled, confused, shocked or unable to speak etc., So it is important that the humans understand the ways of working of the universe and acquire knowledge about the dimension-2 to guide them better in their after-life phase.

I presume that the below may be true:
An astral body or ghost is an intermediate state. Hence it will not be able to have sex, eat or sleep. Most of the ordinary souls cannot even think. Thus, it is by design that they will be driven to their next stage/skin soon after its death in dimension-1. Sometimes due to actions like suicide (Karma not exhausted fully for this birth and hence this existence in a intermediate suffering state (ghost) continues) and due to some ADHRSTA natural accidents, they spend more time in this intermediate than they should and becomes visible sometimes.

It helps to think that the physical form is akin to a hardware, the ghost & layers 3 of Panchakoshanas are an advanced interface system to this hardware and the other end of the interface (layer 4) is 'plugged' into the MAHAT for power and direction.

The AHANKARA or 'I'-ness forms the root of the human's existence.

From Chittam (store house of all impressions)/manas (locus of all thoughts), the thoughts raise for an individual and the buddhi considers the VALUE SYSTEMS that the person subscribes and then allows only certain thoughts to be executed as actions. So, it is important that we build a range of strong value systems covering our existence as
   - an individual person
   - as part of a religion/any other significant group(s)/country/community
   - as citizen of this world
   - as actors in this universe.
   - etc.,

The combination of these value systems should guide the individual to realize his maximum human potential and make him aware of his real purpose of existence.

The experience of a human, good or bad can happen from an outside to inside or an inside to outside perspective.
Examples:

1. Some diseases start in the astral body and progress to the gross/physical body.
2. An accident may result in damage to the gross/physical body and then the astral body is hurt too because of that.
3. Based on how a person uses his Karmendriyas and Gnanendriyas, he may take in lot of bad qualities (drug abuse, alcohol abuse etc.,) or take in a lot of good qualities (wisdom, physical/mental health etc.,)
4. An outside to inside practice like meditation, can make a person a better citizen of this world.

11 THE DOMINATION OF ASTRAL BODY OVER GROSS BODY

We have to note that upon death of the human, the astral or ghost body leaves the human body and then the human body decays upon time. If you are lucky (!), you may spot the ghost body!! On contrary, just for a satirical line of thought, if it happens that upon death of a human, the ghost body dies and the gross body lives, we may really see lot of zombies amongst us!! Consider this for the other living species too! What a morbid, ghoulish and ghastly scene it would be on planet earth! Fortunately, the divine energy is intelligent enough to design better.

Now extend the same idea to other non-animate objects. The difference between animate and non-animate objects are that animate objects will have soul and non-animate objects will not have soul inside - they are inert with a mass, part of Prakruti. So, every living object in dimension 1, will have a astral body in dimension 2 which in turn will have a soul in dimension 3 (MAHAT). Similarly, every non-living object may have a astral body in dimension 2 which has directly derived from the dark matter of MAHAT with no soul in it.

Consider the below act to understand better:
1. Mr.X takes a stone and hits Mr. Y

Now picture this:

1. The physical body of Mr.X takes a stone of mass from dimension-1 and hits the physical body of Mr. Y - Dimension 1
2. The astral body of Mr.X takes a stone of mass from dimension-2 (having perhaps, the exact shape) and hits the astral body of Mr. Y - Dimension-2

3. The soul of Mr.X moves some dark matter towards the soul of Mr. Y using dark energy- Dimension 3 (MAHAT)

In a hypothetical situation, consider that a brilliant scientist dies in his laboratory with all his lab equipment in working condition. And let us consider that he is also a transcendental meditation practitioner and a spiritualist with good understanding of the ways of working of the universe. If he is extraordinary in his intelligence and has promising intuitions on the afterlife, he may do the ultimate thing as a learner - that is to observe himself dying and understand the process of dying. Since he is considered as a advanced soul, due to his intelligence and spiritual practices, it is fair to assume that he will retain his intelligence and knowledge in his astral body too in dimension-2. Since he is an advanced soul, he may build a body in dimension-2 over his astral body in dimension -2. Because of his exposure to science field, he is knowledgeable in the current gaps of science as a body of knowledge, and he decides to live in dimension-2 to explore science in dimension 2. Let us suppose, by providence and divine intervention, he is not harmed by anything or anybody in dimension-2 and he is still in his lab with all the tools now seen to be made up of mass from dimension-2. Say for convenience, he moves one of his tool, a microscope to another part of the lab in dimension -2. But the microscope in dimension-1 remains in the same place- which means the microscope's dimension-1 body and dimension-2 body are separated - Looks like the microscope has died (!), since if the same thing happens to a human, i.e. if his physical body and astral body are separated , it means that human has died in dimension-1.

By extrapolation of the fact that in a human if the body in dimension-2 is separated from the body in dimension-1, the body in dimension-2 (ghost or astral body) continues in its journey of life till his astral body is peeled off and dispersed by the law of karma which also directs the unmasked soul to a new womb (I call this process as 'THE SILENT AND INVISIBLE STORM'). Here the new womb may be present in a part of universe (STAGE) where the karmic load of the soul can be expended better for that soul. If we look at the proposed representation of the construct of the universe, we may see that the similar forces/laws are operating in the dimension-1 and dimension-2 but has different qualities. Thus, it should be possible for the scientist's astral body to use the microscope in dimension-2. He may continue his work as scientist in dimension-2 and, with his inference and knowledge from dimension-1, he may understand the scientific principles of dimension-2 as well. Since stranger things may happen in dimension-2, we have to be ready for any number of surprises that the study of that scientist produces. Since he is an advanced soul, he should be able to transfer this knowledge of dimension-2 to the body of knowledge in dimension-1- but this time he may be seen to be transferring his knowledge to the spiritual body of knowledge and not the scientific body of knowledge!!

I see a similar line of concept in Ayurveda where there are statements related to the health of an individual, which claims that all diseases of a human body in dimension-1 have corresponding one or many root manifestations in the astral body in dimension-2!

12 MY VIEW ON AFFLUENCY

In the larger scheme of things, if we simplify, we know that, we all are after a multitude of experiences in a given life time by the grand design. And we all know what a vital role that the law of karma plays in an individual's life before, during and after his lifetime.

Converging on the above two vital concepts, we can easily deduce that for some of the humans, it is really a 'blessing(?)' in disguise that they are born into a wealthy setting! We do not know the circumstances that led to an individual striking a fortune during his lifetime or an individual being born into wealth. So, we should not be really judgemental about how these individuals live rich- collecting rich experiences.

But the catch here is, I consider money/wealth to be a very potent weapon in the hands of the antagonist. Its accumulation, with a careless 'high society' humans may lead directly to lowering of their guard as decent, unselfish humans. It is easy to get buried in the so called 'rich' experiences that directly leads to depravity and insensitivity towards fellow human beings. Wealth is a double-edged sword - You can play the role of an angel if you wield it the right way or it can make you play the role of an accomplice of the antagonist.

I do not take a moral high stand towards people experiencing richer experiences as long as it is coming of their personal wealth/affluency. At the same time, it should not be garish and considered as insensitive towards the lesser fortuitous people. That is why I recommend wealth distribution as a function of an iron-clad constitution. We should fix the salary ratio of highest pay to the lowest pay and that should be adjusted based on emerging situations at some cadence. Besides, the constitution should guarantee universal basic income for the adult population as long as they are under a certain poverty related criterion. A third major step will be to reign in corruption - the constitutional building blocks should be seen like a ring of hands holding each other at the wrist.

By design, constitution should prevent an individual from becoming 'filthy' rich. I tend to look at a simple calculation that can be enforced in the constitution. A person may at best be able to see his great-grandchildren in his lifetime -may be four generations. So we should calculate the wealth required for the four generations of a family and add some percentage of bonus and benefits part (based on the wealth his enterprise generates) and calculate the money required for a rich individual to support 4 generations comfortably and put that as a cap on his personal income. Rest all of the earnings of this individual should flow into the government coffers to be administered later by one or more sharp wealth distribution schemes. As with respect to wealth of companies, an effective, efficient, revamped and adjustable tax system should be sufficient as we cannot possibly know their growth plan and the time-horizon that they are looking at as part of their growth plans. I also recommend some way-off schemes where an insolvent individual who has made significant money contributions in the past is taken care of by the state in a manner fitting of his/her contributions.

I recommend referring to online reports (such as pewresearch.org/equalitytrust.org.uk) on income inequality to understand the magnitude of this monstrous problem - Richer are getting richer at a faster pace, poor families are staying poor and the median income people are moving towards the being poor state. Life itself has become a big stress - anytime a person can lose his job and be thrown out of his home with his family, old people are being considered as burden to bear and I am seeing people well over their retirement age still working at paltry hourly rates! If you consider the average hourly wage of a fast-food-services company and compare it to the average house prices, I am left wondering how long will it take them to own their nest - called home? The entry criteria into the working class is through university education where it is really depressing to see youth taking on the big burden of educational loans. The exit criteria of the same working-class people is that you have to work till you are completely worn out and also bend at your hip to finally have a death with dignity!! If these grave economic, on-the-edge-living of millions of people is not visible to these so called rich people who are also power players and decision makers directing or influencing the economy of the country that they are living in , they are nothing but the exponents of the
antagonist and therefore the divine force will look down upon them grimly.

13 FORMATIVE YEARS OF A HUMAN

By formative years, I refer to the child when it is born till it reaches adolescence. What it experiences in this period has enormous ramifications through its life. It is in this period of time, that the child is actively learning to understand and interact with its surroundings. It is also experiencing the profound feelings related to its important relationships like mother and father. By nature, and especially due to the protection provided by mother/father, this is the period of a child in which it is expected not to have any exposure to any negative/abusive experiences. I cannot stress this point enough - it is tremendously significant! I would like to point it out that, when the anatomy of human body and carnal knowledge is imparted to an individual, it stays with him/her life long and cannot be shaken off easily. It is such a dominant factor throughout one's life that if channelled in the wrong way in an individual especially during the formative years, it will prove to be very disruptive and unsettling and can cause long term psychological damage and can make his/her life miserable. It is crucially important that this (approx.) 12-14 years learning window without crude carnal knowledge/experiences is available to every child in their formative years. Hence the society should tighten up the necessary laws to act as deterrent and to protect the formative years of every child. If a country wants admirable top-class citizens, it should provide the right protection to all the children in their formative years.

I like the statement which goes - 'Since God cannot be present everywhere, he created parents to support him to protect the children!'. Protecting the children from unwanted experiences should be at the top of the minds of parents. By unwanted experiences, besides any physical injury/trauma, I also mean the mental shocks/trauma that can come from exposures to certain events, electronic media, unpleasant behaviours of family members and those living close-by etc., The most damaging of all is the sexual abuse, a child may face if not protected properly. It is in these formative years that lot of brain development (synaptogenesis) leading to memory formation, learning, adaptation etc., happens, ideally this is the time, when the child should be taught about the desirable value systems and strengthen his/her character that will become a bedrock of his personality during his entire life.

Thus, the transition from being child to adolescence to adults should be carefully guided. Even the formal sex education including physical anatomy should be taught by the right experts at the right time to these adolescents, preferably in the school setting itself. At this time, I am unable to avoid the thought as- how our electronic media - TV, mobiles, tabs and computers is imparting undesirable knowledge with utmost ease to the unsuspecting minds. This is not only creating learning obstructions but also is damaging to the children in long run. Protecting the child is not just the responsibility of parents but also the responsibility of the society, since the child interacts in so many environments besides home. Just imagine the picture of a boy in the bubble - that bubble is akin to the protection received by the children from the society and the parents from the unwanted experiences till it crosses adolescence. This bubble should only be removed carefully after the child gets the necessary knowledge to handle what is to come - especially so when they begin to understand what sex is about.

Also, besides the parents, the most interactions that a child receive in its formative years is perhaps with the teachers (besides friends). Hence, I cannot stress enough how important the profession of a teacher is during the formative years of a child. These teachers should not only be the subject matter experts but also should be well versed in child psychology and social psychology. They need sharp intellect to observe the children in the whole context surrounding the children, and carefully impart the right knowledge (need not always be related to subject matters but also about value systems), and counselling at the right time and guide them towards becoming adult. They should also pay extra attention to the language skills at this time since I think communication skills are vital and should be taught in early years with great care. I would recommend a pedagogical degree for these teachers from a university that specializes in the development of children in the right way to enable them to become the ideal citizen of the country. Thus the profession of teaching, because of the significant value add that it imparts to the society, should be one of the top paying professions.

If the experience of feeling love and being loved is revealed to the young people as devised by the divine and properly guided by the society by the proper implementation of the value systems, they may tend to experience what I call as the 'magic-carpet' experience. Unpolluted by unworthy media related exposures and mentally and physically draining traumas, just at the right time in the adolescence, if a guy or a girl fall in love for the first time, they may feel one of the strongest of the naturally blessed euphoric state. It may seem to the guy/girl that they cannot get enough of each other ever! This is the 'magic-carpet' experience that I wish the blossoming young adults, experience at least once, in their lifetime on their own and this state depends on them not experiencing any disruptive events including undergoing sexual exploitations from nefarious persons in their early part of life. So the society and the parents have the responsibility to see that the bubble we talked about earlier remains intact till the young adults are ready, in a gradual manner, to step into the next significant phase of their life.

Also, we as adults, should take efforts to remove any carnal feelings at least under the below 4 circumstances:

1. When we are in certain places (like temple or school where our intelligence is nurtured and grown)
2. When we are in our family setting (certain relations are blessed upon us for experiencing higher feelings/emotions)
3. When we are in certain times (generally 12 am to 3 am when it is generally considered as time for deep sleep or when it is an eclipse)
4. When we are doing certain activities (like worshipping or teaching etc.,)

14 THE EXPERIENCES THROUGHPUT

Insert We talked about the gaining of experiences by different living beings throughout their life/many-lives leading to higher intelligence and finally leading them to find the answer to the ultimate question about life itself. These experiences are sensed by their sensory organs through different impressions created by the many different tanmatras (essence or potential). Advanced souls like that of humans, deploy science to build a a body of knowledge around these tanmatras and use them to build comforts of lives.

Let us look at the experiences throughput in a human context and ignore the animal(!) kingdom for the time being.

If we consider the advanced state of our being as citizens of this world or as actors in this universe, some of the (life/soul changing) positive experiences, that we as humans undergo, which can be physical or mental, can be
1. Our experience as a student learning his/her subjects
2. Our experience as a scientist making path breaking discoveries
3. Our experiences in excelling in our other professions
4. Our experiences in nurturing our family
5. Our experiences in cherishing friendships and other relationships
6. Our personal experiences like love, lust, euphoria etc., from many different socially accepted reasons
7. Our experiences in some heart-felt sad moments
8. Our experience of us rising up again and rebuilding our torn lives (if applicable)
9. Our experiences in accepting the rewards of the above activities
10. Our experiences through soul-enriching virtual media

If we consider the decadent state of our being as a citizens of this world or as an actors in this universe, some of the negative experiences, that we, as

humans undergo, which can be physical or mental can be :
- Drug addictions and the resultant induced experiences
- Porn/sex addictions and the resultant mentally/physically wrecked statuses
- The experiences of avarice and the resultant apathy for fellow humans and co-habitating species
- The experiences of dominating others by war or ideologies for unacceptable causes
- Experiences of showing or feeling disrespect
- Experiences of being cheated/backstabbed etc.,
- Experiences of being hit by corruption and/or being hopeless

Now on an average, if we accept 75 years as the span of a human life form, and if we count at least 1 soul changing experience a day, the total number of significant experiences that we encounter is around 27375 (75 * 365) - Of course, it can be more if we consider a student who is learning more in subjects in each passing day!

Consider the distortions introduced by money accumulation on the sum total of all experiences of all humans. It is a non-sensical idea that accumulation of money, whether it is by legal or illegal means, leads to a partying mindset more than a serving mindset. Of course, I acknowledge that there are really essential parties too - especially that builds cohesion, and which gives a sense of belonging like the ones hosted by families or colleagues in an office. That apart, partying in the current context, probably means - more drugs, sex and alcohol consumption. If this is repeated (consider all the parties by all the people and the repetitions of the same), the money accumulation is in-fact leading to stagnation of experiences of the souls. When more and more people experience the same things again and again - they become more like blunt robot/effigy objects and hence they are not becoming the finely adorned and embellished soul as expected by the divine! This is a tragedy, and which leads to stagnation of human evolution/involution. Hence it is important that wealth distribution should be enforced in the constitutions of nations to multiply experiences throughput.

On the other hand, if the money accumulated is used with a serving mindset, it has a chain effect that not only touches and transforms lives but can also lead to myriad of good experiences by many varied humans in multitude of settings! For example, instead of a multi-million-dollar party for the rich few, if the business leader bumps up the bonus part of his employees from his legal gains, the experiences gained thus will be varied and in diverse settings. For example, If some of the money is in the hands of a good family man, probably it may result in tourism related activities leading to rich transforming/soul-healing experiences. Of course, the business leader can also have a scaled down party to celebrate his achievements. Perhaps, some of rich people don't even realise that they are saturated with all the experiences that they expect of a party and that they have to look beyond just money powered parties for some soulful experiences. Why not contribute and participate in touching and transforming the lives of other less fortunate people, if you can? (It is 'contribute' and 'participate' - not just 'contribute'!)

Unfortunately, most of us as humans relate all our good experiences to money! And to add to this - a significant part of us, humans, are still in Maslow's lower hierarchical order due to, primarily - lack of money! It is high time we set a desirable equilibrium through proper efforts around wealth distribution.

15 VARNASHRAMADHARMA – IN MY POINT OF VIEW

The Sanskrit word 'varnas' means - to classify or to envelop or to describe or to attribute and the Sanskrit word 'asramas' means 'stage of life'

The stage of life or 'asrama' is easy to understand. The stages usually consist of 5 stages and is time-divided considering the average life of a human. They are:

1. Balavastha (0-12 years) represents childhood where it is generally considered that the child's actions do not inherit sinful karma due to presence of ignorance
2. Bramacharya (12-24 years) represent teens and young adults. This age is ideal for the 'magic-carpet experience' discussed in an earlier chapter. This term means 'Celibacy', which is usually the case in the guru-shishya Parampara in ancient times in India. Primary purpose of this phase is to get educated and gain intelligence that will become a bedrock of his/her persona.
3. Grihastha (24-48 years) represents married life. This is where the person is procreant/childbearing and indulges in economic activities and supports his family thus.
4. Vanaprastha (48-60 years) represents the beginning of retreatment from hyper-active life. Things begin to slow down in life. The next generation takes over. The person gets worried about spiritual ignorance, life-after-death, unspent karma etc.,
5. Sannyasa (60+ years) represents the beginning of renunciation. I would probably expect the person in this phase to avoid eating meat/heavy foods and slowly transition to a liquid diet. Mental activities like talking/meditation and physical activities like walking

can avoid long term health issues related to forgetfulness and mobility etc., Ideal phase to consider, meditation and spiritual guidance, as important.

The above number of years are indicative and should be slightly adjusted keeping in mind the average age of human life in the region and any other good cultural aspects.

But the word 'varnas' is tricky! I think, one of the biggest mistakes that happened in the past was to associate varna with birth. The 'varna' or 'quality' of a person is decided by the value system the person adopts and not inherited by birth.

Since 'varna' means a system of classification, what possibly can be classified here? I think, It is the duty or responsibilities that a person grooms/educates, himself/herself to be in, while serving the society.

In my opinion, in the new world consisting of global economy, interconnectedness and technology, there are possibly 3 varnas only. I consider them only based on a person's contribution to the betterment of society/world through his job/duties. This is indirectly reflective of his education and general intelligence and his/her qualities like empathy, service, sacrifice, promoting freedom, fighting for justice etc.,

The first one is the highest varna consisting of jobs that makes the person in charge, **capable of transforming lives of a large group of people in his sphere of influence in a positive way**. They should demonstrate the highest form of integrity and honesty at all times and should take the proverb - 'Work is Worship' to the heart. This varna people should be given preferably the highest remuneration among all of the varnas since they are likely to ensure the execution of all or some of the below activities -

- Proving education and higher intelligence (Teaching related jobs)
- Providing a sense of security and freedom (Police, Army etc.,)
- Providing health care (Doctors, Psychologists, Nurses etc.,)
- Providing new R&D and related products or knowledge for the betterment of humans (Economists, Scientists, Inventors etc.,)
- Providing good governance and execution (genuine NGO workers/Government workers)
- Establishing justice (Judges, Lawyers etc.,)
- Providing vital information without distortion and thus providing a general sense of direction in which the society is proceeding

(News(wo)men/Journalists)
- Providing spiritual guidance and direction when there is chaos/suffering in the society (God(wo)men/Gurus etc.,)

NOTE: There are many grades of the above job type. And on the last one, society should have stringent criteria on who can be accepted as Gurus since they will eventually guide them in times of distress and chaos. Some professions like NGO workers may not work for remuneration/or take less remuneration. They, perhaps, may work for self-satisfaction. The best possible brains should vie for the above jobs since the general progressive direction of the society in general is set by these people.

In my opinion, the second varna is for the enablers and change-agents. They may not directly come into contact with a large set of people. They also sometimes provide efficiency and effectiveness in resource management. They consist of people of the following professions or similar:

- Business leaders, Farmers, Planner, Architects
- Artists, musicians, writers, poets, other creative artists etc., (The good ones among the artists as evaluated by some stringent standards, should be patronized by Government as they capture the zeitgeist of the society and serve as an important safety valve and also play a role in preservation and presentation of current times to the future generations)
- IT professionals

All other jobs including jobs that are in trading, production, stocking, distribution. logistics or providing services of luxurious experiences are of the third kind.

Together, the terms - 'varna', 'asrama' and 'dharma' means - 'Varnashrama Dharma'- the idea of people living by the sense of responsibilities/dharma and being cognizant of the stages of their life. The stages of life and expected transformation may impact the duties/responsibilities. Thus, retirement from professional life is in some way important. Society should ensure that the retirees are properly taken care. The society should ensure dignity in the natural death of their elders.

16 KALACHAKRAM OR THE WHEEL OF TIME

Insert I firmly believe that the manifestation of the universe- all the wonders, forces, beings, energy, mass etc., and the interactions, combinations, effects etc., are there to be discovered while the actors of the universe are in pursuit of excellence. Looks like, more than any other species, anywhere in the universe, humans are advanced in this pursuit by excelling in building the scientific body of knowledge and of course - in building the spiritual body of knowledge especially in areas where science is currently lagging primarily because of the limits imposed by the grand design of the universe. It does not mean that we will not be able to know the still unknown truths in the universe. The above belief is a very foundational belief that I am rooted in and which is also the raison-d'être, why I am writing these chapters.

One of the beliefs that I have is about the shape of the universe itself. I believe the grand design of the divine energy has left enough clues in nature in different realms of the universe for the beings of the realm to discover the unknown including the shape of the universe. If we consider, some of the most preferred shapes of nature, those that are abundantly present in the various locational contexts, and that which is not usually associated with any negative context in the culture of the location in a long time, then we should be wondering what those shapes signifies or hint at us.

At this point, considering what is implied in the first paragraph, it is alright to assume that those visual effects of shapes of different naturally occurring things, are clues for the humble humans to understand the larger-than-life aspects of the grand design of the universe.

STRANGER THAN FICTION

I am thinking about the following shapes that are appearing abundantly in nature and which seems to be created with some extra effort (going the extra mile) to produce the final shape. We are able to see at least some or all of the rules of symmetry, balance, geometry, aerodynamics etc., in those shapes. Some of the effects are not physical but more like a splurge or a sign of flow of energy.

1. Sphere - as seen in the manifestation of many space objects including planets.
2. Snowflake carrying intricate design
3. Conch/Shells seen in the beach sands (dextral and sinistral)
4. Crystal formations
5. Saligrama stone seen sculpted in some riverbeds of India
6. Colourful effects of the polar glows - aurora australis and aurora borealis
7. Flowers
8. Shapes of chakras in the human body
9. Shapes and colours of corals

From this point on, It can be considered that, I am just trying to derive the shape of a larger body like the universe from the naturally occurring shapes of many naturally occurring manifestations.

Generally, the space-time is considered as a continuum. I consider them as 2 different continuums but interposed. When I think that all universal effects have frequency derived from some form of entropy as a basis, I tend to think the effects of frequency on space and time. I, then, co-relate this with the knowledge that I gained from certain spiritual artefacts like the Upanishads and Puranas where it is claimed that there are upper realms and then the lower realms in the universe, if we define the universe from the point of view of the earth realm. Consider a band of frequency of space from the topmost realm to the bottom most realm. Within this band there could be multiple bands of space like the spectrum of colour. Each of these bands of 3-d space fabric can have its own localized effects similar to density, viscosity and mass systems and any other that we are not able to detect with our sensing faculties. The top realms are likely to have relatively lower frequency entropies as compared to the bottom realms and hence they desolate more slowly than the bottom bands.

On the other hand, the Upanishads and such spiritual texts also talk about the effect of time difference in the different realms of the universe. One such text claims that a single day of Brahma (referred as 'Kalpa') is almost equal to 4.32 billion earth years!! On extrapolating this understanding, we can assume that time should be faster in the lower realms. So, I mentally form a band of frequency of time in different realms. Since time is slow in the topmost realms, I assume that a slow-moving time flow that can be associated with low frequencies is in effect in those top realms, and the fast-moving time flow is in effect in the lower realms that can be associated with the high frequencies.

So, combining the above designs, there may be bands of spaces from top to bottom of the universe and there may be bands of time from the top to bottom of the universe. Assuming that space is relatively static and time flows forward, if we look down from the top most reference point of the universe, we can assume that both bands are infinitely varying and cannot be considered as discreate bands.

I think that this circum-ambulating flowing effect of time in different bands is is called as 'Kalachakram' or 'Wheel of Time' in Hindu scriptures. The effect of flow of time on the masses of the space is evident when we consider, as an example, how our body ages with time!! I assume at this point that, by grand design, flow of time affects all the physical and mental properties of all the living things. Your current physical form may block you from reaching this peak capacity hence it needs to be desolated over time to give you new body to understand newer things till the point where the physical body is completely lost, and the grand merge happens. All the understandings/learnings/knowledge/experiences etc., of the journey may form impressions on the soul, which I, earlier pointed to that, it is indestructible.

As the soul progresses, it undertakes journeys through the different 'elastic' band of space that acts as the stage of action and the 'law of karma' provides the physical body (actor) or the skin for the soul. The soul is expected to not only exhaust its negative karma but is also expected to evolve continuously till the grand merge ! The time flow relentlessly desolates the physical universe consisting of Prakruti and all souls. Again, the time flow desolates everything in dimension-2 too.

Considering the bands of spaces and time and the different realms, I am assuming that the shape of the universe may not be a simple sphere or cylinder. Other imaginations are also welcome till we get convincing evidence.

This model also explains some of the claims in the Hindu texts that gods live longer since the space is resisting time flow and both time/space perhaps, have lower frequencies in their realms. Thus, when a protagonist looks at a person in earth realm, from the upper realm, all things appear to mature fast - something like a fast-forward living. Thus, the protagonist may see the whole life of a human within a fragment of time!

Let us consider how time, Prakruti and soul acts together while the great cosmic dance of creation, maintenance and dissolution is enacted.

1. The 1st body sheath (koshana) - gross body is desolated by time and we grow old.
2. The 2nd koshana - ghost body is desolated by time as we grow old and can sometimes be attrited independently post death.
3. The MAHAT keeps track of the karmic load (It is presumed that no matter how healthy an individual is at the completion of the set karmic load for this birth, that individual is expected to drop dead)
4. To perform all the activities, the body complex receives the instructions from karmic load and free will. The energy for this will come from the food we eat(the first 2 koshanas are sustained by food we eat and this eating may generate karmic load since it is based on free will and choices) and also from the MAHAT as the pranic energy sustaining the inner koshanas.
5. When the karmic load of this birth is expended, the process to power the inner koshanas from the MAHAT will gradually stop.
6. Thus, attrition by time and stopping of the drawing of energy from MAHAT is in sync for all the souls.
7. At the time of death, since there is no more pranic energy (life force), time quickly desolates the gross body by decaying it. (It is best to cremate it in fire).
8. The ghost body sometimes, if left over will also be attrited by the time (I called this as the Great Storm that peels off the ghost body to reveal the soul itself)

Time is a powerful tool in the hands of the great divine energy. While dispensing justice, the Law of Karma as such may use time or space or both to produce desired effects.

17 THE 3 - IMPERFECTIONS

Though I do not agree with the choice of the word -'Imperfection' here, since it helps to understand the context and the idea in a better way, I stick with it. Otherwise - Creation is just beautiful! The Sanskrit/Tamil term used to describe this imperfection is called 'Malam'.

From the spiritual inferences, 3 imperfections (mummalaas) are associated with a soul. They are

1. Anavam - Imperfection that is identified with the 'I-ness' of the soul or 'the spiritual I-ness'. This, in my opinion, is a 'I'-state that gives you a feeling as rooted in your existence itself in any form! This is the "I"-ness that gives you, your name, when you look into the mirror. This is the same "I"-ness that is responsible for the fight/flight responses and generally makes you feel scared of life & death cycle and specifically make it fearful about death itself.

2. Maya- Imperfections associated with the mental models and intelligence. This comes out of our imperfect knowledge, incorrect interpretations out of imperfect intelligence and from the imperfect interactions (imperfect experiences) with Prakruthi itself. Beliefs in false political systems, falsehoods, ideologies, value systems etc., come under this Malam. For a more practical example - A girl is said to be in this Malam if a guy that she loves successfully gaslights her! (Web definition: Gas-lighting is **a manipulative tactic in which a person, to gain power and control of another individual, plants seed of uncertainty in another person's mind**. The self-doubt and constant questioning slowly cause the individual to question their reality.)

3. Ganmam - Imperfections associated with actions arising out of self-identification with the materialistic world. The existence of greed, avarice, excessive lust etc., and the related actions refer to this Malam called as 'Ganmam'. For a human, all activities - validated by their inner belief systems and acted out using the physical body - contributes to this malam.

Thus, most of the times, the 'Ahankara' or "I"-ness, under the influence of maya (instead of true knowledge) , acts out and carries out gross activities out of ignorance, resulting in a sea of karmas that, perhaps, will take several lifes to exhaust.

Consider the below soul states from left to right with cross reference to the 3 malams mentioned above.

Soul States

THE GREAT BLISSFUL & INTELLIGENT DIVINE ENERGY

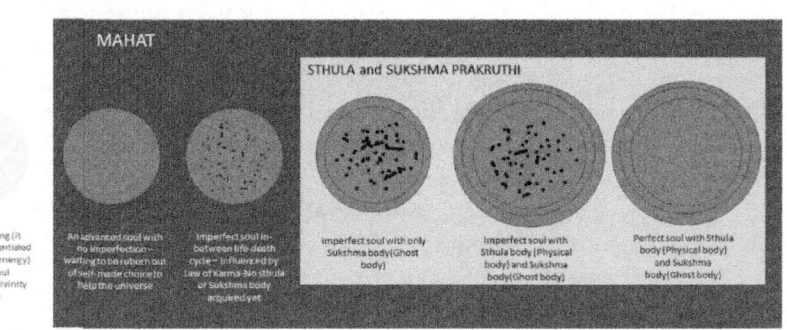

MAHAT

STHULA and SUKSHMA PRAKRUTHI

- SHAPE indicating (it cannot be differentiated from the divine energy) a merged soul - Merged with divinity or Mukthi
- An advanced soul with no imperfection - waiting to be reborn out of self-made choice to help the universe
- Imperfect soul in-between life-death cycle - Influenced by Law of Karma-No sthula or Sukshma body acquired yet
- Imperfect soul with only Sukshma body (Ghost body)
- Imperfect soul with Sthula body (Physical body) and Sukshma body (Ghost body)
- Perfect soul with Sthula body (Physical body) and Sukshma body (Ghost body)

State 1: The soul that has achieved Mukthi
This soul no longer exists as an independent entity. It removed all the 3 malams (I will use this term to denote imperfection) while on its soul-journey (i.e in pursuit of excellence). It might have taken 1000s of gross bodies, life forms while pursuing excellence and finally reached this state where it understood its true nature and merged itself with the infinite and intelligent energy. Thus ended the grand journey of the soul !!

State 2: An advanced soul that removed the 3 malams but it wants to help the universe out of compassion and hence did not merge into the infinite and intelligent energy.
This soul understands the strong influence of the malams and the hurdles that these malams impose on the soul's journey. These souls wait for the right opportunity to emerge to take a right form/stage in the universe to effect a profound change that can set many thousands of souls in the right direction while in-pursuit of their excellence. For example, these souls can decide to be born as a great thinker, spiritual leader or as a warrior (to offset injustice) or as some change agent that can introduce profound changes in a society in a positive way. They keep being born again and again (sometimes called as Avatars) to help the universe to avoid sufferings before they themselves merge with the great divine energy (attaining Mukti).

State 3: This is a soul that has lost both its sthula and Sukshma bodies.
This is an imperfect soul that is caught by 'The Storm' of the Law of Karma.
We saw in our earlier post that, when a human dies, his Sukshma body (ghost body) leaves the gross body (sthula body). This Sukshma body is sometimes (depends on the karmic load and the next immediate destination) peeled away by forces of law of karma (which I would like to refer to as 'The Storm') to reveal only the imperfect soul. This soul according to its karmic load is moved to the next stage and skin by The Storm where it enters a womb and acquires both a new Sukshma body and a new sthula body.

State 4: A soul that has lost its gross body.
This is the ghost body of an imperfect life just after its death and before its next skin/stage. Since it is imperfect (it might have committed sins as influenced by 3 malams of his stage/skin, and acquired negative karmic load), it cannot escape The Storm. Sometimes accidents happen in Prakruthi (nature) and these in-between state souls are left in their Sukshma body for a little longer time!

Stage 5: A soul that is alive and kicking with both its sthula and Sukshma bodies.
This is when the soul is in its journey and has currently taken a skin/stage to exhaust its karma (at least some part of its balance). While doing this it may acquire new karma. These new karma gets added to the store house of karmas and is attached to the soul and will be influenced by the law of karma in its next birth.

Stage 6: An advanced soul with no imperfection that has taken birth to the benefit of the cosmos.

While understanding the souls' journey, thus we have to consider the 3-malams seen in them in various stages as different actors.

18 FORMATIVE YEARS OF A GROUP

Insert We saw in Chapter 6, some samples of groupings such as:

- Country as a grouping with constitution as the value system
- Scientists as a grouping with the principles of science (integrity of knowledge, collegiality, honesty, objectivity, openness etc.,) as the value system
- Students as a grouping with the value system imposed by the learning institution
- Local Community as a grouping with the value system imposed by the local culture and so on.

In the same chapter, we also saw about the concept of defence in depth as seen being used by different groups and individuals in their adopted value systems.
So when I refer to 'the formative years of a group', in a broad context, it also means formative years of a new groups like a group to be formed for climate protection. But in a specific sense, I would like to focus on the group context and value systems that was present and evolving at the time of the dawn of the civilization in the various parts of the planets in this universe. Because this is where some of the early constructs of the society was put in place that is reverberating in some forms, even in the current modern societies.

What comes to one's mind is the confusion on the authority figures that can set value systems for the society. In the dawn times, it is like a melting pot of ideas, prejudices, bias, judgemental errors and possibly sheer brutality that corrupted or influenced the creation of group value systems. Adding to the conundrum is the idea of nature, God, purpose of human and other lives, position of a women in the society (refer to my early Chapter on equality). We all know, that when we undertake an effort, to create a new group such as creating a new company or a software or a global group/trade-blocks etc in the current times, the most difficult times are in the beginning stages even when we are amply supported by knowledge from areas like science, management science, behavioural science etc., . Now, consider the same difficulty multiplied by several magnitudes - that was most likely to be the zeitgeist during the troubled times of the dawn of civilization in various geographies, when important decisions on topics such as religion, god, stature of women etc., were decided in a state of complete ignorance, with lack of scientific knowledge or based on fear of natural elements or clan-strength or by charlatanism or persuaded by wealth/strength. Hence, I think, if any old ideations/customs do not appeal to a new modern society built upon a formal educational system and with abundance of common-sense/intelligence, there should be a way to discard them!

When a very wrong person like a king or a chieftain or a politician, with lots of bias and ignorance, assumes leadership and sets direction for a group, a morally corrupt value system is set in place that may travel several centuries , as part of legacy, as guidance from the elders, customs, traditions and history till it is completely uprooted by phenomenal events like global disasters, dawn/discoveries of the science, clashes of the civilizations or any black swan events.

Hence, it is important for a group, that such verified, truthful signal events are detected, during the group's existence over a given timeline, by any or all of their adopted value systems to amend their existing value systems. We have to consider the biases mentioned above before moving ahead. These changes should be recorded appropriately in the history with proper justification and immense efforts should be taken to preserve the truths that influenced the change of the value systems.

For a truth to be vetted, all bodies of knowledge of the time such as politics, science, philosophy, medicine, spirituality etc of each and every group should be deployed without undermining the other's effort by any bias. Hence it is important for a modern society to acknowledge the role of significant groups and devise a time-tested, fool proof process (may itself change based on new truths discovered) to detect significant events in time and initiate the change process for the betterment of the not just the mankind but for all the lives.

19 THE LAW OF KARMA

In the earlier chapters we saw, how The Law of Karma appears to be on an universal scale. We also understood the 3 super-imposed layers - MAHAT (where souls are embedded), Sukshma layer (the 3D-spatial-canvas that holds the ghost bodies of living beings) and the Sthula layer (the 3D-spatial-canvas that holds gross bodies of living beings).

I also liberally assumed that MAHAT may be the embodiment of dark matters and dark energies in which souls are embedded. Thus the composite structure held in position by MAHAT (with souls), is seen to have the sthula Prakruthi and Sukshma Prakruthi as stages and the related Sukshma bodies and sthula bodies as actors.

The actions of gross bodies (and therefore ghost bodies) will have an imprint on the soul in an outside to inside manner. The imprints of past actions of the soul will also have an force on the gross body of the soul in an inside to outside manner.

One of the definitions of Karma is as follows:

Karma is the sum of a person's actions in current and previous states of existence, viewed as deciding their fate in current and future existences.

Some of the ideas related to karma are -

1. The Karma generated by the actions of the souls is stored for release later.
2. The Karma can be generated by the individual (e.g. act of ploughing in the field) or a group (e.g a country going to war) or from a part of Prakruthi itself (e.g. like star formations)

STRANGER THAN FICTION

3. The stored Karma can be released later, and it can enforce the kind of skin/stage that an individual will acquire. (e.g. the soul is now a cow in the planet Earth)
4. The stored Karma can be released during the journey of the soul and thus affecting his choices in the life (e.g. will he become rich or will he lose a limb etc.,)
5. The stored Karma can be released to form a new group and set its direction (e.g. birth of a country)
6. The stored Karma can be released to erase a group (skins/stages) (e.g. mass extinctions on planet earth).
7. What appears to be sacrosanct is the finality of the Law of Karma - no actions go without repercussions - as you sow, so shall you reap!
8. We may not know the intricacies of how the Karma of a soul is stored. But it is interesting to imagine how the dark matter, dark energy and Karma interact and produce and effect upon a soul/souls or a group.
9. The reverse is also interesting to imagine -how the actions of the soul travels to inside layers and produce an effect on the Karma of the soul and the dark matters and dark energies immediately surrounding the soul effecting some kind of storage (Karma as potential karmic energy).
10. It appears as if, the souls bounce as nodes in a lattice diagram in a sea of dark matter/dark energy called MAHAT whose intelligence (from the great divine energy) governs the law of Karma.
11. There is a term in Sanskrit called - ADHRSTA describing the law of Karma (Wiki: The Sanskrit term, Adrsta or Adhrsta, as an adjective means - not seen, unseen, unobserved, unforeseen, unknown, invisible, unexpected, not experienced, destiny, fate, luck, not permitted or sanctioned, illegal, virtue or vice as the eventual cause of pleasure or pain.). Thus, anybody is free to assume a model of their own at this inner layer and wait for the blessing of the divine energy for their eureka moment!
12. A Karma can generate a result which can be good (green coloured arrows in the below diagram) or which can be bad (red coloured arrows in the below diagram).
13. If you do an action - without expecting to partake of the result, then such actions will not generate Karmic loads (e.g. a soldier going to war and killing an opponent as it is his duty as imposed by the country (as a group))

The various types of Karma is given in the below diagram:

STRANGER THAN FICTION

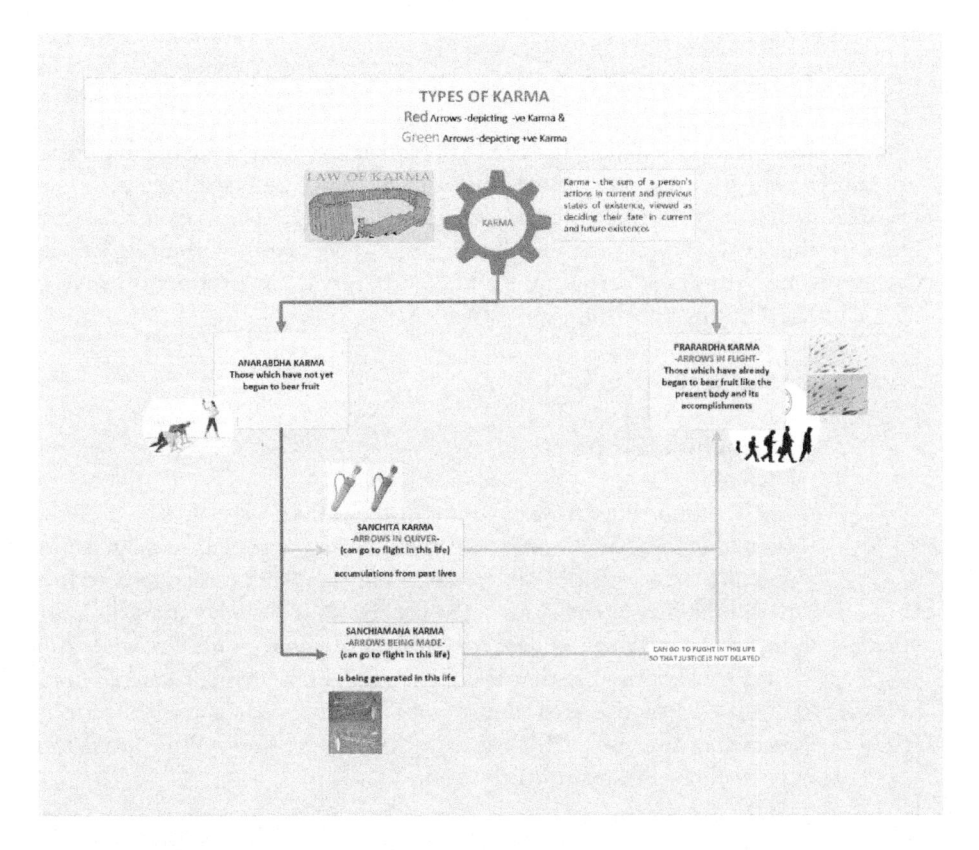

TYPES OF KARMA
Red Arrows -depicting -ve Karma &
Green Arrows -depicting +ve Karma

LAW OF KARMA — Karma - the sum of a person's actions in current and previous states of existence, viewed as deciding their fate in current and future existences.

ANARABDHA KARMA
Those which have not yet begun to bear fruit

PRARABDHA KARMA
-ARROWS IN FLIGHT-
Those which have already begun to bear fruit like the present body and its accomplishments

SANCHITA KARMA
-ARROWS IN QUIVER-
(can go to flight in this life)
accumulations from past lives

SANCHIAMANA KARMA
-ARROWS BEING MADE-
(can go to flight in this life)
is being generated in this life

CAN GO TO FLIGHT IN THIS LIFE
SO THAT JUSTICE IS NOT DELAYED

Some further clarifications on Karma are taken from the references mentioned in the bibliography section of this article.

Karma can be classified into 2 types in a broad sense.

We can consider the different types of Karma and visualize it as the journey of a set of arrows taken from a quiver and shot at its target. The difference in this allegory is that the maker of the arrows, and the receiver of the arrows is the same soul. The launcher is the Law of Karma at its own time of determination!!

Since we firmly believe that 'Justice delayed is justice denied', as much bad karma (from past lives or current life) as possible should be set on a wrongful/erroneous/criminal person by the law of karma in his/her current life, and the corresponding punishment should manifest swiftly for him/her, to reinforce the faith of the good people of this universe.

STRANGER THAN FICTION

1. Anarabdha Karma

Anarabdha Karma is akin to results of Karmas - those which have not yet begun to bear fruit. Besides, sometimes the karma of a person or a group is so powerful that it is destined by the great divine energy to expend this karmic load in this current life/times itself. This also takes care of the need to have swift justice. (thus, the arrow in quiver or the arrow in production may also get launched in this 'life'/'times')

Again, this can be of 2 types.

1.1 Sanchita Karma

This is akin to the arrows waiting in the quiver.
When the Law of Karma considers setting a soul in a stage/skin, it probably may consider all the large karmic loads (green and red) into one bundle to set the skin/stage for the soul and give it an directional indicative push called fate/destiny (and also it is a 'cow' and not 'horse'). It is possible that there may be some unspent karmic load of the soul from the past that is not yet relieved in the current/new journey of the soul. These are still in storage and will be used in the next cycle of life-death of the soul.

Or in case of any breakthroughs in the journey of the soul in the current life, these unspent Karma may take effect in the current life itself.

What we can only feel awe at is the infinite scope of evaluations done by this great divine energy on countless souls in various skins/stages without making any accounting mistake in packaging the Karmic load! So, if our suffering is seen endless, we can hope that all our negative Karmas of the past is being vacated and by doing good in thought and deed, we can improve our life and remove the sufferings ! That is why we have to strongly advise/counsel those who have suicidal thoughts, to remove that self-harming thoughts and think positive. I believe that if a soul commits suicide, it is only pushing the sufferings to the next skin/stage in some form instead of exhausting it with a positive outlook. Besides, one of the best skins to have is the human form, in which (with the help of its intelligence), one is expected to remove big negative loads of Karma effortlessly (e.g. by prayers). It is prudent to imagine that the Karmic effect can be felt as short-time/high-magnitude impact or as a long-time/less-magnitude impact. Thus, it is safe to assume that your free will, aided by good thoughts and deeds, can deflect/attenuate high impact negative karmas in a variety of ways.

We also considered the role of free-will over fate in our earlier articles(s).

1.2 Sanciyamana Karma

This is akin to the arrows in the making.
Sometimes, by the efforts of free will, these arrows can be expected to not only be completed but also set in its path immediately. (to take care of the problems like - 'Justice delayed is justice denied')

One should make sure that we collect/make more green arrows and no red arrows in the soul's journey!

These are the Karmas in making in the current life as we do our duties as guided by our free will and intelligence. This is where our focus should be on being in pursuit of excellence and becoming a gentler and caring soul.

2. Prarabdha Karma

This is akin to the arrows in the flight.
Thus, this arrow cannot be recalled (as we are born already!). We can only hope to make it useful.

We saw how infinite and divine energy resolves the karmic load of a human form or a blade of grass or any other of the countless souls as the souls pursue the excellence path. There is saying in a Tamil literature that - It is extremely rare to be born in a human form. Even rare is to be born without any bodily defects! Fortunately, we are blessed with this human form and thus we should strive our best to get out of the life-death cycle using our free-will guided by our intelligence and good heart. We should be afraid of causing harm to anybody in mind or indeed.

We have an indicative destiny which is being corrected by our free will. Aided by our good deeds, thus we may be able to remove most of our past negative Karmas in this journey and aim to accumulate good Karmas that will relieve us from the cycle of life and death.

Bibliography:

1. Satishchandra Chatterjee & Dhirendranath Datta , An Introduction to Indian Philosophy (Rupa Publications 2016)

2. Pandit Rajmani Tigunait , From Death to Birth, Understanding Karma and Reincarnation (Himalayan Institute Press)e.

20. THE FIELD OF KARMA

In this chapter I am sincerely attempting to portray the field of Karma. i.e the modus operandi of how karma is created and how it is resolved. Though I have considered the field in the context of a human (as the most evolved and capable species), generally this field of interactions will apply to the animal/plant kingdoms as well with appropriate contextual considerations.

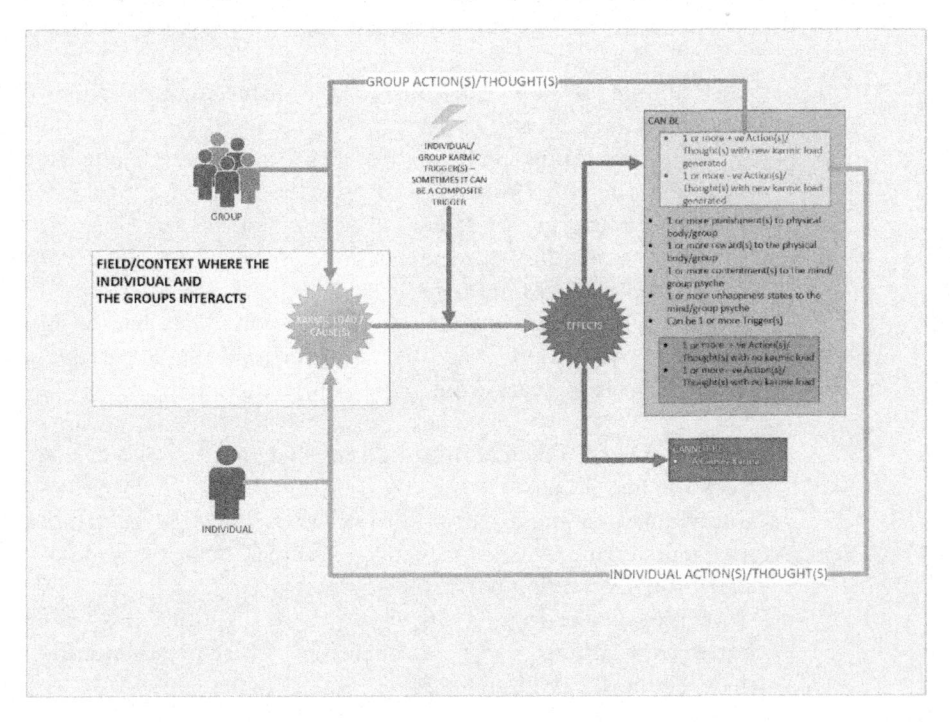

Please note the below set of interactions that can happen in a local or group context or in a focussed context with cascading or ripple effects:

- Karmic load will be there for all humans
- Karmic load will be there for all group identities (explicit or implicit identities)
- Karmic interactions will happen between individuals and groups producing composite cause(s) and/or trigger(s).
- Sometimes it is possible to see the cause and trigger as one congruous unit of execution and trigger and effect as another congruous unit of execution.
- Sometimes it is possible that the intended effect is big enough to introduce delays in between cause and trigger and then in between the trigger and the effect.
- Karmic load transfer (partial or full) may happen from groups to individuals and from individual (as a person of influence) to group

    o Example of how a karmic load transfer may happen to an individual from the group:
    - By any influence from the likes of a protagonist (say god accepting the outcome of sins on of others. Accepting is the transferring/trigger effect and suffering is the execution/expending part. This is mentioned in the Charama Shloka in Bhagavat Gita too)
    - By punishment meted out to the individuals by the justice system(s) (judgement is the transferring/trigger effect and punishment is the execution/expending part)

    o Example of how a karmic load transfer may happen to a group from the individual:
    -Individual goading a nation into going to war (war declaration is the transferring/trigger effect and actual acts of war is the execution/expending part)
    -Individual creating a new ideology (publishing is the transferring/trigger effect and receiving widespread attention is the execution/expending part)

- Karmic load transfer (partial or full) may happen between individuals.

STRANGER THAN FICTION

This usually happens when the relationship is close and pure.
- o Examples: between mother/father and children, between grandparents and grandchildren, between ancestors and progeny, between husband and wife, between guru and shishya, between God and devotee etc.,

- Consider the Karmic field in the context of a field consisting of individuals and groups. It is impossible to precisely pinpoint the exact cause of an effect or the trigger event to the individuals or the groups because of this complexity. The great divine energy resolves both the load and trigger in a ADHRST manner.

- When karma is expended by 1 or more group(s) or the individuals, the following happens:
  - o 1 or more punishment(s) may happen to the group(s) or to the individual(s).
  - o 1 or more reward(s) may happen to the group(s) or to the individual(s)
  - o 1 or more contentment(s) may result in the individuals' mind or the groups' psyche.
  - o 1 or more distresses/unhappiness states may result in the individuals' mind or the groups' psyche.
  - o 1 or more action(s) may be taken with new karma being generated by the individuals and/or groups.
  - o 1 or more thought(s) may be generated with new karma being generated by the individuals and/or groups.
  - o 1 or more action(s) may be taken with NO new karma being generated by the individuals and/or groups.
  - o 1 or more thought(s) may be generated with NO new karma being generated by the individuals and/or groups.
  - o A cause or a karma will not be the outcome of a karma being expended but the outcome can serve as 1 or more trigger(s) leading to a chain of events.

- Thus, in life, individuals/groups should aim to create effects that are positive - i.e. effect(s) that produce no -ve karma or effect(s) that produce positivities.

21 LIVING AN ORGANIC LIFE

Insert This Prakruti is, as we know, is made up of Panchabhootas – earth, air, water, fire and sky. Anything you physically see/feel with your eyes/senses are direct products or derivatives of these elements. We have to get adequate exposure to these elements in its naturally occurring state, as relevant, to have a healthy body and pleasant life. This is my understanding of living an organic life.

Think about the below:

- How many times have you walked on a grass patch with your bare sole? (earth)
- How many times have you taken a dip in water in a lake or a pond or a river? (water)
- How many times have you eaten a wood fired pizza? (fire)
- How many times have you seen the night sky with all its brilliance? (sky)
- How many times have you taken a early morning stroll with it chill air flowing across your face? (air)
- How many times have you felt the burning appetite in your stomach before you started eating it? (fire)
- How many times have you happen to accidentally get drenched in rain? (water)
- Have you played football in mud grounds with bare foot? (earth)
- Have you enjoyed the breeze in a beech? (air)
- Have you visualized/felt cosmic plunge while listening to a transcendental music? (sky)
- So on and so forth …

STRANGER THAN FICTION

But to the contrary we are seeing the below lifestyles especially in mega cities:

1. People living their entire life insulated from the Panchabhootas or used to the poorer forms/representations of Panchabhootas such as
    - Never felt the earth with bare foot (always wearing shoes)
    - Never dipped in a naturally occurring water body.
    - Lived withing the confines of claustrophobic mega cities the entire life.
    - Breathed air laced with poison most of the times.
    - Always relied on fast foods and rapid heating technologies
    - Enclothed with synthetic clothes/footwear most of the times
    - So on and so forth ...

2. A personal fast-paced lifestyle with choking financial circumstances with no breather with an aim to have an own personal concrete nest in a bustling mega city!

3. Night life in dens with hallucinating agents in full use with no recourse to proper sleep filled with happy dreams!

4. Overeating, oversleeping, and overindulgence seems to be the order of the day.

In order to come to a natural balance in life, I, therefore think about the below alternate lifestyles/good practices.
- Building and expanding urban forest concepts in big cities
- Building foot paths – having natural stones (no concrete) and grass paths encouraging bare foot walking.
- Building more sun lit public parks.
- Building abutments and safeguards to support bathing in natural water bodies.
- Encouraging the holding of star gazing events/astronomy events in public parks and schools at the night preferably in the same local communities.
- Eating healthy organic foods most of the times and make/grow it cheap in an affordable way.
- Encouraging gardening
- So on and so forth ...

If we follow this alternate lifestyle, we can accrue long term benefits like being able to move about even at ripe old ages, addressing the mobility/stability related problems faced in old age, avoiding frequent visits to the hospitals and clinics, and believing and benefitting from the practice of considering food(organic) itself as the medicine.

22 THE TRIGUNAS

Insert The word 'Guna' in Sanskrit means "quality or peculiarity or attribute or property".

In our earlier chapters, we talked about the manifestation of Prakruthi and soul. Also, we understood how tanmatras (rudimentary, undifferentiated, subtle elements) exist and how Gnanendriyas (sensory organs) and Karmendriyas (action organs) generate/interpret tanmatras and that some special senses can exist in other species of this universe sensing tanmatras that, we as humans, may not know yet!

The wholesome experience of the above in the context of Prakruthi and soul can be graded into 3 attributes or gunas. In some ancient Sanskrit texts these 3 gunas are called as -
1. Sattva Guna
2. Rajo Guna and
3. Tamasic (Tamas) Guna

Please note that under different philosophical systems of India, several other concepts are described as Gunas. But, in this chapter, I am only referring to the above 3 - so called fundamental - attributes.

Though I tend to quickly equate it to the good, the bad and the ugly (!!), I resist the temptation and try to analyse it further.

For that matter, all 3 exist in all forms of the Prakruthi and soul. It is an amalgamation of all 3 attributes. Let us consider some raw examples to understand this -

1. Food can be organic (sattva), spicy (rajas) or putrefied (tamas)

2. Music can be peaceful (sattva), energetic (rajas) or screeching (tamas)
3. State of mind for a person can be balanced (sattva), aggressive (rajas) or sad (tamas)
4. A painting can be euphoric (sattva), or about a war (rajas) or something macabre (tamas)

In the above examples, we saw how subjective these qualities can be with respect to a person! I have liberally used a few adjectives (An adjective is a word that modifies or describes a noun or pronoun.) and for some other person, the choice of adjectives can vary!

But the essence is to convey the property that we feel when we act/perceive in the Prakruthi as part of our living - in terms of sattva, rajas and tamas gunas.
I urge the reader to consider the paragraph - "Samkhya school of Hinduism" in the wiki site for Guna (given in reference section below).

It helps if we equate Sattva with balance, harmony, goodness, purity etc.,
Similarly, it helps if we equate Rajas with passion, activity, neither good not bad, egoism etc., Likewise, it helps if we equate tamas with imbalance, chaos, anxiety, impurity, delusion etc.,

Please consider the scenario when 2 kings are at war - the winning king may be perceived to be in rajasic state and the losing king may be perceived to be in tamasic state. We cannot generalize that war is a rajasic activity! But a neutral person observing the war can consider that act as rajasic or tamasic!!

And then there are these explicit conditions too:
- Putrefied food is tamasic for humans
- Person under the influence of drugs/intoxicants are said to be in tamasic state
- A spiritual guru in a deep state meditation is said to be in sattvic state
- A sprinter/runner is said to be in a rajasic state

Hence, we can infer that, in anything we do or perceive, using our Karmendriyas and Gnanendriyas, all these 3 gunas keep appearing in a intertwined state. An advanced soul will aim to maximize the sattvic experiences while an ignorant soul may thrash about in a sea of rajas and tamasic experiences with little or no sattvic experiences and look forward to the help and guidance from the sattvic souls (such as Gurus, Acharyas and Masters) for balance, peace and liberation (nirvana). Sometimes this travel can be self-guided too.

A reference to Bhagavad Gita is given in the below wiki site, which I faithfully reproduce:

> *Action that is virtuous, thought through, free from attachment, and without craving for results is considered Sattvic; Action that is driven purely by craving for pleasure, selfishness and much effort is Rajasic; Action that is undertaken because of delusion, disregarding consequences, without considering loss or injury to others or self, is called Tamasic.*
> —*Bhagavad Gita, Chapter 18, verses 23–25*

The above meaning, to me, is very profound! Please refer to the 2nd link given below for the actual script and translation.

In another way of interpretation, as per the wiki site on Guna, the following is also a profound statement:

> *The balance of Gunas of everything and everyone can change and does. However, change in one quality faces inertia from other two qualities in Indian worldview. Change needs internal or external influence or reinforcement, as knowledge and force to transform. The force to change comes from the Rajas Guna, the Sattva Guna empowers one towards harmonious and constructive change, while Tamas Guna checks or retards the process.*

References:
1. https://en.wikipedia.org/wiki/Guna
2. https://www.holy-bhagavad-gita.org/chapter/18/verse/23

23 SOME SYSTEMS OF KNOWLEDGE

Insert Before we start this topic, it helps if we understand that philosophy and maths are considered to be fundamental to any human inquiry through a formal system of knowledge like modern science.

Short Note on the field of philosophy:
The main branches of philosophy are:

1. Metaphysics: The study of the fundamental nature of reality.
2. Epistemology: The study of the nature, origin, and limits of human knowledge.
3. Logic: The systematic study of the form of valid inference and reasoning.
4. Ethics: The study of value and morality.
5. Aesthetics: The study of beauty and taste.
6. Political Philosophy: The study of government, justice, and rights

Short Note on Enumeration (Mathematics):
Let us assume a simple thought experiment. When the first man (let's call him 'Adam') woke up for the first time, he saw a deer. He was bewildered. A little later he saw a pack of deer. He was again bewildered, but this time it was different. Why? Perhaps, because he, for the first time encountered the sense of one and many or the need for enumeration. Perhaps, he was not able to explain the difference and his left-logic part of the brain co-related it to a group of sticks seen thrown on the ground.

This sense of 'numbers' is what is called as 'Sankhya' in the Vaisesika philosophy, an old school system of knowledge. In this system, this sense of enumeration is recorded as one of the 24 fundamental- 'Gunas' of the real world.

On the question of why just 24 fundamental gunas and why not more or less, the answer given is as below (excerpts from the book given in the bibliography section):

> *Why should we admit just this number? Can it not be more or less than that?*
>
> *To this we reply that if one takes into consideration the numerous subdivisions of these qualities, then their number would be very great. But in a classification of objects, we are to reproduce them to such kinds as are ultimate from a certain standpoint, i.e., do not admit of further reduction. So, we come to the simplest forms or kinds of qualities. Thus, while one compound colour like orange may be reduced to red and yellow, or a complex sound may be shown to arise out of the combination of other sounds, it is not possible for us to reduce colour to sound or any other quality. It is for these reasons that we have to recognize colour, sound, touch, taste and smell as distinct and different kinds of qualities. The Vaisesika classification of qualities into twenty-four kinds is guided by these considerations of their simplicity or complexity, and reducibility or irreducibility. The gunas are what the Vaisesikas thought to be the simplest, passive qualities of substances.*

A thought on the act of creation itself:

I believe that the divine energy prefers order, symmetry, geometry, balance, repetition (just not in the shapes but also in designs/models/processes such as in how the planetary system is set as compared to the way how atoms/sub-atomic particles manifest) etc., in the act of creating the real world called Prakruti, on an infinite canvas called MAHAT.

This is evident in the way a leaf or a snowflake or the planets are shaped or by the fact that we have a whole body of knowledge called Geometry as part of the Mathematical field of study. The special shape of human species or any other species can then be defined as additional work by the divine energy, to gain functional efficiencies and to enable activities (to generate karma) and to support the act of perceiving and therefore setting the stage for interactions (thus life happens!). Again, to generate motion/karma (to answer questions such as – Why something and not nothing?) and to disturb the inertia (from initial equilibrium) the divine energy might have created several sub-designs and adjustments, on both Prakruthi (the stage – including the great forms of forces) and the actors (all the living forms) anticipating and enabling all the interactions needed to resolve their respective karmas. The field of modern science probably has not yet discovered all the puzzles, that the divine energy, has thrown at us when it has implemented this grand design.

STRANGER THAN FICTION

Looks like the purpose of this creation is to also unravel the mystery behind the creation itself!

We should also try to remember the scientific method of investigation as followed by modern science:

1. Make an observation.
2. Ask a question.
3. Form a hypothesis, or testable explanation.
4. Make a prediction based on the hypothesis.
5. Test the prediction.
6. Iterate: use the results to make new hypotheses or predictions.

I think that the problem with modern science is that it is limiting itself to the manifested world of the human species only - mostly!

Now, have such an inquiry covering all the dimensions of the universe been undertaken in the past? Maybe yes, and maybe we have lost some of them in the tides of time!

But we could see that some systems of philosophies are still existing at least in an academic sense.

I have created the below data of such systems of philosophies for consideration. We can see the natural human interest to know nature and the purpose of life behind all these intense inquiries. Some of these principles and philosophies went on to become great religions later on. Eventually the ideas around the protagonist and the antagonist too emerged.

STRANGER THAN FICTION

S. No	Name of the system	Some highlights:	Founder(s)	Other Related Eminent persons	Remarks
1	The Carvaka system	1. The word 'Carvaka' means a materialist. 2. Says perception is the only valid source of knowledge.	Sage Carvaka		This is straight hedonism
2	The Jaina System	1. The Jainas admit, in addition to perception, inference and testimony as sources of valid knowledge. 2. Perception reveals the reality of material substances. 3. Perception, as well as inference, proves the existence of souls in all living bodies.	24 - Tirthankaras	Sage Vardhamana or Mahavira – a contemporary of Gautama Buddha and the last Tirthankara	Mahavira's time was 599 BCE to 527 BCE
3	The Bauddha System	1. There is misery. 2. There is cause of misery. 3. There is cessation of misery. 4. There is a path leading to the cessation of misery. 5. The Madhyamika and Sunyavada school, The Yogacara 6. First 2 schools belong to Mahayana Buddhism and the last form to Hinayana Buddhism.	Gautama Buddha		Buddha's time was 563 BCE to 480 BCE
4	The Nyaya System	1. It admits 4 separate sources for true knowledge viz perception, inference, comparison, and testimony. 2. It talks about objects of knowledge such as the human body, mind, intellect, senses, and soul. 3. It also talks about 'mukthi' or liberation	Sage Gautama		Set in prehistoric times.
5	The Vaisesika System	1. Allied to Nyaya system. 2. It brings all objects of knowledge under the 7 categories: Substance (Dravya), Quality (Gunas), Action (Karma), Generality (Samanya), Particularity (Visesa), The relation of Inherence (samavaya) and non-existence (abhava) 3. The atoms are made to compose a world that benefits the unseen moral deserts(adrsta) of individual souls and serves the purpose of moral dispensation.	Sage Kanada (or Uluka)		Set in prehistoric times.
6	The Sankhya System	1. Supports dualistic realism – purusa and Prakruthi. 2. Prakruthi is the cause of the world. 3. Talks about karma and Karta (action and doer) 4. Talks about Karmendriyas, Gnanendriyas, Mans, Ahamkara (ego) etc., (totally about 25 principles)	Sage Kapila		Set in prehistoric times.
7	The Yoga System	1. Accepts the epistemology and metaphysics of Sankhya system with its 25 principles 2. Talks about the system of yoga leading to discriminative 3. It talk about the 8 steps of yoga – Yama (Don'ts), niyama (Do's), asana (Postures – popular in the west), pranayama (Breath-control), pratyahara (Withdrawal of senses), dharana (Attention/Concentration), dhyana	Sage Patanjali		Set in prehistoric times.
8	The Mimamsa System	1. Based on Vedic ritualism 2. Espouses the theory of knowledge. 3. Mentions that the soul is immortal. 4. It identifies the 5 outer senses and mind as the organs 5. It identifies 5 sources of knowledge – perception, inference, comparison, testimony, and postulation. 6. Talks about law of karma	Sage Jaimini	Prabhakara	Set in prehistoric times.
9	The Vedanta System	1. Arises out of the Upanishads 2. Talks about unqualified monism and the liberating 3. Subsequent commentaries were written by Adhi Sankara (Advaita principles), Madhvacharya (Dwaitha principles) and Sree Ramanuja (Vishistadvaita principles)	Sage Badarayana	Adhi Sankara (c.700 – 750 CE), Madhvacharya (c. 1200-1278), Sree Ramanuja (c.1017 – 1137)	Set in prehistoric times.

Reference:

Epistemology | Definition, History, Types, Examples, Philosophers, & Facts | Britannica
Metaphysics - Problems in metaphysics | Britannica
The philosophy of science - Understanding Science (berkeley.edu)
The scientific method (article) | Khan Academy

Bibliography:
1. Satishchandra Chattterjee & Dhirendranath Datta, An Introduction to Indian Philosophy (Rupa Publications 2016)

24. THE PANCHAKOSHANAS OR 5 SHEATHS

It took me considerable time to map the koshanas concept to the human form with all the functions. So let me explain the Panchakoshanas as I understand it.

The 5 sheaths of a human existence are:

1. Annamayakoshana - The physical sheath
2. Manonmanyakoshana - The astral or ghost sheath
3. Pranamayakoshana - The Pancha prana sheath
4. Vignanamayakoshana - the soul itself as sheath
5. Anandamayakoshana - The 'existence' (?) after the great merge
or
    the bliss sheath

Let us look at their functions briefly.

1. Annamayakoshana:

This is the external form of a human, this is manifested (also as eating action by mother - while the child grows in the womb) and maintained by the action of eating once the individual is born. Please note that it is said in some scriptures that, just before entering the birth canal, a newborn experiences a special type of prana - called - 'Vaishnava Prana', that passes over the brain in a down to up manner, and completely erases any past memories. Thus, the baby starts with a clean slate - ready for worldly inputs. It is sometimes thought that this is the same prana that causes the water to break, in a 100% natural birth.

This body exists to expend karma in the external world. The below organs of actions (5 Karmendriyas) are used to expend karma through this sheath:

- Speech or Vak – Mouth
- Grasp or Paani – Hands
- Move or Paada – Foot
- Excrete/Expulse or Paayu – Anus/Rectum
- Fornicate or Upastha – Sexual organs

In nutshell, this is the conveyor of actions to the external world. Food nourishes this sheath. Somewhere,

2. Manonmayakoshana:

This is the astral or ghost body of a human. This is manifested at conception and grows as the body grows. Sometimes they may stay for some additional time after the physical form is destroyed. In the ordinary souls, the Annamayakoshana and Manonmayakoshana, together act to feel the effects of internal sense organs or the 5 Gnanendriyas. They are as given below:

- Sight or Chaksu – Eyes
- Hearing or Shrotra – Ear
- Smell or Ghraana – Nose
- Taste or Rasaana – Taste
- Touch or Sparshana – Skin

Please note how the senses are sensed by our brain/mind complex to produce the intended effect.
In nutshell, this is the conveyor of senses to the internal organs. The related astral body is a transient state and hence there is no ability to eat, sleep or have sex.

3. Pranamayakoshana:

This is the third sheath consisting of 5 main and several sub Vayus. You may imagine this to be a flexible/fluidic sealed bottle containing 5 primary gases each maintaining their individuality/functions by flowing through the Nadi systems (like the great barrier reef of the human body !. I tend to imagine that the complex personality of each human is being reflected here as a multi-facetted arrangement of fluidic-sealed bottle and perhaps the multi-coloured reef occurring naturally is reminding us this complexity). They convey the senses from the first two sheaths to soul as effects of tanmatras. The five pranas or Pancha pranas are listed below with their auxiliary functions. The auxiliary functions are adequately explained in the link provided in the reference section.

- Prana Vayu – Vayu flowing and operating in head and thoracic region.
- Apana Vayu – Vayu flowing and operating in lower abdominal region.
- Samana Vayu – Vayu flowing and operating in the upper abdominal region.
- Udana Vayu – Vaya flowing and operating in the throat, head, and face regions.
- Vyana Vayu – Vayu flowing, operating, and permeating the whole body.

Please note that some Gurus consider the process of death as compete, only when the Vayus are completely withdrawn by the MAHAT. When the accounted/set karmas of the life are exhausted, MAHAT withdraws these Vayus and completes the process of death. There is more to these Pranamayakoshana and perhaps when the time comes, I may write another chapter just on this third sheath.

4. **Vignanamayakoshana:**

This is the fourth sheath – the soul. (also called as causal body or 'Karana Shariram') This is indestructible till the great merge happens. When the pranas convey the senses (while performing the karmic activities) as tanmatras to the soul, it faithfully transfers the sensations to the great divine energy. This feedback required by the divine energy is caused by the primordial question that originated in the divine energy – "Who am I?" Imagine the infinite commits (of sensations) by the various life forms to the divine energy – all culminating finally in the great merge after its journey through many types/forms of bodies-thus committing/reinforcing the answer to the primordial question as "I am God"!!

5. **Anandamayakoshana:**

This is the divine energy itself – the final "Mukthi" state of an individual soul. This is bliss itself as existence.

STRANGER THAN FICTION

Another important consideration is how the actions of Karmendriyas can impact pranas and how it is consequently converted as tanmatras and transferred to soul and then to the divine energy. Similarly, the sensations of Gnanendriyas too are imposed upon soul as tanmatras. And the thoughts/free-will, themselves, from the mind/intelligence complex are imposed as "Chittam" right into the soul itself - and they become the locus of all impressions for that soul. They remain as impressions affecting several forms that the soul may take in its journey through countless life-death cycles, or such thoughts cleansed in hellish situations as part of dispensing justice or expending karma. But note that our regular physical breathing is not the same as these Pranas. Controlled breathing, a smaller number of breathing cycles leads to- (means -less activities), less agitation in the koshanas and hence less agitation in Chittam. The reverse is true too - a smaller number of thoughts (alpha state of mind - say for example, 4 thoughts in a minute), leads to less energy consumption and helps us present a calm disposition. Please note the act of brain too as part of mind-body complex. The sensations from the sense organs are felt by brain, processed, and then transferred to the pranas by mind. On the inside-to-outside transfers, the Chittam presents thoughts relevant to current context to the mind, and it is the brain that converts these thoughts into actions by activating the Karmendriyas. Also, note that the mind as captured in statements like - "love felt in the heart", "a hearty laughter", "a brave heart", etc., is centred in the heart but the intelligence is centred in the brain (when someone emphasizes advanced concepts to their students and ask them to think, they unconsciously point to their head while speaking about it). Thus, intelligence acts as an effective filter to mind in an outside to inside manner (have you heard 2 people verbally fighting, and at the end when they make up- they sometimes say - "I hope you have not taken it to the heart !!"). And it acts as effective filter to control actions in an inside to outside manner. In a cosmic sense, thus, mind dominates over intelligence and the purpose of intelligence is to generate super refined higher thoughts in mind - in an outside to inside manner. Conversely, when mind processes only higher intelligent thoughts, in an inside to outside manner, the resulting actions, become great and commendable!

Please note the mind itself acts as an internal sense organ - that passes, unexpressed thoughts (through Karmendriyas), and feelings such as jealousy, greed, rage etc., to the "Chittam" and as the same as tanmatras to the divine energy.

So, we can consider our brain (intelligence/thinking) to be our tool that is essential for survival. But mind(feelings) is some part of you - yourself!!

Having said that and since we are constantly fighting for justice/freedom/success etc., we cannot underestimate the importance of our tool- the brain, since it, the intelligence, is a fundamental requirement when we are in pursuit of excellence. After the Great Merge, it is said that we FEEL bliss for eternity, but as long as the brain of a soul, as part of survival instinct, differentiates the divine energy and THINKS it as a separate God, Great Merge may not happen for that soul.

I presume that for the last 3 koshanas, the energy comes directly from MAHAT. When the intake of this energy stops, (a related term is 'Prana left the body)', death happens- this is the real death and not the medical death observed in the 1st and 2nd koshanas.

We also must think about how the 3- imperfections.

The first imperfection, 'Anavam' – operates in the soul itself.
The second imperfection, 'Maya' – operates in the first two sheaths.
The third imperfection, 'Ganmam'- operates in the first sheath.

Sage Patanjali has similar classifications called Kleshas which are five in number.

1. Avidya or ignorance – I consider this as Maya as above.
2. Asmita or I-am-ness – I consider this as Anavam as above.
3. Raga or Attachment – I consider this as Maya as above.
4. Dvesha or Repulsion – I consider this as Maya as above.
5. Abhinivesha or Will to live or survival instinct – I consider this as Anavam as above.

Thus, we can see how Sage Patanjali considers the Ganmam to be a by-product of Maya and Anavam, and thus has treated it as such.

Reference:

1. Pancha Prana Vayu - The Five Energy Flows in the body (yogicwayoflife.com)
2. https://www.yogabasics.com/learn/the-cause-of-suffering-the-kleshas/

25 ABOUT THE NEXT PROTAGONIST

Why should we be good?

And why, I think, it pays, being good in having a humane heart.

The Low of Karma is nothing, but a value system adopted by the divine energy on a universal scale to dispense justice. The necessary mass and energy (necessary to create karma and Prakruthi) comes from MAHAT.
The divine energy then created countless souls from itself and set them into this stage to provide the answer to the primordial question – "Who Am I?"

So, when all the actors(souls) act out at the stage (Prakruthi), they commit various experiences – good and bad, and everything in-between, to the divine energy. All these experiences finally culminate in the great merge for the soul and thus, it provides, part of the definitive answer to the primordial question to the divine energy over its infinite existence.

This creation happens in cycles. And I believe, that in the past, several such cycles may have completed, and each cycle may have had its own protagonist(s) and the antagonist(s).

In the past and in the current, the protagonist and the antagonist may have fought it out for the establishment of the appropriate value system (as per their perspective). But, based on the knowledge about how the Law of Karma operates now, we can be sure that the divine energy has also blessed the protagonist's view of adopting the right value system for dispensing justice. We see how the Karmic value system, has trickled down and resulted in different Legal systems of the Universe in general and in this world in particular. To put in layman's terms – people still have faith in the legal systems and in living a good, decent life!

We may not know who the current protagonist(s) is/are. But, since the goodness is still appreciated in this world, perhaps the current protagonist is winning wherever he is!

What may be his essential characteristics?

Since he is the God/Protagonist, he is expected to understand the Law of Karma better. This means he shall bear witness to all the activities and should intervene only to maintain justice i.e. when the nature of the value system adopted by the universe in itself is threatened by the protagonist and his/her cronies.

Since, he is expected to bear witness to the various activities, he should not taint himself with Raga or Dvesha. He should be mindful about the 5 Kleshas or mental afflictions.

Thus, in case he is born into this world as an avatar, he is expected not to become jealous of others who are leading a better and prosperous life. Hence, he should be free of greed, avarice, jealousy, excessive lust, frenzy, mindless rage etc., At the same time, he cannot allow the Law of Karma to be taken for granted and hence at times he should be warrior/punishing God and at times he should be Wisdom/benevolent God. At the same time, he should be razor focussed on the goals and objectives of the avatar as part of establishing justice and peace. It is like the association between the leaf of the lotus plant and the water – fully immersed and still not wet!

As we discussed earlier, the advanced souls, in their compassion to help, may be taking birth as avatars to help the world alleviate its sufferings and to help the world to regain its faith in the goodness of the world.

Then there is the concept of hell and its functions. This should act as deterrence to those who have a evil bent of mind. There may be realms of hell too, where the antagonist has won temporarily.

Over and above everything, I think the divine energy, while collecting the various experiences from the souls is also aware of the great commits by some souls – a commit that has resulted in profound good changes in the world, where it was committed. When such great souls become advanced souls in their journey towards the great merge, and present themselves as avatars to help the universe, - again and again and again, they may present themselves to the great divine energy, unknowingly as the next candidate for being the protagonist!

Hence, it pays to be a good soul in the long run! The good soul gets grand purpose of life, not just in this birth, but also in several other future avatars and also in several other future cycles!!!

26 COMMUNICATIONS FLOW BETWEEN ASTRAL & PHYSICAL BODIES

In one of the earlier chapters, we talked about astral and physical bodies and how they are related (in chapter 12).

In this chapter, I dwell and try to ruminate a little more on this topic. While a person is living, his physical or sthula body is playing a dominating role. After death, the astral body may live a little more and thus is considered more dominating than the sthula body.

Let us understand how the different apparatus of an integrated human body plays out. This is purely my assumption of how the 2 bodies interplay while a person is alive or when he is dead.

1. **Outside to Inside communication:**

    - The Karmendriyas or organs of action does the actions necessary driving from free-will. The action and the outcome is processed by the brain based intelligence and then is felt by the heart based feelings, if necessary, in different intensities as demonstrated by the emotions.
    - The Gnanendriyas or organs of senses converts its inputs which are processed by our brain and again it may be converted into heart-based feelings if necessary.
    - The intelligence-based inputs and heart-based feelings are then converted into tanmatras and is passed by the 3rd koshana-Pranamayakoshana to the chittam
    - This tanmatras impinges on the chittam (locus of all impressions)

2. **Inside to Outside communication:**

- From the chittam, based on karmic inducements or other interactions, selected impressions climb into manas. Few of the selected, may, then climb into buddhi. A person may experience a glimpse of a impression, while it is residing in chittam, as a feel and undefined by a language construct. Intuition is also a feel from the chittam. (The vak system consisting of para, Pashyanthi, Madhyama and Vaikhari will be taken up later in a separate chapter)
- Those thoughts from soul's impressions can be of 4 kinds:
    - Conscious/Sub-conscious 'acts of thinking' processed by the brain (Tamil word for act of thinking is 'sinthanai').
    - Conscious/Sub-conscious thoughts processed by the manas (Tamil word for the thought is 'ennam').
    - Conscious/Sub-conscious thoughts that lead to some actions through Karmendriyas
    - Conscious/Sub-conscious thoughts that lead to some sensory feelings through Gnanendriyas
- These thoughts in manas can again induce some sensory perception. This is different, in the sense that it is not as strong as those from the sensory perceptions coming out of Gnanendriyas (in the outside to inside process).

Now if we break-up the above process into its constituents and map it the first 2 layers of the human bodies, we obtain the below mapping:

Karmendriyas – Present in sthula body and astral (Sukshma) body. The Karmendriyas in astral body is not as fully defined as in the sthula body.
Gnanendriyas – Present in sthula body and astral(Sukshma) body. The Gnanendriyas in astral body is not as fully defined as in the sthula body.

In fact, the basic 3 functions – FOOD, SEX and SLEEP are not attainable fully in astral-body only existence and hence this transient condition propels it to the next stage naturally. Hence this astral-body only existence is considered as not sustainable.

Intelligence or Buddhi – Present in sthula body (brain centred)
Manas or thoughts – Present in astral body (heart centred)
Chittam/Ahankara – Present in the soul.

STRANGER THAN FICTION

Now, while we are in pursuit of excellence, and expend our karmas, this outside to inside communications and vice-versa takes place continuously.

From the chittam (holding all past and current impressions), a real-world person can get the required information/wisdom through intuition, beliefs/assumptions and facts. Sometimes a known fact from chittam can be converted into an assumption by the same person due to doubts arising from his intelligence. The reverse process - a real-world person's scientific knowledge, beliefs, facts and assumptions can get stored in chittam as impressions. These impressions of chittam are generally believed to last over several life cycles of birth that soul may probably undertake.

27 ABOUT THE CHAKRAS

Chakras are residents of the astral body. The physical body has several systems like the skeletal, muscular, respiratory, nervous etc., The astral body has the Nadis and chakras in which the Panchapranas manifest.
Though there are several big and small chakras, generally we set special interest on the 7 basic ones.

They are as below:

1. Muladhara - controls the ahankara and basic instincts like fight/flight/fear and is located near the coccyx.
2. Swadhistana - controls sexuality and creativity and other such and is located near the genitals.
3. Manipura - controls will, personality and self-esteem and other such and is located in the stomach region.
4. Anahata - controls love and higher ideals and is located in the thoracic region.
5. Visuddha - controls communication and intelligence and other such and is located in the throat region.
6. Ajna - controls intellect, awareness and other such and is located between the eyebrows.
7. Sahasrahara - leads a living human to enlightenment and is located at the crown.

You can relate the chakras to Maslow's hierarchy which consists of needs centred around physiological, safety, love and belonging, esteem and self-actualization. It helps if you map the Muladhara chakra to the base layer in Maslow's hierarchy which is on the needs surrounding physiological aspects.

Like how, knowledge and practice is propelling a human to self-actualization (in Maslow's hierarchy), transcendental/chakra meditation leads a person to enlightenment and also helps that person acquire higher ideals. It is generally said that life energy is lying in a coiled manner in the Muladhara chakra and by transcendental meditation a person is lead to enlightenment by moving this life energy to the crown chakra. This life energy is called - Kundalini.

Knowledge and practice gained by humans' aid in this journey to self-actualization and higher ideals. Similarly focusing on astral body by practising transcendental meditation arises the kundalini and gives not only great clarity and heightened sensitivity (of all senses) but helps a person become more humane and loving as the kundalini force crosses the heart/Anahata chakra on its way to the crown.

I believe that, these chakras are probably the centres in which the gross or sthula body, the astral or ghost body and the soul (is believed to be in the centre of Anahata chakra for an average good person) are pinned. The process of death, hence, can be analysed from this understanding and surely is a topic for another time.

But briefly, if you can consider the process of death with the above understanding - the following can be reasonably expected to happen. I have not separated the actions of time and karmic forces in my earlier chapters. But here I do differentiate based on my new understanding.

1. Time induces aging in the sthula body. As long as karma is waiting to be expended the body lives and thus the sthula body ages as time progresses.
2. Astral body leaves the Sthula body. (sometimes it is immediately attrited)
3. Time induces attrition in the astral body. As long as the karma is waiting to be expended (say for instance the unspent karma of a unfortunate soul that committed suicide or a soul that had encountered premature death through some events) , the astral body

is attrited by the time.
4. Pranas are sucked in by MAHAT
5. 1-4 activities can happen all at once or with some delta time difference.
6. The soul needs to be sucked in too and may need a new stage. If the soul was sucked in via the Muladhara chakra, then it may be placed in the lower realms of the universe where basal life quality is expected to exist. If the soul is sucked via the crown, MAHAT places them in the higher realms of the universe where higher ideal beings are expected to be existing.
7. Finally, the Karmic forces again move the soul to the new womb to begin a new life.

It is interesting to note that the chakras are well defined in humans only and not in animals or plants.

The below is my thought on the MAHAT and Karmic forces.

MAHAT is the dark energy/matter responsible for providing energy/mass for the construction of the universe with its dimensions and for sustaining the various physical laws/processes in different dimensions.

Karmic force is different because it has to intelligently decide a course of action based on the goodness (good karma)/ badness (bad karma) attributable in an entity like human or an entity like an animal in this universe.

Withdrawing a soul and placing them in a stage is a basic action compared to the action of placing the soul in a certain womb (as an example - plant seed or human womb).

Hence, I tend to think that the withdrawing and propelling the soul of a human is done by MAHAT but placing it in the right womb is done by the Karmic forces

Recommended Read:

Kundalini - The Evolutionary Energy in Man by Shambhala publications and written by Gopi Krishna.

28 TRI-DOSHAS OR 3 - MALAISES

This chapter is based on my concern that ayurvedic system is not getting a clean focus as one of the mainstream system of medicine. I am not a Subject Matter Expert in Ayurveda and hence any unintended mistakes in this chapter are purely coincidental that I am willing to correct.

I looked up the proper definition of the western system of medicine – allopathy. Here it goes (from https://www.cancer.gov/publications/dictionaries/cancer-terms/def/allopathic-medicine).

> *A system in which medical doctors and other health care professionals (such as nurses, pharmacists, and therapists) treat symptoms and diseases using drugs, radiation, or surgery. Also called biomedicine, conventional medicine, mainstream medicine, orthodox medicine, and Western medicine.*

The allopathic medicine derives its knowledge from the body of science. In this regard it is purely focussing on the representation of human body and mind in the dimension-1 (the manifested universe).

Let us now look at the definition of the ancient ayurvedic system of medicine primarily originating from the Indian sub-continent.

A western definition from the same cancer.gov site above goes like this –

> *A medical system from India that has been used for thousands of years. The goal is to cleanse the body and to restore balance to the body, mind, and spirit. It uses diet, herbal medicines, exercise, meditation, breathing, physical therapy, and other methods. It is a type of Complementary and Alternative Medicine (CAM) therapy. Also called Ayurveda.*

STRANGER THAN FICTION

From a knowledge source deeply rooted in ayurvedic principles (e.g. https://ayurveda.com/ayurveda-a-brief-introduction-and-guide/), the same definition goes like this –

> *Ayurveda places great emphasis on prevention and encourages the maintenance of health through close attention to balance in one's life, right thinking, diet, lifestyle and the use of herbs. Knowledge of Ayurveda enables one to understand how to create this balance of body, mind and consciousness according to one's own individual constitution and how to make lifestyle changes to bring about and maintain this balance.*

This is expected to be balanced by balancing vatta, pitta and kapha constituents of a human body.

> *In Ayurveda, body, mind and consciousness work together in maintaining balance. They are simply viewed as different facets of one's being. To learn how to balance the body, mind and consciousness requires an understanding of how vatta, pitta and kapha work together. According to Ayurvedic philosophy the entire cosmos is an interplay of the energies of the five great elements—Space, Air, Fire, Water and Earth. Vata, pitta and kapha are combinations and permutations of these five elements that manifest as patterns present in all creation. In the physical body, vatta is the subtle energy of movement, pitta the energy of digestion and metabolism, and kapha the energy that forms the body's structure.*

But there are some issues in the current practice of Ayurveda as seen from an Indian context. Some of them seems to be the below ones:

1. They are treated as complimentary system of medicine and not as one of the major ones.
2. At least a significant portion of the practitioners of Ayurveda has been subconsciously forced to accept that their practice is an extension or addendum to the allopathic system of medicine.
3. Because of the ease with which allopathic system medicine can be reached out to along with the 'swift' results, general public has largely gravitated to this system of medicine and hence potential practitioners of ayurveda do not possibly have a strong supporting revenue generating mechanism or incentive to practice ayurveda.
4. At least in India, there are quacks and charlatans who masquerade as ayurveda healers, and the liberal use of the term 'Ayurveda' is not strictly regulated like the term M.B.B.S – the title

given to persons graduating from the allopathic system of medicine learning in India.

5. The ayurvedic body of knowledge is not well developed and curated or organized like the body of knowledge that exists in allopathic system of medicine. R&D operations/data, documentation, creating a unified body of knowledge etc., is perhaps, still rudimentary, or unintegrated in the system of ayurveda even in India. Variations in the form of treatment is not properly explained. I wonder if, even, somebody has collected all the good **ancient** literatures that espouse the ayurvedic principles and the body of knowledge.

6. In Ayurveda, primarily certain types of food and herbs are identified as the medicines for consumption for addressing malaises. Besides, the patients are taught to practice certain yogic practices like pranayama and meditation to heal the mind. But I fear that a lot of information on herbs, and on the styles of administering food as medicine are lost in time. Moreover, I am deeply concerned that, lot of species of medicinal herbs may have been lost from the gene pool itself or is not identified still or whose information is also lost over time.

I think the below may be true:

1. Allopathic system of medicine is primarily focussed on physical body and mind.
2. Ayurveda system of medicine is supposed to be focussing on physical body, mind, astral body, consciousness (am not talking about the sub-conscious mind) and chittam too.

Please note that there are other herb/plant based medicinal systems practiced around the other parts of the world - like in China-that are not covered in ayurveda. I think it helps if we integrate these knowledge bases into a unified ayurveda body of knowledge post proper due diligence to benefit the whole mankind, since we now consider ourselves as citizens of a global village!

Having said that, we can now look at the concept of Tri-doshas or 3-Malaises.

The idea of diseases in ayurveda is given below-

> *The cause of disease in Ayurveda is viewed as a lack of proper cellular function due to an excess or deficiency of vatta, pitta or kapha. Disease can also be caused by the presence of toxins.*

Diseases can also originate in the mind.

About Vatta, Pita and Kapha:

The 3-doshas does not mean or refer to vatta, pita and kapha. The 3-doshas are related to the imbalance that comes out of these 3 effects because dosha is a Sanskrit term which means – fault!
In the reference-1 site, the concept of Ojus, Tejas and Prana is also referred to while talking about Vatta, Pita and Kapha.

It is given as below:

> *Prana, Tejas and Ojas are subtle forms of Vatta, Pita and Kapha respectively and they have influence over the mind. The same factors that create 3-doshas can also disturb these mental forms.*
>
> *Ojas is responsible for immunity, Tejas is the heat and light energy of Ojas and Prana is the energy and strength that comes from Ojas after it has been kindled into Tejas.*
> *In the physical body, vatta is the subtle energy of movement, pitta the energy of digestion and metabolism, and kapha the energy that forms the body's structure.*

In general, it is believed that a health human body will have the vatta, pita and kapa properly balanced.
The supposed effects of a balanced and unbalanced vatta, pita and kapa effects are given below. Sometimes it is thought that some diseases manifest internally in astral body before showing up in physical body. Similarly, an injury from accident may cause external body injury and this may damage the astral body too. We do not have any data or corroborating evidence as of now.

STRANGER THAN FICTION

MENTAL FORMS	In-Balance supposedly creates or is responsible for:	Increased State / Out-of Balance supposedly creates/diminishes	Decreased State / Out-of Balance supposedly creates/diminishes
PRANA (relates to subtle form of Vatta, wind and sprit)	Strong immunity, life force, breath of life, supports functions like respiration, digestion, circulation, excretion etc.,	Hyperactivity, impulsivity, inattention, mood instability, outbursts, impatience, restlessness.	mental energy, enthusiasm and curiosity, inhibited receptivity and creativity, makes our mind and senses dull, lack of motivation, leads to overly conservative attitudes
TEJAS (relates to subtle form of Pita and Agni/ inner radiance or the fire of the mind)	Intelligence, reasoning, inquisitiveness, focus, self-discipline, perception and mental clarity. It also imparts glow or aura, lustre in eyes, courage and fearlessness	Doubt, anger, irritability, enmity, hard to please and short tempered.	Ability to distinguish, unwilling or unable to criticize, loses power to learn from experience, makes a person passive, easily influenced, and may lead to lack of purpose of life.
OJAS (relates to subtle form of Kapha, defined as primal vigour)	Mental strength, immunity, stability, endurance, patience, calmness, good memory, sustained concentration, happiness, content and bliss	Heaviness, dullness in mind, complacency and unwillingness to change, High OJAS is much less a problem than excess prana or tejas.	Fearful, weak and worried, lack of confidence, difficult concentrating, poor memory and mental fatigue

PHYSICAL FORMS	In-Balance supposedly creates or is responsible for:	Increased State / Out-of Balance supposedly creates/diminishes	Decreased State / Out-of Balance supposedly creates/diminishes
VATTA (Space and Air)	Governs breathing, blinking, muscle and tissue movement, pulsation of heart, and all movements in the cytoplasm and cell membranes.	Any disease in physical body due to imbalance, toxins, lifestyle and body type	Any disease in physical body due to imbalance, toxins, lifestyle and body type
PITA (fire and water)	Digestion, absorption, assimilation, nutrition, metabolism and body temperature.	Any disease in physical body due to imbalance, toxins, lifestyle and body type	Any disease in physical body due to imbalance, toxins, lifestyle and body type
KAPHA (earth and water)	Forms body structure – bones, muscles, tendons – and provides the "glue" that holds the cell together.	Any disease in physical body due to imbalance, toxins, lifestyle and body type	Any disease in physical body due to imbalance, toxins, lifestyle and body type

Thus, we can see the benefits of using allopathy and ayurveda in a synergistic way to treat people with diseases aiming for rapid recovery.

References:
1. Prana, Tejas and Ojas - Subtle Forms of Tridoshas (easyayurveda.com)
2. https://ayurveda.com/ayurveda-a-brief-introduction-and-guide/

29 THE VAK SYSTEM OR THE SYTEM OF SPEECH IN HUMANS

Vak is the system of speech present in human form. Just as Sankalpa - a pure thought, has to pass through several stages before it actually manifests as concrete creative force, the sabda also has to pass through several stages before it is fully audible at the gross level.

The below are wise sayings from Vedic era:
1. Tvam chatvari vak padani – (Thou art the very syllables of the four varieties of speech).
2. Ekam sat, vipra bahudha vadant – (Truth is one, the wise express it in many ways).

The below tables try to express the essence of the vak system of humans:

S. No	Degrees/Stages of Speech	Associated Chakra	Type of Body	Powered by	Quick Reference
1	PARAA	Mooladhara (or root chakra)	Transcendental	Adi Sakthi	Intent/Urge
2	PASHYANTI	Manipuraka (or navel chakra)	Karana – Causal body	Iccha Sakthi (The power of will)	Formation/assembly
3	MADHYAMA	Anahata (or heart chakra)	Sukshma- Astral Body	Jnana Sakthi (The power of knowledge)	Mind voice/thinking
4	VAIKHARI	Vishukthi (or throat chakra)	Sthula – Physical body – throat, mouth, teeth, and tongue	Kriya Sakthi (The power of action)	Spoken words

PARAA:
Paraa state manifests in prana.
Paraa vak is the sound beyond the perception of our senses. Paraa is the first stage of sound in its unmanifest stage and is the source of all root ideas and germ thoughts. On the stage of Paraa-vak there is no distinction between the object and the sound. Paraa means the highest or the farthest. Paraa vak is the sound beyond the perception of our senses. Paraa has to go undergo some transformations to manifest as a clear sound at a gross level. It is NOT possible to lie in Paraa state.

PASHYANTHI:
Pashyanthi state manifests in mind.
Pashyanthi literally means observing or seeing oneself. Here sound is neither produced nor heard by anatomical ears. It is more of a mental sound – not words yet – or in crude form. Pashyanthi observes and analyses her impending changes in the heart, throat and the tongue, where the sound finally attains audibility. Its frequency is supposedly less than the high frequency sound of Para Nada. It is difficult but still possible to lie in Pashyanthi.

MADHYAMA:
Madhyama state manifests in buddhi or intelligence.
Madhyama is mental speech, verbalized but unspoken, the internal monologue and dialogue. It also uses intelligence of the brain. It is said that the conversations in dream state (subconscious state) and the psychic conversations between spiritually advanced seers happen through this vak stage even though they are separated by distance.
The Anahata chakra is the domicile of internal sounds called Naada, which can be heard only by our subtle ear (not the anatomical ear). The sounds of Anahata chakra are not audible to the external ears. It is relatively easy to lie in the Madhyama state. Madhyama requires you to pause and think.
I think that certain processes of obtaining confessions from hardened criminals using drugs is the act of directly expressing Madhyama vak as Vaikhari vak.

VAIKHARI:
Pashyanthi state manifests in mouth and throat.
Vaikhari will use intelligence and therefore the constructs/grammar of the spoken language are considered when uttering the sound.

STRANGER THAN FICTION

The sound which has come all the way from the root chakra with the force of vayu, travels further upwards to the throat, mouth, teeth and tongue, to become an articulate sound, audible to the external ear. This is called Vaikhari. The vayu which helps to bring the sound from the Anahata chakra to the throat is called Vikhara and hence the last stage of sound which is the source of all that is spoken and heard at the grossest level, is the Vaikhari. It is easiest to lie in the Vaikhari state. Vaikhari requires you to pause and think too. You are using Vaikhari to read this chapter too!

References:
Sound - Hindupedia, the Hindu Encyclopedia
4 Degrees of Human Speech (yogainternational.com)
.

30 POSSIBLE MODES OF OPERATIONS OF THE GREAT DIVINE ENERGY

The great divine energy undergoes a constant flux because of the gazillions of experiences that various species undergoes. We covered about it in the chapter – The Experiences Throughput

In a possible hypothetical situation, we understood how the protagonist and its supporters, and an antagonist and its supporters of a creation-cycle may fight for domination. Such an epic fight generates a storm of experiences through-put that is evaluated by the divine energy to adjust its justice delivering mechanism, which is also a divine intelligent energy – called as the Karma. I humbly understood that the intelligence of the great divine energy is just not limited to the administration of the karmic engine – given its infinite potential.

We are glad that the protagonist and its supporters are winning and the law of karma (aka the value system of the universe used to deliver justice) is aligning with the good forces of the universe. This is leading to a stable state of bliss as the most preferred state of the divine intelligent energy out of all the infinite variations of the states.

How can the divine energy be expected to save the lessons learnt so that, in the present & future creation cycles, it is able to prevent the win of the antagonists who is trying to set a new diabolic value system?

The answer may lie in observing what surrounds us. As an example, to consider - disruptive technological advances like cloud computing, quantum computing, AI/ML simulations, IoT etc., – which introduces us to new limitless computing/networking and storage experiences not only help us –

humans, but I think in the larger context, these experiences may help the great divine energy to the concepts of storage, networking and processing. Earlier I talked about the potential hints left out in nature from the dance of creational forces of the great divine energy for humans (and other advanced species) to understand its true potential and nature. This reverse may also be true where the creational activities go through the storm of experiences and introduces new understandings to the great divine energy so that it can continue in its pursuit of excellence! While we are at it, it is my personal humble opinion that we also aid the antagonist forces by developing technologies that wreak havoc with our planet and that be-numbs our mind (e.g. GPT software that delegates human excellence to brute force computing!)

Think about the various experiences' throughput (besides the above technology related example) that manifests while in pursuit of excellence from activities that are happening all around in various species and we can understand the tremendous growth of intelligence that the divine energy harvests beyond its default infinite intelligence!!I can only think of kneeling before it and praying for redemption!

When things are not going correct, because of activities of individuals and groups, the great divine energy may let us know that through appropriate karmic reactions - e.g climate change, global warming, poverty, epidemic etc., We do not know which action caused what reaction or which group of actions caused which group of reactions! But, is it not that - we just have to focus on being a decent citizen of this universe as individuals and as members of various groups to solve all our problems including the problems of this planet?

When I think deep, I find that when the great divine energy is processing all the gazillions of experiences – each one in the same fervour, it is using enormous amount of energy to plan and deliver karma and for any other new creations, maintenance and dissolutions – all the while keeping a tab on the reasonable time frame of the context. This is an astounding and unparalleled feat. This must happen at all times so that the karmic engine keeps chugging, and the justice system works as expected.

But in some places/times of the universe the battle/war between the antagonists and the protagonists may be intense. Since these battles/wars have the capacity to hurt the value systems adopted by the good sources of the universe, a swift and extra intervention is required too. Hence, we can think about the additional modes of processing needed by the great divine energy besides the mode of infinite processing.

Hence, I think about the below 3 possible modes of processing of the great divine energy. I have attempted to list them below with a full understanding that, using its infinite intelligence, the great divine energy can spin up new modes that may be completely tangent to the human mind. Perhaps - only God knows certain things!

Please note that the divine energy can run in 3 or more modes simultaneously at any given time in any given context of the creation in this great universe.

Mode 1 – Mode of Infinite Processing:

Here the great divine energy tracks all the souls of the universe and administers the law of karma within a reasonable time frame. Essentially, for every ticking of time, it captures, processes. understands and plans the next executions that are required in each second of this universe's existence for all the souls.

Mode 2 – Mode of Special Processing:

Special attention may be needed in parts of universe where events are affecting large groups and systems of the universe. This span of depth of attention may be much more intense than the focus it keeps in Mode 1.

Mode 3 – Mode of Intense Focus:

Sometimes the great divine energy may need to focus much more deeply and intensely, especially when situations arise in a surprisingly fast manner introducing de-stabilization of the whole universe such as when the antagonist forces are trying to wreak havoc with the law of karma. In such cases, the great divine energy should also don the hat of the protagonist or any such good forces of the universe to understand the nature of the new evil so that it can quickly extinguish the emerging threat. The actions of the protagonist may also extinguish this threat, but the intervention of the great divine energy may give permanent resolution to re-occurring problems. We can possibly link this mode to the various good avatars that happen from time to time.

Thus, while operating in the 3 or more modes simultaneously, and by the countless activities and effects of the dances of creational forces, the great divine energy may identify new ways of dealing with old problems.

31 NETI-NETI (NEITHER THIS …NOR THAT…)

Net-Neti means – neither this …nor that.

Further elaboration on this can be found at -
https://en.wikipedia.org/wiki/Neti_neti

What does this mean to a focussed spiritual inquest?
It means that our inquest to know the divine energy fully will never end. In fact, in a different context we can only address that divine energy as a 'Divine Manifest', because it is wrong to conclude that it is an energy. We are just limited by our constraints imposed by the language and hence I settled for a term called 'Divine Energy'.

> Is it what is proposed in the Quantum Theories? – Neti-Neti
> Is it what is proposed as the god particle? – Neti-Neti
> Is it a central grand intelligence? – Neti-Neti
> Is God a person, a tangible entity? – Neti -Neti
> Is the theory of evolution real? - Neti-Neti

The scientific quest will never end if it is trying to be decisive. That is the beauty of this divine manifest - It will never allow the human (or any other species), in-pursuit of excellence to end.

I have always proposed that for an effect to take place there may be more than one reason, driving the karmic engine and balancing the karmas. Besides, the Great Divine Manifest may also complement by blessing the human endeavour/exertion in discovering new innovations, discoveries, inventions, ideations etc., Hence, I think, it is advisable to seek the blessing of this Divine Manifest before embarking on each of our endeavours.

There may be multiple truthful faiths in pursuit of excellence.

There may be multiple valid truthful theories & proofs of scientific body of knowledge discovered while in pursuit of excellence.

There may be multiple value systems of spiritual knowledge while in pursuit of excellence. That probably is why the principles of Advaita, Dwaitha and Vishishtadvaita - all will make sense in a way.

In the entire span of existence of this universe, and more specifically in the entire history of human existence, there would have been several spectacular awakening moments in the field of science, maths, philosophy, economics, administration, spirituality etc., where a deeply profound truth has been espoused. But what we know is that it is – Neti-Neti too! We will probably never know the full entirety of the Great Divine Manifest – but keep discovering it part by part in an infinitely inexhaustible quest for excellence. here.

32 NETI-NETI – PART 2- MORE ON THE CONCEPT OF ADHRSTA

Life, if we have to sum it up – It is about collecting experiences and committing the great ones (so that others can learn and experience from it) among them while we are in pursuit of excellence with a heart of gold which agrees to all the good value systems (collectively called as Krishna consciousness) of the universe.

In this grand drama, every single soul encounters the unknown in the background. We know that it is impossible to know all the unknowns on the day one or at any one point in life! We keep going!

This unknown has many vivid colours. Some of contexts to explain about this thought process is given below in an attempt to make the reader understand the concept of ADHRSTA (unforeseen/unobserved) correctly:

- A toddler has many Neti-Neti zones that is continuously cleared when it grows as a normal child. Parents, family, neighbourhood, communities, sensory perceptions etc., imparts new experiences and learnings to the toddler, and makes it a little more intelligent living unit each passing day.
  There are many unknowns, -yet life is not incomplete for the growing toddler!

- A common man knows that the series of numbers are infinite, and he does not wait for the infinity to be resolved before using the numbers for his everyday needs!
  There are many unknowns with the numbers, -yet life is not incomplete for the common man or the scientist or the

mathematician!

- I have written about how universe itself leaves clues about its 'unknowns/knowns' as objects and attributes in this grand spectacle called universe. A spiritualist may take this as clue and see himself as a model of the universe. As a human he knows, there are many knowns & unknowns, but he also knows that he is ably endowed with sensory organs and sprit of learning and exploring that will help him to cross the chasm of unknown.
  There are many unknowns, -yet life is not incomplete for the blossoming spiritualist!

- A student after graduating from the school, looks at the myriads of courses offered in the universities. He knows that he has the passion to excel in studies and learn each passing day. But he also knows that it is impossible to master all the courses in a given lifetime and he has wisdom to know that the life is expecting him to possibly graduate into living as a husband, father, grandfather and as a retired citizen before the grand au-revoir!
  There are many unknowns, -yet life is not incomplete for the maturing young man!

So, the concept of ADHRSTA (unforeseen/unobserved) s supported by the concept of Neti-Neti, is to be acknowledged and understood properly. It is not blindness per-se. It is a field of view that is not yet visible due to our known constraints such as space, dimensions and time.

Considering an individual on earth,
    Does he know why there is something instead of nothing?
    Does he know the purpose of life and why he is here in this universe?
    Do we have clear sight into how an individual must organize and explore in his life?
    Does he have the necessary knowledge on how to integrate himself into the various value systems that he must adopt into?
    Does he have adequate knowledge about the ways of working in the universe?
    Does he properly understand the role of science and spirituality to guide him in his life?
    ...

Such questions above tries to address the basic things needed in one's life. For that, I think we as an advanced civilization, have built a vast repository of knowledge and practices! We are not blocked by the things unknown in order to lead a decent life, while in-pursuit of excellence!

But when we look at the largely unknown subjects of the universe such as with the concepts of space, dimensions, time, energy, mass, quantum space, etc., we know we are looking at the ADHRSTA realms of those subject areas and manifestations! We also know that the cosmos may have its little secrets in its objects of creation to give us the right clues when are unable to move forward.

Similarly, as a spiritualist, we have the well-established concepts of thoughts and thinking, mind, intelligence, consciousness, tanmatras, impressions etc., yet we know we have much to cover. There are ADHRSTA realms in the mind/consciousness too.

Even God/protagonist may have his limits of wisdom and knowledge. But as long as he is able to function as the preserver of the universe and as the progenitor, for the betterment of all souls and to ensure that the right justice is upheld, he should also be comfortable with the idea of ADHRSTA! He is also probably willing to learn for other's experiences.

We need to keep moving and improving on each passing day. It is OK even if it is only a minor improvement from the previous day! We gain by self-exploration, established knowledge bodies, self-experiences and experiences of others. Even the protagonist may be doing this to dispel ADHRSTA as much as possible. For him, currently, establishing order and justice and promoting equality may be far more important on immediate terms than exploring the quantum or deep space realms or anything in-between! This is same as how a government prioritises public spending for security, education and health over
spending on military and space research.

33 THE EXPERIENCES THROUGHPUT – PART 2

I am adding my further thoughts on this topic in this Part 2.

Generally, it is safe to consider that the state of this universe is tending to be towards being in a blissful state. Sufferings have to be eliminated and replaced with content, happiness and bliss.

This is exactly the reason why, as individuals and groups we have to assume the role of the angels on earth, and promote content, happiness and bliss.

Consider the experiences throughput that can happen while we all prescribe to this idea and devise our living and purpose as per this expectation.

1. Increase in kindness and therefore leading to charity giving way to life altering experiences.
2. Increase in inquisitiveness and therefore leading to inventions/discoveries giving way to the expansion of bodies of knowledge.
3. Increase in self-discovery and therefore leading to self-awareness giving way to enlightenment.
4. Increase in pursuits-of-excellence and therefore leading to the knowing the purpose of living giving way to Mukthi!

We may be ordinary mortals today. By becoming an angel on earth for somebody or a group, you can possibly defeat the negative karma of the past and transcend the life-death cycle and take a higher and finer responsibility. If one-by-one, we start to change, our group takes a different outlook and when this tendency becomes contagious, this earthly realm possibly may become a heavenly realm!

While we are at it, we will have to be mindful about acquiring negative karmas that has the tendency to put us back into the life-death cycle. Some simple rules help while we gather our experiences:

1. Don't give up trying.
2. Be righteous when you pick your fight.
3. Be on the good side and be quality conscious while you are selecting a book,
   or a movie or an outing or a friend in your life etc.,
4. Always react to the event in a commensurate manner. If you have to react in an excessive manner, may you be guided by the goodness in your heart. If you have to act first, let you be guided by the abundance of goodness in
   your heart and the good value systems surrounding you.
5. Acknowledge that there is always a time for everything and everything occurring has one or more reasons.
6. Acknowledge that based on the past you have been placed in this current field of karmic energy and your acts now on will decide the new field of karmic energy in future.
7. Acknowledge with profound gratitude the existence of this Great Divine Energy that is making all of this happen in a grand cosmic scale.

34 WORKS OF MAYA ON OUR INNER FACULTIES

We read about the 3 imperfections in one of the previous chapters.

In this chapter, I am going to focus only on the second type of imperfection, called Maya- the maya that affects mental model and intelligence.

Usually the forces of the antagonist, deploys 3 strategies to create this, Maya. They are as follows:

1.   **Misinformation**: This is deliberately presenting misleading information for public or target's consumption. This is spreading falsities.
      Some of the examples are:
      - A journalist accepting payment and promoting a marketing pitch of a product or company in the name
      of establishing truth.
      - Lying about credentials to land an admission into a university or to land in a job.
      - Blatant lies of conmen with vile effects on unsuspecting people.
      - Recording falsities in history and spreading false bodies of knowledge.

2.   **Mal-Information**: These are half-truths.
      Some of the examples are:
      - Presenting only a part of the whole story to make the target or public believe in an alternate version of
      truth.
      -Altering the sequence of truth so that the emotions/understandings of unsuspecting people are raised in the very wrong moment or in a time and place that favours the perpetrators.
      - Joining an existing condition of suffering or elation to an unrelated

cause and effect.
- Making people believe in feelings that are not theirs as their own and that are created by use of unjust causes and theatrics.
- General gas-lighting techniques/social-engineering tactics
- Recording partial truths in history

3. **Hiding the truths**: In an attempt to elicit or supress a certain reaction or to change time aspect of the reactions, some forces of antagonists, use this technique – to hide the truth or to allow that to emerge in a choice of their time/space.

Some of the examples are:
- A defected/betraying war-load using the popular sentiments related to uprising to trigger a war while making sure that the armament is empty.
- Reports from front lines on losses making it look like wins for the consumption of the top leadership.

There may be other strategies/tactics used by the antagonist forces, but the above 3 gives a good coverage on their basic tactics. Our personal value systems play an important role in protecting us from these evil influences. Besides our sincere attempts to gain knowledge and intelligence will go a long way in improving our mental capabilities such as our abilities to co-relate information, our ability to probe to the desired depth and breadth and to strengthen our intuition etc.,

If we look at the state of our ancient literature, we can understand how a very determined force of the antagonist in the role of an historian, philosopher or statesman or such can weave a Maya that stays unremoved for thousands of years! May the forces of the protagonist win and remove this kind of Maya to spread truth and enlightenment.

The effort to collect and record knowledge is important and the process should be meticulous and formal. The people involved in this effort to create or enhance the knowledge bodies should be of the right calibre and thoroughly professional and their output should be vetted by relevant experts to the right extent. The related bodies of knowledge should then be dispensed through formal academic institutions.

35 CHITTAM OR THE IMPRESSIONS OF THE SOUL

Earlier, in one of my chapters, I quoted that all the learnings of the soul are never lost. They stay as impressions.

These impressions are different from the higher level of knowledge represented say for instance -in the books. The knowledge in the books, as presented as a sequence of words and sentences, is structurally and grammatically correct with the choicest of the words used. In the 'Chittam' they are stored in a different form that is understandable to the divine energy but ADHRST to us -humans.

In the 398th Thirukural, Sage Thiruvalluvar has presented the below couplet:

Orumaikkan thaan katra kalvi oruvartku
Ezhumaiyum emap pudaithu.

Which means – 'The learning acquired in one birth protects a man in the next seven.'

The acquired knowledge has to be stored in a local context for presenting it to the new skin of the soul post death. It is widely believed that it is stored in the soul itself and is called as 'Chittam'. I call 'Chittam' as loci of all root impressions.

What can be stored in the Chittam?

STRANGER THAN FICTION

I believe the below forms of knowledge are stored (storing not just the alphabets in library but all the prose and poetry and other knowledge representations too) in the 'Chittam'.

1. Knowledge acquired in pursuit of excellence in education
2. Outer world experiences as part of living
3. Sensual experiences
4. Experienced emotions/feelings
5. Experienced tanmatras
6. Any degrees of punishments endured by the souls as part of corrections imposed by the law of karma
7. Any degrees of blissful experiences endured by the souls as part of blessings
    from the law of karma
8. Some remnants of the process of death- which I believe is the root cause of
    fear of death in all living beings

We then have the below logical question.

How can this stored knowledge surface in the current birth?

1. As an intuition
2. As a sudden thought (please refer to my chapter on the vak system -
3. As an ability to learn fast, assimilate fast and in excelling in what was acquired in the past.
4. Feelings of familiarity and quick co-relations

With divine blessings, there may be other interventions that I do not know of yet.

But the below may not be stored in chittam but which may be easy to learn and master:

1. Full language capabilities - like the full grammar/style of English language
2. Full subject matter expertise -say like in the contents of a scholarly book.
3. Knowledge in fine arts
4. Professional knowledge, skills and practices

Reference:
398 - ஓரமைக்கண் தான்கற்ற கல்வி ஒருவற்கு எழுமையும் ஏமாப் புடைத்து. - Learning - Wealth - Thirukkural

36 WORKINGS OF THE CONSCIOUSNESS-MIND-BODY COMPLEX – PART 1

I thought it is time to clarify how the mind-body complex along with consciousness works. The Intelligence or Buddhi is related to the brain organ of the gross physical body (Annamayakoshana). The Mind or collection of thoughts is related to the chakras of the astral body (Manonmayakoshana). The Consciousness is what remains further inside – in the Pranamayakoshana, Vignanamayakoshana and Anandamayakoshana as tanmatras, impressions, intuitions, enlightenment etc.,

Let me write my understanding of certain terms before I try to explain the inner workings.

The terms are lined up from deep inside (Ahankara) to the outside (physical gross-body) basis:

1. **Ahankara:** This is the 'I' ness rooted in the soul. This is the strong basement upon which the super-structure of consciousness-mind-body complex is built.

2. **Chittam:** Locus of all impressions. It operates in both the modes – pull and push. Please refer to my other chapter -

> **Pull mode:** Sensory organs (both Karmendriyas and Gnanendriyas) in the gross body pulls thoughts from the chittam into the mind and then the intelligence (processing by brain with co-relations and context building), possibly commands an action out of it.

Push mode: The karmic store creates and raises thoughts into the mind. This can be aided by certain triggers released 'inside' by the sensory organs of the gross body.

For example, if a person is karmically destined to be in USA in a certain phase of life, a sensory act of seeing a bird in flight, may trigger a thought to buy a ticket to USA that raises up into the mind. Then the brain-based intelligence adds additional context related to schedule, visa proceedings, expenses, outcome etc.,

3. **Mind or Manas:** This is centred in the heart and related to the astral body (not gross body) and literally for an ordinary person, it is a storm of thoughts that constantly plays out in the mind (conscious or sub-conscious) because of constant pull and push functions mentioned above. Hence meditation can help such persons to calm down a stormy mind and therefore to have a calm external disposition. A stormy mind (say with repetitive same stressful thoughts) can lead to an agitated-stressful brain organ.

Conscious thoughts: These are thoughts that are actively processed by the brain. This can again be of 2 kinds – that which is accompanied by a mind-voice (also raised while reading a book), or that which just remains as a thought in working. In the vak system this occurs in the Madhyama phase.

Sub-conscious thoughts: These are the thoughts that has manifested in the Pashyanthi phase and briefly felt in the Madhyama phase in an abstract manner or in an out-of-focus manner. Psychologists have to curate these thoughts from Madhyama to understand the psyche of a person because it is difficult for an ordinary person to lie in the Para/Pashyanthi phases, but it is easy for that person to lie in the Madhyama/Vaikhari phases.

The above conscious or unconscious thoughts (tamil word for this is 'ennam') can come from brain-based-cache like memory system or Chittam-hard storage like impression-based system.

Please note that - at least some of the brain based superficial thoughts that originated in an outside-to-inside manner - can never reflect in Pashyanthi (or the stored tanmatra for that Pashyanthi) unless it is meant to be stored as an impression in the chittam. It depends on the intensity of the thought (or the physical experience that resulted in the thought) to get registered in the Chittam. I think this tanmatra of a powerful thought stored as an impression in the Chittam, and the 'Adhi sakthi' (dark energy) from the MAHAT is the Para form of the speech when this is raised again from stored impressions into the mind.

4. **Buddhi or Intelligence:** This is centred in the throat chakra and the brain part of the gross body plays a vital role in this function. This is where a thought is processed and additional information, additional contexts, plan of action etc., are decided. I think the current body of science related to biology has to enhance based on the new understandings coming from the consciousness-mind-body complex.

What thoughts are processed by the brain from the manas is decided by the value systems adopted by the host. Sometimes the actions expended from thoughts are challenged by the same value systems adopted by the host. This act of thinking (tamil word for this is 'sinthanai') in the brain can also be in a Conscious or Subconscious manner.

5. **Action by Karmendriyas/ Gnanendriyas:** Based on the finalized thoughts, commands are issued by brain to the Karmendriyas to either turn or walk or take or speak or excrete or copulate. The brain can also issue commands to the Gnanendriyas to smell (to process the smell entering the nose) or taste (to taste the food placed on the tongue) or see (followed by processing of the sight) or touch (to feel the temperature) or to hear (to focus on a particular feeble sound).

The actions in the brackets above are the follow-up actions of the brain!

Please note that these Gnanendriyas based action can be conscious or subconscious. Sometimes the Karmendriyas based action can also be subconscious (like in driving).

To put everything in the perspective let us recap the above concepts through a simple exercise. This time we will revisit the above concepts through an earthly example in an outside-to-inside manner.
Let us say Mr. X is walking along a downtown street.
1. His eye sees a Red-Velvet cake.
2. His brain picks up the information and by co-relations, it immediately adds some context – like – 'It looks good!', 'It looks hygiene' etc.,), Here, I believe in the modern science which talks about a cache memory system operating out of the brain organ. The immediate reactions may be coming

from this cache system. Imagine brain-based memory as a 'cache memory system' and the 'Chittam based impression' as a 'hard drive storage system').
3.   Now because of the thought flux, some thoughts based on additional but related contexts are elevated into the mind from the Chittam. As an example, these can be the below ones:
-   Conscious thoughts: About 'his age', 'his heath', 'his calorie adds' etc.,
-   Subconscious thoughts: About 'his scare on the last visit to the clinic', 'his deceased wife likes it too', etc.,
4.   Let us say, there is a + ve karmic load on Mr.X at this juncture in his life. So, one of the +ve karma is related to the 'joy' of moving to a higher position with higher remuneration' that further leads to a multitude of pleasant experiences. It is waiting to materialize based upon a trigger event.
5.   Mr. X's brain quickly analysis all pros and cons and decides to intake the Red-Velvet cake into the gross body.
6.   Mr. X's brain orders his feet to walk towards the bakery, orders his hands to pick up his wallet, and certain subconscious thoughts triggers his light salivation at the thought of eating this delicacy and so on. Thus the Red-Velvet is purchased and eaten.
7.   The Law of Karma may decide this action of soulful eating to be the trigger and arranges certain happy sequences of events to happen in Mr. X's life.

Consider- a normal person who was immersed in earthly activities in the past, and at the time of retirement, say, he turns spiritual and seeks peace and becomes a recluse. His life is then considered to be consisting of 2 grand phases   -   Evolution   and   Involution.
Evolution: This is when he goes through the first 3 phases of the 'asrama' dharma. This is heavily dominated by physical activities.
Involution - This is when he goes through the last 2 stages of the 'asrama' dharma. This is heavily oriented towards mental/meditational activities.

While it is possible that a single life may contain remnants of both evolution and involution, It is also possible that a soul's progression from being in evolution and then further into involution may span several births. To give a very crude example, a soul starting as a fish can evolve successfully by birthing into higher organisms in multiple births before it takes the human form (as a great guru or rishi) and attains mukthi. Probably, I will write more about evolution and involution as it applies to a soul's journey later. For now, it is good to know that the 'asrama' dharma talks about this concept in a single human's life.

37 WORKINGS OF THE CONSCIOUSNESS-MIND-BODY COMPLEX – PART 2

Our objectives to excel as humans, if simplified and distilled, will become the below 2 –

1. Be good at heart and
2. Whatever you do, be in pursuit of excellence and in every passing day, build your knowledge and intelligence and if possible, at least occasionally, commit great experiences.

The experiences that a human goes through -can be one of the 3 possible states- grouped as tri-gunas – Sattva, Rajo and Tamas. Each of these states will generate its own

1. Physical effects
2. Mental Thoughts
3. Soul Impressions

Sattvic experiences does good to body, mind and soul. Rajo experiences create action and sense of purpose/pursuit and challenges status quo. Tamasic experiences retards the progression of a soul. Based on the intensity of these experiences and the related thoughts, impressions are created in the soul which may drive the destiny of the soul eventually.

It helps if a person has accepted several layered virtuous value systems. Because of a series of good, layered value systems the below may happen:

1. PHYSICAL EFFECTS: An accepted/well-integrated value system may give directions to the host on what to smell, what to taste, what to see, what

to touch and what to hear. Further, it may help him decide on where to go, what to take/accept, what to speak etc., Thus the physical effects are filtered by the adopted value systems into manifesting externally or to get stored internally in the impressions of the soul.

2.   MENTAL THOUGHTS: Similarly, an accepted/well-integrated value system may give directions to the host on whom to accept as a Guru, which knowledge base to build, which profession to take or to choose hobbies and habits.

3.   SOUL IMPRESSIONS: Further, prolonged sattvic experiences like kundalini practices (as part of Kriya/Raja yoga practices), deep professional mastery/acumen (as part of Karma yoga practices), meditations/Bhakthi/Bhajans (as part of Bhakthi yoga) and passion to acquire soul enriching knowledge (as part of Gnana yoga practices) – can lead to a super stoic state where the in-built/strengthened value systems can prevent the storage of disturbing tamasic experiences into the soul impressions. Thus, a super soul is born. These super souls might have evolved/involuted over time which means, they may be storing past tamasic experiences as impressions in their soul. These super souls can supress any such impressions from emerging or they can even expel it from their store house of impressions as part of purifying their souls.

We know from part -1 that the brain-based cache memory storage system and Chittam based hard memory storage system – both throw up conscious and subconscious thoughts into the manas and we know that few of them will get selected to be processed in the buddhi as conscious and subconscious acts of thinking.

Consider, 2 people both eating and watching television. Based on their adopted value systems, for one person the observing the television becomes a primary activity and related thoughts become the conscious thoughts, and the act of eating becomes a secondary activity with its own subconscious thoughts. For the other person with a different adopted value system, his primary activity and conscious thought may be set on the food and his secondary activity and subconscious thought setting may happen on watching the television!

Here we should also be aware that a stoic/seasoned super soul (say a protagonist) may have several strong built-in good value systems that operate in the conscious/subconscious layers of the mind/buddhi. And he may be having several conscious/subconscious thoughts all at once in a related flux in his Consciousness-Mind-Body complex that for the ordinary people it may be impossible to know his intent or next action by merely observing this flux of thoughts!

Now, I sincerely believe that an accepted/well-integrated value system may control what gets thrown into the mind (manas) as well as into the intelligence (buddhi). Which means the right value systems can operate in both conscious or sub-conscious manner. After all, these value system principles also operate like a meta-level conscious/sub-conscious thought!

These meta-level conscious/sub-conscious thoughts need great deal of reinforcements (possibly by all 4 margas or paths – Kriya yoga, Karma yoga, Bhakthi yoga and Gnana yoga) to become a guiding meta-level principled thought system that can help vacate tamasic thoughts (and allow the desired rajasic thoughts) in the system before it takes root.

Based on what we experience in our total consciousness-mind-body system, imbalances may get created in the physical and astral bodies creating a tamasic base for various kinds of mental and physical diseases to form.

So the foundational principle for being in a good state of health means to avoid tamasic experiences totally and to have rajasic experiences with good control and to binge on sattvic experiences.

STRANGER THAN FICTION

In order to avoid the confusion that may happen, I recommend the below:
- Use the terms - 'conscious'/'subconscious' in modern science literature as before.
- When referring to the 3 deep layers, use 'Chittam' as it is by incorporating this Tamil word in English.

39 THE 3-TYPES OF DEATHS

At least among the humans, I think there are 3 major types of deaths that can manifest for an individual.

They are:

1. Internally Induced Death:

Post the previous death (of any type), the karmic engine recalculates the karma for the soul and decides upon a particular skin and stage. Please remember that at this point of entry to the womb, the Karmic engine may have done the below:

· Decide a suitable skin/stage for the next birth of the soul and allocate the karmic load to be expended by the soul for that skin/stage. It is prudent to expect that the Karmic engine would make the soul expend its most significant loads to be emptied first. This Karmic load that is attached to this skin/stage, that is expected to be expended in this birth-death cycle, is called **Prarabdha Karma**.

· The remining karmic load (+ ve or - ve) if any, will be set in the Karmic account of the soul that is expected to be expended later. This Karma is called **Sanchita Karma**.

It is possible that because of the choices made by the soul or by divine intervention in the current skin/stage, some of the Sanchita Karma can also be released in the current birth-death cycle.

It is possible that because of the choices made by the soul in the current skin/stage, some of the new Karmas may also be added to the Karmic account of the soul. This new Karma in the new skin/stage is called **Sanciyamana Karma**.

It is possible that, even some of the Sanciyamana Karma may get released in the current skin/stage phase, due to the soul's actions or divine intervention.

Together, the Sanchita and Sanciyamana Karmas are called **Anarabdha Karma**.

Whatever is the karmic load for that birth-death cycle, at the end of the expending, the below happens:

- The time, by now, may have stared the desolation of the gross physical body (old age) and the ghost body (if the being is ignorant) of the soul.
- As the final karmic load (as set at the birth or as modified during the birth-death cycle) of the soul is expended, the karmic engine stops feeding the dark energy from MAHAT into the consciousness.
- Panchapranas are withdrawn too.
- Physical death happens to the current being however good the health of the gross body is.

In my opinion, this is the best form of death for a health-conscious human, because there is definitely dignity in death as the person is possibly healthily living independently till the last moment. So, it is important that, we keep our good health in our mind always and change our food habits and lifestyle suitably as we age.

Good actions and certain faith based and meditative spiritual practices can definitely help in reducing the store of negative karma and suffering. And certain sacraments like chanting, fasting, personal sacrifices (like giving up meat eating) can also help in healing the soul.
I also firmly believe that, if the divine energy foresees benefit to the mankind/other species, it may intervene and extend the life of a good soul. After all, the collective goal of all the souls is to realise the blissful state of the divine energy and to get to the awakening moment at which it's consciousness cries out of joy that- 'I am God'!

2. Externally Induced Death:

This kind of death may happen due to capital punishments, sabotage operations, accidents or sudden adverse health conditions. Several reasons can be behind this event, and we cannot possibly know the exact reasons as the inner workings of the Karmic engine remains **ADHRST** (unseen) to us.

But I think some of the reasons for this sudden death event may be the below ones:

- Unacceptable accumulation of negative group Karma in a certain place/time in a given context.
- The souls karmic account being adjusted (as mentioned in the 1st point) due to its current actions or divine intervention.
- Capital punishments meted out to certain souls due to the workings of the criminal justice systems. (I do not believe that Karmic load is planned with an execution by criminal justice system in mind, as the related criminal actions by the perpetrator violate one or more value systems that the karmic engine may regard in its workings and hence cannot be a pre-planned set of actions)
- Abuse of the current gross physical body by overindulgence and poor lifestyle.
- I think that, rarely, sometimes, certain deaths happen due to cyclical nature of applying karma with retribution. Sometimes, due to the nature of karma, some souls are made to meet this type of death too.

The sudden deaths happening in this type of dying, results in the condition where the gross body is dead but the full karmic load (possibly set at birth and corrected during the birth-death cycle) is not fully expended. Hence the ghost/astral body may live a little longer before the desolation is complete.

I believe that the existence as a astral-only ghost body is a state of suffering since,
- it is just a transient state not capable of performing any useful karma and
- it is not possible to experience even the basic functions like thinking, eating, sleeping and having sex.

3. Suicidal Death:

This is the worst kind of death a soul can suffer. As neither the full karmic load is expended, nor it relives the soul from the current suffering. Besides, I believe that, if any soul commits suicide, it may possibly live longer in its astral body which is again a state of suffering.

I also believe that the quality of living and death is decided by the soul's thoughts/actions in the current life. So, one should be good at heart and be in pursuit of excellence and in the modern economic setting, should be mindful about where his source of money is coming from. Also, the karmic engine is believed to reverse the role of souls sometimes to expend karmas. We should, therefore live decently as much as possible and not harm any living beings by thought or deed. We should also be mindful about our group affiliations and the group karma that is incurred.

Hence, we should have a fresh look at our meat consumption habits too and I, for one, strongly recommend, stopping of mechanical mass culling (automated means of killing) of animals/birds meant to feed the meat industry. We, as humans, should not have rampant consumerism habits in meat consumption and indulge in mindless/excessive (say, by using monstrous fishing trawlers) killing and wastage.

Another important take away, is that I believe that the great divine energy always plans for the 1st type of death, for all souls when they start a new life. (for argument's sake I am ignoring the effects of manifested evil designed by the antagonist to keep the idea simple and clear) Being a benevolent blissful energy, how can we expect the other 2 types of deaths (2 & 3) to be part of the plan to release the soul in a new womb? Then comes the logical question on the violence that we see in this world. I believe that the other 2 types of deaths (2 & 3) are due to either group karma or self-inflicted or both.

If the reason is group karma, the following holds true:
1. The value systems adopted by the group is not good. (implementation faults) and/or
2. The justice system adopted by the group is either weak or ineffective or both (enforcement faults)
3. The group, to which the individual belongs is not fair in treating its individuals (participation and integration related faults)

4. More individuals in the group are not aligned with the good value systems at various levels. (identity faults)

If the reason is self-inflicted, the following holds true:

1. The personal value system (or lack of it) of the individual is weak or corrupted.
2. If the individual's value system is strong, perhaps it diabolical and/or does not accept any other value systems and hence the individual becomes vulnerable to take wrongful decisions.
3. The group, to which the individual belongs is not fair in treating its individuals and the group is perhaps providing convenient stages for confrontation (like a crime filled neighbourhood activities)

Hence, by the above groups of reasons, other types of death (2 & 3) happen which may be - death by violent confrontation, death by state, death by unhealthy lifestyle, death by self-harm etc.,

As mentioned before, I also think that, rarely, sometimes, certain deaths happen due to cyclical nature of applying karma with retribution.

Then, finally we are aware that, humans and certain wild animals/birds kill for food and evil always plans for mayhem. and death. These deaths do not fall under the 3 types mentioned above. I vaguely remember that the dharma of wild animals is blessed by nature and hence they will not incur karma when killing for food.

40 ABOUT THE LAYERS OF THE DIVINE ENERGY

We saw in my earlier chapters on how the 'divine'/'blissful' energy came to be referred as such. I was able to express my thoughts on the common denominator that exists between the structure of the universe and the structure of the human in other chapters.

I expressed my thoughts that the nature of this true infinite manifest (since the use of the term 'energy' in itself is limiting) can never be completely explained. We will come across the concept of 'ADHRSTA' or the unseen if we attempt so. As we cross frontiers after frontiers in the science, we understood how the concept of 'ADHRSTA' is staring at us at every breakthrough!

Since we are not able to define the vast, intelligent, infinite manifest as anything but 'GOD' , let us look at the manifested universe and try to understand the tangible portion of this divine energy!

We can term this divine manifest as the 'ADI SAKTHI' or the 'PARASHAKTHI'. ADI means 'root' and Parashakti translates as "The Eternally Limitless Power". In my opinion, this primordial continuum consists of, but not limited (Since we come across the concept of 'ADHRSTA) to – infinite energy and infinite types of energies in infinite range of intensities, infinite intelligence and infinite types of intelligence in infinite range of intensities and infinite feelings/emotions and infinite types of feelings/emotions in infinite range of intensities. But, I believe that with respect to the last factor, the predominant feeling/emotion is bliss as explained earlier. Thus, I believe that the divine energy is not only infinite and intelligent, it is very much alive and kicking! Look at the variety of species and Prakruti, just on earth - I see them all as multitude of ways in which the divine energy is letting us know that it is alive!

For example, in the Vak system of the humans, the innermost (4th Layer) energy form of the speech is called 'Para' (intent/urge).
At this layer, there is no differentiation between Prakruthi and Soul-Body complex.

We have to depend on our mental faculties to understand the inner layers of this energy-mass continuum. Once this manifests in dimension-1, (a.k.a manifested universe), science is able to not only takeover this concept but also is able to direct this knowledge to the benefit of the lives on earth. Spiritualists on the contrary are not interested in dimension-1, but in the inner 4 layers of the Panchakoshanas.

Once MAHAT is formed in the process of the creation of this universe, the 1st derivative of the 'ADI SHAKTHI' is seen as permeated in this layer. There may be several other 1st derivatives of this energy. This energy at the MAHAT is termed as 'ICCHA SAKTHI' or the 'Energy of the will'. The concept of 'Dark Energy' in contemporary science comes close to this. Karmic energy repositories for groups and souls, intelligence related to the governance of this Universe etc., lies in this layer. Thus- 'ICCHA' meaning 'will', means – 'the will' of the intelligence deriving from this great dark energy and dark mass continuum (MAHAT) where all the created souls are seen embedded like a lattice.

For example, in the Vak system of the humans, the 3rd innermost-layer energy form of the speech is called 'Pashyanthi' (formation/assembly).
Thus 'ICCHA' Sakthi exists for both the Prakruthi and the Soul-Body complex.

The next layer of the universe laid over MAHAT is the Sukshma Universe where the ghost bodies of humans/Prakruthi exist. This Sukshma Universe is powered by the 'JNANA SAKHTHI' or the 'Power of Knowledge' which is the 2nd derivative of 'ADI SAKTHI'. There may be several other 2nd derivatives of this energy. Whose knowledge are we talking about? This is the knowledge of the Prakruthi which in turn is waiting to be explored by the science. When you consider the humans in this light, we may see a slight disconnect. A ghost of a dead man may have feelings but will not have intelligence (the act of thinking). Hence is it right to call this as 'JNANA SAKTHI'? The answer is that this is term used with reference to the Prakruti and not the human embedded in it. For a living human, whose ghost body and physical body, coexist, while the person is alive, this JNANA Sakthi is what is powering his 'act of thinking'. It is possible, that the ghost bodies of other living things in this dimension may have a different dimension-1 body/prakruthi in their context other than what we, humans have.

For example, in the Vak system of the humans, the 2nd innermost energy form of the speech is called 'Madhyama' (mind voice/act of thinking).
Thus 'JNANA' Sakthi exists for both the Prakruthi and the Soul-Body complex.

Finally, emerges the manifested universe. The 3rd derivative of the 'ADI SAKTHI' is called 'KRIYA SAKTHI'. 'Kriya' means – action. So, all the energy powered actions – visible/invisible can be attributed to this energy. All the other derivatives of this energy has been adequately explored by science and we have not stopped with our current understandings. Again, this is the 'KRIYA SAKTHI' of the Prakruti.

With respect to a human or a living thing, this Kriya Sakthi is primarily designed to be provided by the food that is eaten since some part of intelligence and karma has a play in this activity.

For example, in the Vak system of the humans, the manifested, expressed energy form of the speech is called 'Vaikhari' (Spoken words).
Thus 'KRIYA' Sakthi exists for both the Prakruthi and the Soul-Body complex.

Similar to the 4 layers of energy discussed above we can contemplate about the mass or the combined continuum. Perhaps the vacuum in space is limited only to this dimension!
Similar to the vak system, we, in our endeavour to understand this manifested universe, should explore the other principles that are currently in incomplete state.

41 ABOUT THE LAYERS OF THE DIVINE ENERGY – PART 2

This time, I want to create 2 additional perspectives – the energy layers as seen through the human design and the energy layers as seen through the Prakruti.

First let us consider the perspective as seen from the **PRAKRUTHI** or NATURE.

ADI SAKTHI – the deepest layer with uncountable ADRHSTA mysteries and phenomenon that is the root cause of the existence of this universe. This is perhaps the God itself.

ICCHA SAKTHI – This is the dark energy/dark matter – MAHAT matrix. The karmic forces of interactions and souls with impressions operate in this field. Most other 1st derivative forces from ADI SAKTHI along with tanmatras operate in this field and most of them are ADRHST to us as of now.

GNANA SAKTHI – This is the 2nd derivative forces from ADI SAKTHI. We commonly know this as the world of scientific phenomenon. The laws of science and the related forces operate in this field.

KRIYA SAKTHI – This is the 3rd derivative forces from ADI SAKTHI. We use the various scientific tools, instruments, machines etc., to harness the scientific principles that we have understood to generate various potential and kinetic energy formations.

STRANGER THAN FICTION

Next, let us consider the perspective as seen from a **HUMAN FORM** (since it supposed to be the most evolved of all the species in the universe).

ADI SAKTHI – No change from the above statements. In the Panchakoshanas Tatva as applicable to humans, this Sakthi belongs to the Anandamayakoshana.

ICCHA SAKTHI – As specified in the previous chapter, this is the field in which the will power of the humans operate. It is believed that mantras, penances, yagnas and other sacraments can be used by human forms to harness the energy from MAHAT as some sort of ICCHA SAKTHI to achieve some degree of capabilities with which some 'desirable' effects can be achieved. In the Panchakoshanas Tatva as applicable to humans, this Sakthi belongs to the Vignanamayakoshana and Pranamayakoshana. Hence this body of knowledge related to ICCHA SAKTHI is purely in the realm of the religious/spiritual bodies.

GNANA SAKTHI – This is primarily the energy field attributed to the knowledge present in humans. On one hand, this can be used to understand the potency of various mantras, penances, yagnas and other sacraments and be used for practice and perfection. Hence this part of the body of knowledge related to GNANA SAKTHI is purely in the realm of the religious/spiritual bodies. This SAKTHI in humans is dependent on the strength of the ICCHA SAKTHI present in humans. The strength of ICCA SAKTHI in a person decides whether that person is brilliant or dull.

On the other hand, a normal human- even those not attributed to religious/spiritual bodies exercise this SAKTHI to understand the ADI, ICCHA, GNANA, KRIYA SAKTHIs as applicable to the Prakruti or nature and use it in his daily life. Hence this part of the body of knowledge related to GNANA SAKTHI is purely in the realm of Science. Also, all other knowledges related to formal education, soft-skills training, other specialist physical training etc can be attributed to this SAKTHI in the humans.

In the Panchakoshanas Tatva as applicable to humans, this Sakthi belongs to the Manonmayakoshana. In a way, the mind and other inner faculties are considered by some scriptures as part of this manifested universe!

KRIYA SAKTHI – This is the action part of the human body and the thinking part of the human body and hence this clearly belongs to the Annamayakoshana.

42 THE ESSENTIAL DIVINE BLESSING

Adi Sakthi is something primordial and predominant that we can never understand that fully in human form or in any other form except possibly when attaining mukthi (where a person becomes part of the divine energy itself).

When it comes to Iccha Sakthi or the power of will, I presume that many great clashes between good and evil in both evolution and involution phases has clearly established whose Iccha Sakthi has prevailed which also resulted in a just and sound value system being adopted by the Law of Karma. If we observe the studies on the evolution of mankind since pre-historic times, the focus on science happened, possibly several centuries after we started recording history! The ideas about group entities like nation, civilization, collective benefits, wars over justice, honour etc., is possibly the dawn of the involution phase in the clash between good and evil. I shake at the thought of what might have happened in the evolution phase in the war of good vs evil.

I believe that the Gnana Sakthi is a derivative of Adi Shakthi and Iccha Shakthi (I also count Iccha Sakthi here because of the possible continuous improvements based on past understandings) and is designed and controlled by the prevailing Iccha Sakthis into many manifestations. The Kriya Sakthi is a derivative of Adi Sakthi, Iccha Sakthi and Gnana Sakthi (I also count Gnana Sakthi here because of the possible continuous improvements based on past understandings) and is designed and controlled by the Gnana Sakthis into many manifestations. I presume that based on the string of victories in the past, by the protagonist's side, at least at the Iccha and Gnana sakthi levels, the principles are still mostly acting under the protagonist's ideals/principles (value systems) and I think it is prudent to believe that the antagonist's ideals/principles (value systems) are severely degraded or non-existing. I also believe that science as a body of knowledge started to develop only after the protagonist forces reached this stage and gained significantly and established their ideals/principles.

Thus, whatever is the new disruptive technology that is happening, I believe that there is an implicit blessing by the divine energy to let it happen. If you want to be a successful scientist who wants to invent or discover, I suggest you align yourself with the protagonist's good forces, heart and soul, and seek the divine blessing in ways convenient to you, before you venture and take your first steps.

So, when I see a news bit somewhere that there are people who break coconuts and pray before the launch of a ship or a rocket, I tend to not criticize or laugh at it. Probably, they are seeking divine blessing for their undertaking in ways that they are comfortable with! Who knows – it may increase their rate of success. Hence, I never underestimate or criticize the power of religious rituals/observances/sacraments coming from a good faithful heart. I believe that decent humans do not do that.

Let us take a look at another important aspect of human evolution where the divine blessing manifested either implicitly or explicitly. It is about the development of languages itself.

In the primordial times when there was war between good and evil, and when there were no languages prevailing, the emotions/feelings played a big role in conveying the intentions (imagine a picture of wild animals fighting). In order to reduce the emotions and feelings to a common denominator, so that it can be put through the process of thinking, the idea of spoken (later written) languages became inevitable. Thus, rational thinking powered by one or many languages became an essential tool to understand and adopt the best serving value systems. The protagonist's value systems, thus established, later evolved into the value systems adopted by the Law of Karma.

When the divine blessing was bestowed on some of the languages, those languages, perhaps became adept in addressing several other secondary but nevertheless important functions like describing the ways of working of the universe or to develop prayers, arts and science. Thus, when I see unregulated developments in the scientific world such as in genetic engineering or in the use of AI or in any new developments (leading to undesirable effects like rampant consumerism, piling up of debris of electronic cigars in plastic containers, piling up of electronic debris, floating satellite debris, spread of dangerous use of technologies like internet, etc), I think we are very far away from divine intentions.

It is high time we understand and integrate this divine manifestation into our ways of living so that we all benefit from the new understanding. I sometimes think that currently, scientists are more comfortable to embrace established scientific ethos/principles when they abandon their spiritual side and claim to be a 100% rationality-oriented thinking individual. I hope, I am able to make them see what they are not seeing till now.

So, I think, when we seek divine blessing, lots of unseen good manifestations happen, to influence the goal, design, intention, use etc.,

43 FOOD - AS A SATTVIC CONSTITUENT

As a seeker, I wanted my readers to be aware of the inputs to their system. These inputs may be food, friendships, relationships, other interactions, media, books, music, movies, TV etc.,

Maintain top quality in all your inputs to develop not just intelligence and knowledge but also more sensitivity and humaneness which I think are fundamental traits of a good spiritual person.

I want to write about the 'FOOD' as an input to my system. I am from India and hence I may be a bit biased in my food related writings since I come under the influence of food culture of India. But the idea is to take the learnings and interpret it in your own context.

The first thing I want to emphasise is the idea of the 'STAPLE FOOD'. Wikipedia definition for the term staple food is –

> '*A **staple food**, **food staple***, or simply ***staple***, *is a food that is eaten often and in such quantities that it constitutes a dominant portion of a standard diet for an individual or a population group.*'

Let us consider the staple foods of India:
- Wheat
- Rice
- Pulses (such as chana or Bengal Gram)
- Lentils (dal)
- Whole-wheat flour (atta)
- Pearl millet (bājra)

STRANGER THAN FICTION

- Vegetables
- Dairy products
- Spices

8 out of 9 of the above staple food is plant based.

Let us consider the staple foods of a standard western economy:
In Western Europe the main staples in the average diet are animal products (33 percent), cereals (including wheat and corn) (26 percent), and roots and tubers (including potatoes and yams) (4 percent).

From the 1st link, I extract the below text:
> *Just 15 plant crops provide 90 percent of the world's food energy (exclusive of meat), with rice, maize and wheat comprising 2/3 of human food consumption. These three are the staples of about 80 percent of the world population, and rice feeds almost half of humanity.*

Though a vegetarian, I am not an avid proponent who asks people to avoid meat eating. I think meat-eating is an experience that many people enjoy. But if you want to excel as a spiritual person, at least take some steps to reduce meat consumption.

To this effect, the definition of the STAPLE FOOD should be changed after due consultations with experts representing different cultures of the earth.
I, for one, believe that STAPLE FOODS are PLANT-BASED primary foods that are consumed in large quantities. Other foods like meat, and other animal produces are only supplementary to the primary staple foods.

I can go through the Indian cuisine a bit to explain this concept.

Primary Staple Food:
RICE: I am quoting from the 3rd reference.
> *Today we still have about 6,000 different varieties of Rice in India, but environmentalists estimate that we have lost tens of thousands of indigenous Rice varieties in the last 40 years. Nevertheless, the variety of Indian Rice varieties is the highest globally.*

WHEAT: I am quoting from the 4th reference:
> *To cater the need of each agro-climatic condition and cultural conditions, around 294 varieties of wheat have been released and notified by the Central Sub-Committee on Crop Standards, Notification and Release of Varieties for Agricultural Crops (CVRC). Similarly, around 154 wheat*

> *varieties released by the State Varietal Release Committee (SVRC) were notified under section 5 of Seeds Act, 1966. So far, 378 bread wheat varieties, 59 durum wheat and 7 dicoccum wheat beside 4 triticale varieties have been notified (Table 1.3).*

So, we are essentially counting about 448 varieties of wheat.

Similarly, we have an astonishing number of varieties in all the staple foods that are plant based in India including protein rich pulses, lentils and vegetables!

Coupled with a deep immersion in spiritual realm as guided by their ancient masters/gurus, the food culture has evolved to be refined and sophisticated. And by the way, India has the highest number of vegetarians among its population.

I am quoting from the 5th reference:

> *The vast majority of Indian adults (81%) follow some restrictions on meat in their diet, including refraining from eating certain meats, not eating meat on certain days, or both. However, most Indians do not abstain from meat altogether – only **39%** of Indian adults describe themselves as "vegetarian," according to a new Pew Research Center survey.*

The full course is laid out something like this – (Please refer to the 7th reference.)

Main Course in a typical lunch (Breakfast and dinner may contain a host of many other varieties called 'tiffin varieties' - please refer to links below for more information):

Rice based (boiled white rice, red rice, flavoured biryani rice etc.,) (Many more varieties) along with any currys/food-potions as given below in detail.
Request for additional portions of boiled rice as necessary when the lunch is in progress. Rice is mixed with the varies curries/food-potions for consumption.

Wheat based (roti, chapati, naan etc.,) (Many more varieties)
Request for additional portions of above breads when lunch is in progress. The breads are teared and dipped in curries for consumption.

Curry:
Vegetarian: Any pulses/lentils based, or vegetable based (see below)
Non-Vegetarian: Any meat based but primarily they are chicken, sheep, goat, fish and some sea foods. (Please refer to links about Indian Cuisine to know the types of meats consumed)

Beside the main dish and curries, Vegetables, eggs, desserts, other food-adjuncts are also present. Sometimes mango (1500 varieties!) and banana (15 – 20 commercial varieties and many more!) are also included in the full course meal.

I quote the below from a popular portal given in the 9th reference.

A typical South Indian lunch might include:

- **Rice**: *The staple of the meal, often served with ghee (clarified butter).*
- **Sambar**: *A lentil-based stew with vegetables and tamarind.*
- **Rasam**: *A tangy, spicy soup.*
- **Poriyal**: *Stir-fried vegetables with spices.*
- **Kootu**: *A thick stew made with vegetables and lentils.*

In South Indian cuisine, a typical meal is designed to balance six distinct Flavors: sweet, salty, bitter, sour, astringent, and spicy. This balance is believed to promote overall health and well-being. Here's how these Flavors are typically realized in a South Indian lunch:

1. **Sweet**: *This flavour is often represented by dishes like* **payasam** *(a sweet pudding made with rice or lentils, milk, and jaggery) or* **banana** *slices served at the end of the meal.*
2. **Salty**: *Saltiness is a fundamental flavour in most dishes, but it is particularly prominent in* **pickles** *and* **papad** *(crispy lentil wafers).*
3. **Bitter**: *Bitter Flavour are usually introduced through vegetables like* **bitter gourd** *(karela) or dishes like* **neem flower rasam**.
4. **Sour**: *Sourness is a key component in dishes like* **sambar** *(a lentil-based vegetable stew with tamarind) and* **rasam** *(a tangy soup made with tamarind or tomatoes).*
5. **Astringent**: *This flavour is often found in* **legumes** *and* **lentils**, *such as in* **dal** *(lentil curry) or* **kootu** *(a vegetable and lentil stew).*
6. **Spicy**: *Spiciness is a hallmark of South Indian cuisine, with dishes like* **spicy chutneys, curries,** *and* **poriyal** *(stir-fried vegetables with spices).*

Taste Name	Action	Sources
English: Sweet **Tamil:** Inippu	Soothing, nourishing, energising and satisfying **Emotion : Happiness**	Milk, Fruits, Cereals, Jaggery
English: Sour **Tamil:** Pulippu	Increases Appetite, helps digestion and produces Saliva **Emotion : Disgust**	Yogurt, Fermented food, citrus fruits, tamarind
English: Salty **Tamil:** Oovaruppu	Increases water intake, gives skin a glow and cures stiffness **Emotion : Fear**	Salts
English: Pungent **Tamil:** Kaarppu	Increases blood circulation, kills worm in digestive tracts, purifies mouth **Emotion : Anger**	Pepper, chilly, ginger and onions
English: Bitter **Tamil:** Kasappu	Blood purifier, firms the skin and antidote to poison **Emotion : Sorrow**	Dark green leaves, coffee, tea, bitter gourd, olives, neem flower
English: Astringent **Tamil:** Thuvarppu	Aids digestion, blood purifier **Emotion : Surprise**	Pomegranates, turmeric, broccoli, cauliflower, betel leaf

*The sources given above are raw foods. we have to also consider the cooked foods that is coming out of these raw foods.

A typical Indian full course meal covers all the 6 types of tastes deriving from the concept that I mentioned earlier in one of my chapters – 'Food as Medicine'.

The 6 basic flavours identified by Indian food cuisine are – Sweet, Sour, Salty, Pungent, Bitter, and Astringent. It is widely believed that a balanced intake of these 6 flavours daily will have a medicinal effect on the whole body.

All the regional variants of cuisines of India tries to present these 6 flavours in a full course meal or by daily intakes by properly deploying the food-aids like spices, onions, ginger, turmeric, asafoetida, garlic, shallots, other condiments, etc., and other composite ingredients like curry/masala powders.

May be, food-experts can take a deep look into the Indian Cuisine and understand the philosophies behind it and how it is mentioned in Ayurveda. Then steps should be taken to spread the various staple foods seen in India but not seen anywhere. Together with less meat consumption, a high quality food input can do wonders to your body and soul!

References:

1. Staple food - Wikipedia
2. Indian cuisine - Wikipedia
3. Top Varieties of Rice in India: Hybrid, Types, and Production States (agrifarming.in)
4. cover.cdr (aicrpwheatbarleyicar.in)
5. In India, 81% limit meat in diet and 39% say they are vegetarian | Pew Research Centre
6. Banana varieties, Production, and season in India. | ABC Fruits
   1. South Indian Full Meals | Lunch Menu For Guests | Thalai Vazhai Ilai Virundhu | Chitra's Food Book (chitrasfoodbook.com)
   2. South Indian Lunch Recipes | What South Indian's have for lunch | (tarladalal.com)
   3. Six tastes of Food | Arusuvai Unnavu | Nithya's Nalabagam (nithyasnalabagam.com)

PART C

SOME ECONOMICS FOR SPRITUALISTS

STRANGER THAN FICTION

1 AN ALTERNATE VIEW ON ECONOMICS

The movement of tectonic plates is engineered by the divine force but drawing of the borders of the country was/is-being done by humans. So the division of natural resources by movement of tectonic plates may point us to something more fundamental. In a large space like planet earth, if the divine force has envisaged the creation of several species (which is perfected by evolutionary forces) in some geography, it might have already planned for the provisioning of the resources needed to support all of the species in that geography. All species are in harmony with nature and are using these resources in a sustainable way except for one - Humans.

I am going to assume (!) that humans are also, a responsible species and that they understand the needs of the co-habitants of this planet earth, before I write about their economic activities. If the economist of a particular country has to plan for the next 100 years (I believe in ideating long term strategies for the growth of a large economic-activities entity like a country irrespective of its election cycles), then he/she should first take stock of as-is conditions and then focus on the geography in which his country is situated in. He/she has to understand what the nature preferred boundary for the eco-system is consisting of his people and other living beings. Obviously, he has to ignore the country boundaries while deciding upon this. If this eco-system is spanning several countries, then he should take steps to build a trade block consisting of these countries. Also, when such a trade block is formed, the participant countries should understand the basis of the creation of this trade block and thus give it higher priority over any other trade blocks that it is part of aiming at objectives like political support, diplomatic advantages, security etc., . In long run, if these trade blocks are becoming a bedrock for economic stability and ecological sustainability, the participant countries should not be afraid of re-drawing the borders of their trade block as a new, but bigger country. Sometimes we may have to cross water boundaries too while re-drawing the boundaries. In my opinion, the following are the main elements of observation while deciding the boundary of such an eco-system for a hypothetical country:

1. Basic food security of all the living beings of the countries which are part of the trade block
2. Basic water security of all the living beings of the countries which are part of the trade block
3. The above 2 should be understood in the light of the combined effect of weather/climate/seasons and the presence of any natural bodies like a river or freshwater lakes.
4. Enough geography for all the species to move about freely without the limitation of the borders. No native species should get a claustrophobic feeling while moving about in the eco-system.
5. If special resources are available in that eco-system, an economic model to gain from the development and use of those resources which is acceptable to all the participant countries of the trade block should be designed and implemented. Obviously, the country where these special resources are available can be expected to have a strategic advantage in the economic model built to utilize/develop the said resources.
6. The countries of the trade-block can leverage their combined might in exploring better ways of using innovation, R&D, healthcare, space, military, human-capital, tourism, agriculture, education, governance, infrastructure, transportation and technology. Making use of the combined resources of the countries of the trade black in the most efficient, effective and sustainable way should be at the core of any such integration effort.
7. Members of the trade-block should be consulted for any sale propositions of any special resources before considering the export options. While doing so, the 100-year plan (long term) and mid-term and short-term plans of development of individual countries and for the trade block as a whole should be considered. Similarly, imports should also be debated among the member countries before allowing it.
8. Sectors such as Information Technology should be given special attention as this is generating a group of jobs that requires special skills like mental modelling and abstract thinking. The ability to get trained and excel significantly in the metal capacities as part of day-to-day activities is not present in too many job sectors. This should be considered as a critical value adding sector of any trade-blocks.

9. While aiming for the balanced growth of all regions of the trade block, the following aspects should be considered:
    - Start with the human-population distribution map of the in-focus trade block. (It is we, humans that need more help to run with our lives. The animals in the forests seem to be at-peace with nature and all by themselves till we disturb them with our economic activities)
    - Identify the different resources that are economically viable to extract/process in the map
    - Identify ways of sustainably utilizing these resources for the benefit of all the species of the trade block
    - Identify ways of development/use of these resources to benefit local population where the resources are originated while focusing on the equal quality of life for the entire trade block
    - Identify ways of generating jobs in different sectors using those resources and distributing them evenly
    - Plan for the distribution of economic activities based on all the resources and the related use. I compare this to the power sector for an easy understanding. If Power (economic value output) is the value targeted to be generated from the economic activities then, it is better for this power to come from small wind-mills, wave mills, hydro-electric powers and solar plants generating jobs for locals and thus supporting a local buzz of economic activities than from a high risk nuclear plant (or a giant coal power plant) which is importing costly nuclear fuel rods from outside and which is also damaging to local environments through its operations.
    - Based on all of the above, if you could overlay GDP figures (over the population figures) on the map above, of a small region in the trade block, with a possible support of an exclusive micro-economic plan, then those figures should not vary too much from the other such regions of the trade-block map.

STRANGER THAN FICTION

2 IDENTIFYING THE SKEW IN THE COST OF LIVING

A spiritualist should be well versed at least in the basics of managing an economy and how to compare economies. (remember sometimes in the past 'Theocracy' was in reign too).

We, at least the common folks, usually paint the state of economy of world nations with a broad brush under the below categories:
   1.   Developed nations.
   2.   Developing nations and
   3.   Underdeveloped nations

We all know how grey the classification criteria are and we are not clear how it has changed over the period of time.

I have lived in India, UK and USA for a considerable period of time and have come to understand the dynamics of the life events of an average person and its interplay with the larger economy.

Let me compare the cost of living in UK and India and see if there is any 'skew'.

I know that a study like this needs careful gathering and analysis of vast amounts of data. I do not have time or resources to commit to such a study. This article is based on general observations and is subjected to the below challenges that bother all researchers:

   1.   Lack of availability of data
   2.   Data proliferation leading to low quality of data that promotes

confusions
3. Outdated data
4. Lack of sense of period of data collection for the data and lack of idea
   about its relevance today
5. Ability in means/time to verify the data sources
6. Difficulty in even searching for the right data source

I am also constrained by my limited knowledge of statistics and its related tools and techniques.

I used the below sites for my R&D to gain useful insights. They seem to be reasonable. Some of them also specify the time when the data was recorded.

1. www.worlddata.info

2. www.80000hours.org   and several other sites.

But before this let us compare some vital parameters of the country data of the 2 countries to set the stage.

STRANGER THAN FICTION

Table -1:

S. No	Parameters	INDIA	UK	Comments
1	Population	1,425,776,000	67,327,000	India is 21X than UK
2	Annual GDP	$ 3386 B	$ 3070 B	
3	Annual GNP	$ 3023 B	$ 2994 B	Higher GNP (over GDP) is better, as it accounts for investments returning to the country on the long run.
4	GDP per capita	$ 2,405	$ 45,775	UK is 19X than India.
5	Debt (% GDP)	84.68 %	102.64 %	
6	Debt per capita	$ 1,895	$ 46,981	UK is 25X than India. Compare this to GDP per capita
7	Expenditure	$ 263.8 B	$ 1190 B	UK is 4X than India
8	Expenditure % GDP	29.33 %	45.14 %	20% goes to Interest Payments and 7 % to subsidies. About 8% of expenditure goes to Debt Interest in UK.
9	Corruption Index	60 (Bad)	27 (Good)	
10	% Education Expenditure	12.75 %	13.34 %	The average yearly cost of university education is about GBP 9000, and this is a steep expense for a student in the UK. Though Student's finance is providing loans, it is a debt burden on students who are just at the verge of stepping into a new phase of life - work life.
11	% Health care Expenditure	3.38 %	18.74 %	Still there are lots of complaints on ineffectiveness of NHS in UK
12	% Defense Expenditure	8.27 %	4.66 %	
13	% Interest Payment Expenditure	20 %	~7.9 %	
14	% Risk of Poverty	21.9 %	18.6 %	
15	Political Stability	52	77	
16	Civil Rights	46	90	
17	Health	36	78	
18	Hospital beds per 1000 inh.:	0.53	2.46	
19	Physicians per 1000 inh.:	0.78	2.81	
20	Internet Users	430/1000	948/1000	
21	Unemployment rate	7.7 %	4.8 %	
22	Inhabitants per Sq Km	433.7	276.4	
23	Life Expectancy	69	79	
24	Birth Rate	16.57 %	10.20 %	Indian population growing
25	Death Rate	7.35 %	10.40 %	UK population declining
26	Suicide Rate (intentional harm per 100000)	15.59 %	8.2 %	
27	10-year bond yield	7.00 %	3.79 %	India leads

STRANGER THAN FICTION

Let us also look at some other statistics of the 2 countries.(I used numbeo.com, nimblefins.co.uk, google and many others).

Though the below data is usually segregated by cities, regions, and countries, and by urban/rural groupings, I am considering a approximate/guestimate value out of all segregations.

Table-2

S. No	Parameters	INDIA	UK	Comments
1	Annual Median Income (approx.)	GBP 3770	GBP 33280.00	UK is 21 times of India
2	Average food cost as % of annual Income of an average family	12 % (GBP 467)	18 % (GBP 5924)	
3	Average living expenses (without rent) as % of annual income of an average family	Approx. GBP 900 – is about 24 % of the average income	GBP 25000 – is about 75 % of the average Income	Cost of living is very high in UK as compared to India
4	Average rental expenses as % of annual income of an average family	Approx. GBP 710 – is about 20 %	GBP 13000 – is 40 %	Rent in cheap in India
5	General mortgage rate	8.5 %	4.78 %	India is 1.8X of UK
6	General savings account rate	3-4 %	0.85%	India is 4X of UK
7	General savings rate among the population	30 %	7.63 %	2/3 of people in UK believe they wouldn't be able to last 3 months without borrowing money
8	Median housing price as X of annual income	Varies too much by place	Approx. 100 times	
9	Wealth distribution profile	10 % of population holds 77 % of total national wealth, 73 % of wealth generated in 2017 went to the richest 1%	10 % of population holds 43 % of all wealth. The poorest 50 % by contrast own 9% of the wealth	Extreme inequality prevails in India
10	Average retirement age	60	65	
11	Average debt for a person as % of annual income of an average family	(GBP 1128) 30% of yearly salary	(GBP 34546) 105 % of yearly salary	

Let us look at the above tables and the figures sourced from internet given in the appendix:

Some Inferences from all of the above and the charts in the appendix:
1. UK is very well ahead in a number of country parameters and is classified
    as a developed country

2. Cost of living in India, is, on an average, lower than in UK

3. Rent in India, is on an average, lower than in UK

4. By comparing the income distribution curve shapes, I can infer that income distribution is more spread in UK as compared to India. The prices of food and essential goods are governed by the affordability of majority of the people and that is clearly on the lower end as seen in India data (If you are earning INR 25000/GBP 243 per month you are in the 90 percentile !!). This applies to the living expenses including the rental cost.

5. On the contrary, just by comparing median income of an average family to the living expenses (not including rent) and rental expenses separately, I am shocked to see that, in the UK, the fictitious average man is forced to spend beyond his means.
Considering this with the national debt per person, lower savings interest rate and lower propensity to save, it seems life is much more tough to live in UK for an average person. Seems, the economic fluctuations can unsettle people in UK much faster than in India.

6. Considering Figure 3, and point number 5, we get into a false sense of security that the developed countries are doing better. But factors like cost of living, inequality etc., sometimes point to the opposite understanding.

7. On the Figure 4, I am extremely shocked to see how much skewed the Global income distribution is. How horrifying the difference between haves and have-nots!!! Approximately just 75% of all the income in this world is enjoyed by 25% of the people.

8. We noted above that 10% of UK population owns about 43% of the wealth in the UK. I think, this data should be considered as a outlier only. We have to consider the 57% wealth and 90% population to arrive at the average

income. All the national policies, budgets etc., should consider this derived median income as one of the important data while finalizing.

9. Let us compare the debt of the 2 countries and the debt of the average citizen from the 2.
From Item #5 in Table 1, we can infer that the UK has a debt of 102.64 % of GDP (It consumes more than it produces). On the contrary, India has a debt of 84.68 % of GDP.
Debt burden of an average Indian citizen is 1.16 lakhs or GBP 1130 which is 30 % of the median income.
Debt burden of an average UK citizen is GBP 33410 which is 100.5% of the median income!

10. Considering the modified median income from the above point, certain time-tested parameters, indicative of 'affordability' - like
- house price as number of 'times' the medium income
- rental income as '%' 'of 'the median income'
- living expenses as number of 'times' the median income
- Average savings as number of 'times' the median income
- Average pension savings as number of 'times' the median income

etc., should be tracked as macro-economic indicators.

11. If an average person is having a sense of financial insecurity constantly, then it starts to affect him/her psychologically. He starts to get disturbing questions in his mind on a constant basis.
- Will my savings last for my retirement?
- Will I have mobility/energy to continue working post-retirement?
- Will I complete my mortgage on time?
- When will I clear my credit card debts?
- Is vacationing too expensive these days? Should I avoid them?
- etc.,

To overcome these large life impacting issues, I recommend the below 2 suggestions preferably enforced through an iron clad constitution:

1. Wealth Distribution
2. Universal basic Income
3. Free education till any levels so that an average person feels motivated to go to an university to get a higher education that will make him eligible for a high valued high paying job.

3 OBSERVING THE DIFFERENT NODES AND LAYERS OF THE ECONOMY

Often times I use to think about the good design of a sound economy. I observe the large-scale impacts of offshoring/outsourcing/mergers/acquisitions and the related layoffs and shocks to public life.

How can we build a resilient economy that is built with inbuilt safety mechanisms and sound structural design?

The answer to me, seems to be around building it with all around inclusivity and careful central planning. The planning may focus on the integrated trade-block level and/or at the country level with the later given higher priority.

The economic think tanks may consider some simple models (interconnected matrix) as a starting point for visualizing the economic structure and then modify/enrich as more data/inference is obtained. The different layers and nodes should be derived from the underlying knowledge about the below aspects:

· How are the count of jobs of the population mapping to different sectors of economy?

· How are the count of jobs mapping to different sizes of organizations (Global, Large, Medium, Small scale and niche shops)?

· How is the educational scope of the population mapping to the above segments?

- What are the noticeable salary bands of the population and their distribution in the population?

- How are the salary bands mapping to the above segments? (Notice the location of medium income and its related trend over years)

- How are the noticeable age group bands of the population mapping to the above segments?

- What are the Cost-of-living aspects impacting, specifically the local economy and generally the national economy? (studying/researching housing costs, heating costs, food costs, education related costs etc., mapped to median income and studying the trend of the related indexes to unemployment data and/or tracking related indexes by GDP/GNP or to some measure of poverty trend)

- What are the scenarios surrounding outsourcing/offshoring? Please notice the effect of employment outsourced/off shored for purely the reasons surrounding profits of a given organization, but which may be harmful for the greater economy if practised in large scale by several organizations among several sectors.

- How is the deployment of the local economic resources in the same block/country faring in generating employment/GDP?

- How is the import of major resources helping the different economic segments and hence providing direct employments to local population? What are the opportunistic gains (such as products focussing on physical/mental health of the population) of such imports? If the import is not adding to GDP or providing any support to generation of jobs, we should take precautions on those imports.

- How is the export of major local resources helping the different economic segments and hence providing direct employments to local population? What is the cost of not using it locally? Is the opportunity cost of not using it locally exceeding the revenue obtained from exporting? While doing these analyses, we should always keep in mind not only the direct costs/revenues but also other aspects like physical and mental health of the population and the related derived expenses and should not be excessively focussed on a single micro entity like an organization.

- Tracking of any other relevant metrics aiding in the central planning

When the above data points in the highest state of quality is obtained, we can observe/infer the below aspects post careful analysis:
- The segment which is generating the most employments
  - The segments which are generating the most employments for people below or at medium income
  - The interconnectedness of the economic activities possibly crossing one or more boundaries and the cascading effect of any negative impact for sectors having tight and numerous integrations. Here we must be open to avoid any global/regional domino effects and hence should take meaningful measures for isolating and barricading the segments and blocks of economy, especially for those areas that provide maximum employment to the population or is based out of any local economic resources.
  - Ideas around how sustainability be obtained for the economic activities while focussing on the growing population and depleting resources.
  - The economic usefulness of any sectors or organizations vis-à-vis its impact on sustainability and any potential long-term issues.
  - The risk and reward potentials.
  - A reflection on the health of economy on the long-, medium- and short-term horizons.

In the last step of the analysis, we should create an economic model that is resilient, self-healing and is sustainable. A sample reference model can be a matrix/node model where the below aspects may manifest:

1. Strong nodes Layer: A bedrock of organizations that is providing for maximum job employments/stability. Efforts should be made to increase the quality of life at this layer by increasing the efficient and effective involvement of government in social schemes such as free healthcare, free education and the implementation of the universal basic income scheme etc., These steps should have a drag effect on the economy and should pull more and more population out of poverty and into acceptable living standards.

This bedrock of organizations should be identified as systemic institutions and hence should be protected with adequate measures from any global/regional negative domino effects.

The above organizations'/sectors' impact on the state of physical and mental health on the jobseekers should be studied with carefully curated metrics on a continual basis. Possibly the calculation of the median income of the country should be weighted more in this layer. Outsourcing/offshoring/mergers &

acquisitions should be carefully controlled in this layer.

2. Medium nodes Layer: The organizations are possibly not as resilient as the above nodes and can consist of organizations of any size. Probably we may expect the business leadership to steer it appropriately than being influenced by any focussed central policies.

3. Layer with niche nodes: If the nodes are practising something niche, then the IPR related concerns should be addressed. If some of these nodes are dependent on local resources, then special care should be taken to keep these organizations/sectors alive. Sectors like defence, telecom, finance, infrastructure etc., are to be treated carefully so that national interests are kept intact all the times above and beyond profitability concerns.

The economic principles should be created based on the model designed and should cover the below points:

1. The different layers are efficiently integrated.
2. The different layers/segments are adequately designed for resilience.
3. The failure of any part of the model is largely/quickly insulated and contained and should not be producing any domino effects.
4. The failure risks of the different aspects of this model should be adequately distributed and sharp risk handling mechanisms should be put in place.
5. The use of economic resources and the related logistics are very efficiently planned across the layers.
6. Different steering mechanisms to navigate the economy in choppy weather should be in-built by design. It may not be just the fiscal and monetary measures taken by the central banks. We can be innovative and thus provide the sector wise number of jobs (new and old) generated and sustained in each locality and nationwide and publish this metrics in publicly viewable dashboards energizing the public and to influence its spending habits. For example, suggesting them about spending in local shops more and less in online shops till a certain targeted recovery is made.

Thus, it helps if the government creates a macro level fictitious organizational structure (like the Basil org structure in Banking sector) or which can also be termed as the economic meta-model as discussed above. All the different organizations should be mapped to this meta-model for effective planning, governance and resource optimizations. The central planning should carefully study the active metrics designed for this economic meta model and should be used as significant input to direct the economy in general.

The central planners should also track the use of resources in long, medium and short terms over this meta model for its effective and efficient use and should derive its significant metrics (on inputs, outputs and WIPs) on a real time basis. This model should be carefully controlled and optimized, and the planners should not be afraid of redesigning this meta-model if the situation warrants.

4 TRANSFORMATIONS OF MONEY

Money has been a very fascinating invention of man. Its initial purpose was to enable easy flow of goods and services. It replaced the barter system which was very difficult to implement where the matching of goods and services was at the best hap hazard. The economic value of a good or a service was not really the focus of a barter system in most of the cases, but it just served as a method of exchange. The invention of money changed all that. It became a very effective intermediary for exchange of goods and services.

At the beginning, the modern-day economists pegged the value of a country's currency to the gold stock that is in reserve in that country. It made sense till the concept of fiat money was adopted.
That is the point at which, I think, money transformed into an "EVIL" entity.

This mindless printing of money resulted in the below:

1. Money became a proxy for the political power.
2. It supported large scale hoarding and corruption.
3. The real value of money was not deducible since the printing was made on a mere promise and also it is generally believed that the stock markets and currency exchange markets can be effectively controlled by those needy "experts", and hence it is believed by some that both the purported use and value of money can be bent!
4. Fictional money generation started by means of stock/currency/commodity derivatives (laid out as several layers) where the value of money generated did not fairly represent the underlying stock! This generated all sorts of burstable economic bubbles affecting lives of millions of ordinary people!
5. Even when the practice of new generation of electronic transfers of money is very much in vogue, there is a general perception that large

sets of printed currencies are being hoarded and subsequently being used for funding illegal activities that also primes up unspeakable crimes.
6. The fair money representing salaries of common people, revenue from business operations etc., pales in comparison to the money generated from hedging, fictional stocks and crime.
7. It was also easy for crime syndicates to organize their activities (even like some private hedge funds) all around the globe in a manner that does allow them to be at NO loss all the time – It is bullish – they win; it is bearish and still they win! This scale and efficiency cannot be matched by governments and legitimate international businesses.

Thus, to make the money turn GOOD again, I suggest doing the below after thoroughly consulting other experts in the field. Of course this may not be a conclusive list of controls.

1. Remove fiat currency concept and peg the value and printing of currency to gold reserves, verifiable/certified GDP value of the nation.
2. Since we have identified precious metals other than gold, we can also consider the national reserves of other metals like platinum and other economically promising rare metals while printing the currencies.
3. Instead of printing the currency, we can consider creating the currencies in some digital (national cryptos) formats too. The national crypto currency should have equal value to the national currency at all times and they should be complementary to each other.
4. Make all transfers as electronic transfers and make the relevant technologies an easily available/implementable commoditized technologies.
5. Credit cards should be replaceable by a person's biometrics to identify his credit/savings.
6. Borrowing based on a sovereign nation's promise (by entities like bonds) without considering its real economic potential is not a good practice. This is evident in the huge deficits/loan obligations that we shift from current generations to the future generations. Why should our kids be born in debt??

5 ADMINISTRING THE ECONOMY IN NOVEL WAYS – PART 1

Generally, for quick categorization, the countries of the world are divided into 3 segments – Developed (Developed Economies), Emerging (Economies in Transition) and Frontier (Developing Economies).

Please refer to the below links for a quick refresher:
https://www.investopedia.com/updates/top-developing-countries/

Excerpts:

A wealthy nation isn't synonymous with a developed one.
The International Monetary Fund (IMF), on the other hand, takes several different factors into account when determining whether a nation is an advanced economy, an emerging market and developing economy, or a low-income developing country.
The World Bank uses gross national income (GNI) per capita for its measurements, and it has four different categories: high-income economies, upper-middle-income economies, lower-middle-income economies, and low-income economies.

Developed countries typically share several other characteristics:

- *Their birth and death rates are stable. They do not have very high birth rates because, thanks to quality medical care and high living standards, infant mortality rates are low. Families do not feel the need to have large numbers of children in expectation that some will not survive.7*
- *They have more women working. These career-oriented women may have chosen to have smaller families or eschew having children altogether.8*
- *They use a disproportionate amount of the world's resources. In developed countries, more people drive cars, fly on airplanes, and power their homes with*

electricity and gas. Inhabitants of developing countries often do not have access to technologies that require the use of these resources.

- *They have higher levels of debt. Nations with developing economies cannot obtain the kind of seemingly bottomless financing that more developed nations can.*

https://www.investopedia.com/terms/d/developed-economy.asp

Excerpts:
- *Countries with relatively high levels of economic growth and security are considered to have developed economies.*
- *Common criteria for evaluation include income per capita or per capita gross domestic product.*
- *If per capita gross domestic product is high but a country has poor infrastructure and income inequality, it would not be considered a developed economy.*
- *Noneconomic factors, such as the human development index, may also be used as criteria.*
- *Developing economies are often helped by globalization to reach improved levels of income and increased standards of living.*

The classification is based on complex indicators which are primarily the below:

1. Per Capita GDP (Gross Domestic Product)

From the 2nd link above, we could see that,

The most common metric used to determine if an economy is developed or developing is per capita GDP, although no strict level exists for an economy to be considered either developing or developed. Some economists consider $12,000 to $15,000 per capita GDP to be sufficient for developed status while others do not consider a country developed unless its per capita GDP is above $25,000 or $30,000. The U.S. per capita GDP in 2019 was $65,111.

2. HDI – Human Development Index

Please refer to the below link to know the full list of indicators of HDI:
https://hdr.undp.org/sites/default/files/2023-24_HDR/hdr2023-24_technical_notes.pdf

STRANGER THAN FICTION

I could extract the following indicators of HDI from the above link:

Life expectancy at birth, Expected years of schooling, GNI per capita (PPP $), (HDI- Human Development Index from the previous 3 indicators), (Inequality-adjusted HDI from the previous 3 indicators)), (GDI or Gender Development Index from the previous 3 indicators), Maternal mortality ratio, Adolescent birth rate, Female and male population with at least secondary education, Female and male shares of parliamentary seats, Female and male labour force participation rates, (GII or Gender Inequality Index from the previous 5 indicators), Nutrition, Child Mortality, Years of Schooling, School Attendance, Cooking fuel, Sanitation, Drinking Water, Electricity, Housing Assets, (MPI – Multidimensional Poverty Index from the previous 9 indicators), Carbon-di-oxide emissions per capita (production) and Material foot print per capita.

Please refer to - https://worldpopulationreview.com/country-rankings/hdi-by-country for visual display of HDI state.

Excerpts:

A country's Human Development Index value is determined by aggregating the country's scores in a vast assortment of indicators including life expectancy, literacy rate, rural populations' access to electricity, GDP per capita, exports and imports, homicide rate, multidimensional poverty index, income inequality, internet availability, and many more. These indicators are compiled into a single number between 0 and 1.0, with 1.0 being the highest possible human development. HDI is divided into four tiers: very high human development (0.8-1.0), high human development (0.7-0.79), medium human development (0.55-.70), and low human development (below 0.55).

3. GII - Global Infrastructure Index

One way of measuring infrastructure index, the Ipsos study is based on surveys which has a Likert scale to collect responses.

This considers the ranking/rating of infrastructure of countries such as Airports, Motorways/Major Road Networks, Local Road Networks, Rail Infrastructure, New Housing Supply, Flood Defences, Digital Infrastructure, Water Supply/Sewage, Renewable Energy Infrastructure, Electric Vehicle Charging Infrastructure, Solar Energy Infrastructure, Wind Energy, Pavements-Footpaths & Pedestrian Areas, Cycle Routes/Lanes/Facilities & Nuclear Energy

STRANGER THAN FICTION

Source: Ipsos/GIIA Base: 19,514 adults (online), July-August 2021

The top 4 priorities as per 2023 study were:

1. Solar Energy Infrastructure
2. Water Supply and Sewage
3. Flood Defences
4. New Housing Supply

4. Levels of Industrialization:

One way of measuring levels of industrialization, the MVA per capita is an indicator of a country's level of industrialization, adjusted to the size of its economy. It is widely used to classify country groups according to the stage of industrial development

Indicator 9.2.1 - UN Statistics Division/More information at:
https://www.unido.org/resources-publications/industrial-statistics-guidelines-and-methodology

Though there may be many more complex indicators to categorize a large economy, the above 4 are comprehensive.

Now let us analyse how the governing entities like the government of a country can build some processes to administer ways to organize the economy with an intent to improve upon the above indicators.

To be effective, I think a global body like the UN should publish a data collection and management framework and prescribe it to member countries to source high quality data on the above 4 complex indicators. If necessary, the indicators should be designed to enable the member nations to collect data without ambiguity and the possible presence of derived indicators should also be acknowledged here.

A nation can have some possible meta-structures based on the idea proposed in other chapters-

Let the major (not all - only the primary ones) governmental departments (as per the mappings suggested in the above link) that are primarily responsible to collect the data pertaining to the above 4 complex indicators be assumed to be the below ones:

- Central Planning Commission (CPO)
- Central Statistical Organization (CSO)
- Central Bank (CB)
- Ministry of Environment and Sustainability (MES)
- Ministry of Finance (MoF)
- Ministry of Infrastructure and Industrialization (MII)
- Ministry of Human Welfare (MHW)
- Ministry of Education (MoE)
- Ministry of Water Resources (MWR)
- Ministry of Power (MoP)
- Ministry of Governance, Risk, Compliance, Audit, Quality and Training (MGRCAQT)
- Ministry of Land, Agriculture, Husbandry and Forestry (MLAHF)
- Ministry of Marine and Blue Economy (MMBE)
- Ministry of Information Technology (MIT)

Here I envision that there will be a close match of the above central/federal departments to the state/provincial departments and that their operations will be synchronized, optimized and fully integrated for maximum efficiency and effectiveness. (Mostly, because of the party affiliations and local concerns this integration may remain as a pipe dream in a lot of countries leading to suboptimal use of economic resources that is detrimental to the nation's population as a whole).

6 ADMINISTRING THE ECONOMY IN NOVEL WAYS – PART 2

Let us look at the proposed functions of the above departments. I am not exhaustive in my listing of the relevant functions but sincerely hope I have added the major functions. Any additions as feedback is welcome.

1. **Central Planning Commission (CPO)**

    - Develop, execute and continually improve and check the strategic (e.g. 100 Years), tactical (e.g. 20 years) and operational plans (e.g. 5 years) of the nation.
    - Make sure that when Government changes (i.e the party in power changes) , there are no impact to at least the strategic and tactical plans)
    - Draw up the nation's economic grid model – i.e Focus on the development of all the areas (grid) of the nation. Identify the economic factor(s) that will power a administered node (e.g. at the lowest level of focus this node can be the district or county of a nation) and draw up and development and integration (to the national economy) plan.
    - Identify those resources that should be nationalized and hence should be centrally administered for the benefit of the whole nation.
    - With appropriate liaison with the state/provincial governments ensure that the economic "buzz" is healthy in the nodes.

2. **Central Statistical Organization (CSO)**

    - Align the organizational objectives with the objectives published by the CPO.

- Develop and store governance and operational framework for collection of data to be used for the nation's development and improvement.
- Be the central authority for data management – assuming the roles of Data Steward (Strategic), Data Steward (SME) and Data Custodian/Controller (IT/Infosec)
- Publish the collective results of the data analysis over the above listed 4 complex indicators
- Post appropriate data scrubbing, this data should be shared with the global bodies like UN to track the progress at the global level at a regular cadence.
- Supply data for the various governmental entities including the other departments dependent on data for planning and evaluation.

Central Statistical Institute (CSI) under the ambit of CSO

- Align the organizational objectives with the objectives published by the CPO.
- Lead on the cutting-edge technologies needed for the CSO for the betterment of the nation.
- Design and operationalize the technical and management frameworks related to the national data collection exercise to support CSO.
- Design the various technical models (AI/ML, heuristic) needed for tracking the development/progress of the nation and continually improve it.
- Design the service management interfaces to the CSO and other data dependents.
- Aid the other government entities in the above 3 requirements.

3. **Central Bank (CB)**

- Align the organizational objectives with the objectives published by the CPO.
- Administer monetary policies (cash reserve ratios, interest rates, strategic reserves like gold)
- Administer fiscal policy (government spend-direction, time and quantum, tax rates)
- Aid the government to convert from fiat currency to a

commodity-based currency
- Develop a verifiable process to print currency based on strategic reserves and GDP.
- Advise the central and state governments on the implementation of the universal basic income program.
- Track the flow of currencies in the various parts of the nation's financial eco-system.
- Lead on the effort to digitize the financial systems of the nation (including promotion of electronic payments over cash payments)
- Identify intelligent ways to use the block chain systems including crypto currencies.
- Supply the relevant data for the complex indicators tracking the nations progress.

4. **Ministry of Environment and Sustainability (MES)**

- Align the organizational objectives with the objectives published by the CPO.
- Supply the relevant data for the complex indicators tracking the nations progress.
- Develop a nationwide ESG plan from sources like UN SDG as applicable to the nation.
- Develop a blueprint for converting to green economy and continually improve it.
- Track the ESG indicators of the nation

5. **Ministry of Finance (MoF)**

- Align the organizational objectives with the objectives published by the CPO.
- Supply the relevant data for the complex indicators tracking the nations progress.
- Budget, direct and control the deployment of funds
- Evaluate the performance of the funds deployed in terms of economic returns and other economic performance indicators.
- Track the sources and application of funds of the strategic and tactical plans of the nation
- Develop the tax regimes relevant to the nation
- Oversee the tax collection

6. **Ministry of Infrastructure and Industrialization (MII)**

    - Align the organizational objectives with the objectives published by the CPO.
    - Supply the relevant data for the complex indicators tracking the nations progress.
    - Create and R&D institution that will pioneer the latest technologies and identify ways to operationalize the learnings. This institution should also take care of the concerns of the MES.
    - Create an industrial base to support strategic infrastructure and industries
    - Operationalize a system of bases and networks holding strategic equipment and personnel that aid in rapid construction and deployment
    - Implement plan around GII and Interface with MoE on all critical aspects of GII.
    - Develop high end operational research oriented central IT systems that can support transport networks and nodes covering roadways, railways and waterways. The nodes can be container exchange stations, markets, distribution centres, ports, harbours, bus and railway stations, ware houses, food storages, cold storages, storages of other economic resources. etc.,

7. **Ministry of Human Welfare (MHW)**

    - Align the organizational objectives with the objectives published by the CPO.
    - Supply the relevant data for the complex indicators tracking the nations progress.
    - Develop a nationwide sustainable, economic healthcare plan.
    - Develop a nationwide health care infrastructure consisting of public and private bodies.
    - Develop a charter for all healthcare workers and other tier-1 workers who have public interface responsibilities.
    - Track the EHS aspects of the nation
    - Ensure that there are processes that verify if the salaries paid to population are in tune with the laws and regulations.
    - Track and control the highest to lowest salary ratio among various salary bands.

nations progress.
- Develop a nationwide plan to integrate water ways with ingenious designs for example by taking advantage of geography and topography.
- Develop marine resources (e.g ships of certain tonnage), industrial bases and organizational structures to leverage the transportation by waterways.
- Develop reservoir lakes in numerous to take in excess water and to supply water on demand to the water ways canals.
- Cover the canals with solar panels in appropriate places to reduce water evaporation and to generate local employment.
- Develop tourism ideas around the water ways.
- Build desalination plants, dams, tank bunds as appropriate to retain water for economic purposes
- Build a stringent environmental policy towards water conservation, pollution and use and enforce it legally with punitive fines on infringements.
- Create and R&D institution for harnessing water resources of the nation

10. Ministry of Power

- Align the organizational objectives with the objectives published by the CPO.
- Supply the relevant data for the complex indicators tracking the nations progress.
- Focus and invest in non-conventional energy sources.
- Devise strategic plans to lean away from fossil fuels and nuclear plants.
- Continually improve the power infrastructure with the adoption of the latest and the best capabilities.
- Create and R&D institution for harnessing the non-conventional resources of the nation
- Adopt IoT/SCADA technologies to efficiently track power generation, distribution and consumption.

10. Ministry of Governance, Risk, Compliance, Audit, Quality and Training

- Align the organizational objectives with the objectives published by the CPO.
- Supply the relevant data for the complex indicators tracking the

nations progress.
- This department should
  o Design governance processes based on popular management frameworks
  o Plan and execute Integrated Risk Management (IRM) programs,
  o Track compliance to laws, regulations, standards and frameworks,
  o Become external auditors for other government departments and conduct performance audits, security audits, process audits and compliance audits.
  o Ensure compliance to process quality indicators for other government departments.
  o Conduct relevant cross-cutting trainings including quality management training programs like 6-sigma programs for other government departments
    - Track and send early warning emerging risk indicator data to the relevant stakeholders of the other government departments and heads.
    - Publish integrated risk profile for the nation.

12. Ministry of Land, Agriculture, Husbandry and Forestry

- Align the organizational objectives with the objectives published by the CPO.
- Supply the relevant data for the complex indicators tracking the nations progress.
- Ensure programs like crop rotation, livestock immunizations, water conservation techniques like drip irrigation etc., are run as expected. Should liaise with the relevant R&D institutions like the agricultural universities and absorb the latest and the best for operationalizing.
- Should maintain a genetic reserve of all critical plant and animal species.
- Should develop special focus on medicinal plants.
- Create and R&D institution for conserving, developing and harnessing the forest resources of the nation
- Create and R&D institution for developing and harnessing the animal husbandry potential of the nation
- Focus on reducing agricultural loss due to lack of storage of agricultural produce by developing several strategically

located big and small produce storages dotting the nation.
- Develop and maintain ingenious ways to support the poor rural and urban population dependent on agriculture – for example - essentially their financial burden for activities like sale of agricultural produce should be taken care by accepting the sale of agricultural produce in any quantities at the big and small storage locations without any imposing conditions.
- Develop plans for nationwide organic contract forming and reduce financial loss to farmers by leveraging crop insurance programs.

13. **Ministry of Marine and Blue Economy**

- Align the organizational objectives with the objectives published by the CPO.
- Supply the relevant data for the complex indicators tracking the nations progress.
- Have strong measures to tackle rampant exploitation and contamination of marine resources.
- Develop marine harnessing plans that takes care of affected species.
- Develop tourism plans and build structures like aquariums and water sports complexes.
- Develop cold storage capabilities that dot the shores of the nation where sale of marine goods can happen without adding burden to the fishermen population.
- Administer insurance plans for the population that is dependent on marine resources.

14. **Ministry of Information Technology**

- Align the organizational objectives with the objectives published by the CPO.
- Supply the relevant data for the complex indicators tracking the nations progress.
- Develop IT policies, standards and frameworks for e-Governance
- Develop IT policies, standards and frameworks for developing IT Industry - both software and hardware
- Develop and maintain strategic IT resources for the nation including but limited to initiatives like government on cloud, CAT 8 cables, Fiber optic connections, hardware industries, data centres etc.,

8 SOME SUGGESTED FINANCIAL REFORMS

Please note that I am not an economist by education or profession. I think it is right to state that value systems and philosophies are reared and felt at heart whereas scientific subjects and subject dissertations are analyzed in the brain before being presented. Eventually the stronger the dissertations are, the easier it is, for the subject matter to persist in the heart as part of the individual's value systems. I think, for me, the subject of economy benefiting all the species on this planet is something of paramount importance (the right principles can even avoid an existential crisis for the mankind and/or this planet) and not just a critical higher order subject. Based on the convictions of my adopted value systems, I treat economy so and hence I can be considered more as a philosopher tackling economy and not necessarily a SME in the economic field.

1. Cap on Personal Wealth

A properly designed iron-clad constitution should ensure that insane accumulation of personal wealth to an individual is avoided. An inflation adjusted correct cap on personal wealth (represented as sum total of all possible forms of assets that an individual possesses) as a guidance value should be announced by the nation's central bank at a given cadence. This guidance value should be appropriately implemented by legal strictures. This can be a new additional fiscal policy tool since it can generate additional revenue for the government.

2. Affixing top-to-base Wage Ratio

In order to avoid the scenario where the executives pay themselves hefty salaries, in alignment with the above point, a ratio of the top-to-bottom salary in a given organization should also be stipulated by the central bank as a guidance value. This guidance value should be appropriately implemented by legal strictures.

I recollect reading in one of the analytical news articles that the top-to-bottom wage ratio of an average organization in the USA in the 60s was about 60-80 and in recent years it is topping 200! Though I do not recall all the exact details, the numbers were scary enough that it got stuck in my mind. So, this ratio can be used to regulate the basic minimum wages and the top salary.

This can be a new additional fiscal policy tool as it can influence the income tax component.

3. Foreign Investment – Source

For an individual or an organization to explore the investment opportunities, the welfare of the nation and the trade-blocks that it belongs to should be considered to avoid undesirable flight of economic resources including money out of that country/trade-block(s). To this effect government bodies/departments like the national environmental agency, central bank, finance ministry and the planning commissions and such bodies should layout a multi-approval policy for investments destined to be deployed in foreign shores.

This can be a new additional monitory policy tool as it can stop/start the capital flight.

4. Foreign Investment – Destination

Similar to the above point, the nation receiving the foreign investment should be very mindful about the source of the funds (not forgetting the action of law of karma enacting at the group level). Dubious funds always bring its own problems with it. Hence before accepting foreign investments (Yes, I know how difficult it is to say no to an incoming fund), the national environmental agency, , the nation's central bank, planning commission the finance ministry and the foreign investment board and such bodies should carefully consider the proposal before green lighting it. The approval should be based on all-to-approve strategy and not any-one-approval strategy.

Next

5. Cap on Company Reserves

How much can a company hoard resource such as cash reserves citing future growth plans? It should not be to insane levels. The nation's central bank can suggest an inflation-adjusted guidance value which should then formally be stipulated in legal terms as the cap on holding reserves. This guidance value can be absolute or on a percentage basis of some indicator.

This can be a new additional fiscal policy tool since it can generate additional revenue for the government.

6. Wealth Distribution as a National Policy

Ignoring utter poverty is a shame on humanity. Like I said before, I think that

God has not created all the representations of wealth to be enjoyed by a very few individuals. Wealth distribution should be enshrined as one of the founding principles of the adopted iron-clad constitution.

7. Universal Basic Income (UBI) as a National Policy

Similar to the above point, another founding principle of the iron-clad constitution should be the implementation of the Universal Basic Income. Because of its sixth-sense, humans are considered to be a higher order species. Hence, a nation should ensure that all its citizens are in pursuit of a higher order excellence and are not getting stuck in the muck of poverty. I find it strange that a dog can travel in Rolls Royce while a fellow human on the street is worrying about where his next food is coming from. I definitely do not hold any grudge against that dog, but definitely we can do better and take care of such fellow humans. UBI can go a long way in not just sustaining humaneness but also to repel evil manifestations like exploitations, human-trafficking, prostitution and such crimes.

This can be a new additional fiscal policy tool since it increases government expenditure.

8. Tier-1 Professionals to be Salaried by the Government

I talked about Tier-1 professions in my blog on 'Varnashramadharma'. These are the professions that face and impact a large set of public members sometimes running into thousands. I also tried to enlist some of the potential candidate-professions of this kind – Doctors, Nurses, Lawyers, Police, Teachers, Government Employees including Politicians, Church (or any Place of worship) Leaders and Facilitators, Recognized Artists etc., In aligning with the serious nature of these jobs, and its accorded importance, the professionals of this job should be a polymath covering a wide area of knowledge starting with their core competence and knowledge of their profession and covering fields such as psychology, social psychology, constitutional guarantees, economy, project/program management etc., Keep the importance and the strive that comes with the profession in mind, the government should extend them the right salary so that there is a healthy competition to join this tier-1 professions among the general public. To maintain top notch quality of these professionals and the commitment that comes with these professions, it is important that the government have an appropriate screening mechanism/policy.

To avoid misuse of the power that comes with some professions, new innovative roles can be created like – public defender who defends the public from incarceration during the initial stages of the purported crime. Once the crime is wetted, then the public prosecutor can take over.

9. Tier-1 Professional Infrastructure Capacities to be Nationalised

In alignment with the above point, hospitals, schools, universities should be either nationalised or they be funded by the government with appropriate monitoring and control. Government can build professional complexes for lawyers practising law (with appropriate filter criteria) and representing public, living quarters for Teachers, Police men/women etc.,

10. Supporting the High Tax Paying/Contributing Good Samaritans

In tune with the point-1 above, considering the continuous contributions of a good tax paying and contributing (considering point-1, assuming that his excess wealth is given to the nation) Samaritan, appropriate conventions can exist in the constitution that takes care of these Samaritans when they fall in bad times and become destitutes.

11. Supporting the High Tax Paying/Contributing Good Companies

In tune with the point-5 above, considering the continuous contributions of a good tax paying and contributing (giving the excess wealth to the nation) company, appropriate conventions can exist in the constitution that takes care of these companies when they fall in bad times and become debt ridden. Government can also suggest and participate in proper merger with another healthy member. Thus, we keep the cogs of the economy intact. In long run, problems of the companies will become the problems of the nation itself, hence government participation in mergers and acquisitions should be encouraged where appropriate.

12. Financial Investments to Consider Trade Blocks that Share Geographical Boundaries

I wrote about the importance of the trade blocks that share a common geography and an eco system. Hence the planning commissions or any such national bodies should consider not just the nation's interest but also the interest of the trade blocks that it is part of, before allowing any investments to come-in or go-out. The consideration is complete only when the nation has the complete knowledge about the potential impact of the eco-systems that it is part of and about the potential impact of the eco-systems permeating the trade-blocks that it is part of. The latter part is needed to register our respect for the co-habituating species that share the same living space.

13. Tax Credits due to Green/CSR/ Initiatives and for Demonstrating Compassion to Other Species who are Co-habitants of the Shared Living Space

This is also a wonderful gesture on part of us humans to register our compassion to the environment and to the co-habituating other species.

14. Removing Fiat Money

Since fiat money generates fictional money leading to lots of evil manifestations, it is important that we print our currency based on critical reserves like gold and by considering the GDP of the country.

This can be a one-time additional monitory policy tool and hence can be carefully timed for better outcomes.

15. Removing Spurious Derivatives from Exchange Markets

Needless to say, spurious derivatives like the CDOs should be done away with and the national bodies like FCA in UK and the SEBI in India should tighten the norms around the nature of the financial instruments of investments. In fact, a simple sane rule could be to allow only those financial instruments that is backed by a solid asset class/principle.

16. Standardisation of International/National Financial Discipline

By standardising, terms and conditions becomes clear to all and removes any grey areas of operations. This standardisation should be on the vocabulary to be used, processes, frameworks and guidelines practiced in the nation, trade-blocks and in the international community. A global body like UN (World Bank) can lead in this effort of global standardisation and could leverage any solid existing knowledge bodies.

17. Reserves Mandate for Nations

Since we are treating nations like a large organization these days, we can stipulate certain reserve requirement mandate to nations. Probably a UN financial body like world bank can take the deposits from nations that are related to reserve mandate. This can be used to great effect to cure a nation's financial state and also to do a credit check.

9 SOME LABOUR MARKET OBSERVATIONS AND IDEAS

I have mentioned in one of my earlier chapters (On Kalachakram) that, I feel that nature is leaving us important clues about the ways of working of the universe in its manifestations and the reverse (new paradigms like cloud computing) is also possibly true which means, us (all species on earth), are teaching nature about some possibilities to gain efficiency and effectiveness.

In a similar line of thought, I equate the economy with the water cycle.

Water collects/flows at a place, either through rain or through rivers fed by perennial springs/tributaries. Similarly economic value/activities manifest/happen at a country/place, either through employment or through entrepreneurship/ (or by government sector employment).

Let us consider the rainwater:
Rainwater droplets, in trillions, fall on earth, collect into puddles, pick up run and volume, join water bodies like pond/lake and possibly flow as a deluge in a river, finally merging with the ocean.
Similarly, labour class employments, in millions, feed the lower rung of economy, supporting the general population and/or feeding into the business organizations. The economic value of the work nature increases as the feeding/supporting conditions aggregate to large organizations across the 4 spectrum of core sectors (agriculture, manufacturing, services and the harnessing of natural resources) and finally translating as revenue income in the government coffers.

Let us consider the other sources of water:
Under-ground springs from certain locations, snow fed lakes and other

possible perennial sources of water, supply water to ponds/lakes/rivers and tributaries and they too accumulate in small numbers before becoming a deluge.
Similarly, new investment-based employments, break-through related employments (e.g. cloud computing or AI in IT sector), employments from government spending create an alternate form of economic activities and related employments in a given place/country.

I refer to this 'buzz' of activities and related employments in the 6th Chapter on economics for spiritualist, as economic 'buzz' under the topic – Central Planning Commission.

To sustain an economy and to avoid large scale unemployment, the central planners of the government have to focus on both of these catalysts (Systematic maintenance of basic employments and the ones that come by because of sudden investments like foreign -investments/government-spending/innovation-led/technology-breakthroughs that help in generating employment opportunities.

These employments primarily belong to 4 basic sectors:

1. Agriculture (sowing, production, harvesting, transporting, storing, logistics and distribution)
2. Manufacturing (procurement of raw materials, production, WIP, shipping, storing, logistics and distribution)
3. Services (low level – general service jobs to public/ mid-level – front/mid-office service jobs/other blue collared jobs/white-collared jobs)
4. Harnessing of Natural Resources (mining/marine ecology/energy/tourism etc.,)

Employment opportunities will be curbed because of the below possible actions/happenings:

1. Adoption of technology, mechanization and automation (the general trend when this happens is to bring efficiency and effectiveness leading to FTE reduction).
Governments – local and central must consult their planning commissions and strategies to properly regulate the adoption. Reckless adoption of automation/AI will reduce available ground level feeder job opportunities (remember what missing rains can do to a country) while non-action i.e non-adoption of technology driven automation/mechanizing will be leading to

stagnation of conditions and nature of workforce. We have to remember how the introduction of computers greatly lifted the quality of life for a large set of people by shifting a large number of jobs from agriculture/manufacturing (while these sectors were diving into automation and mechanization successfully) to services sector.

When too much rain happens without an outflow or harnessing, this leads to water stagnation and clogging. This is what happens in low-income sub-urbans where population builds without proper investments that provides quality jobs.

Like how a stagnating body of water leads to diseases, low-income sub-urbans leads to the raise of criminal activities.

Considering these analogy, local/central government, backed by data, have to take high-quality decisions fairly quickly that leads to optimal outcomes.

I always consider local/central leaders akin to ship captains whose ships are passing through dangerous waters perennially.

2. Shipping of the natural resources in raw form without analysing possible local uses (may not be suitable under all conditions)

Please refer to the links in the references section.

I think a country should be careful when it is exporting large quantities of raw materials unmindful about its use for itself especially if it is lacking long term planning going even up to 100 years! Since it is true that a knowledge powered society with its able leaders will never miss such an opportunity, one of the basic need for subsequent prosperity is to increase education level of the population.

It may be flawed or may not be true 100% of the time, but I generally think the below is true.

Processing raw materials provide low paying jobs while manufacturing and selling the finished products from these raw materials provide high quality, high paying jobs! Add to this the fact that for at least some of the poorer countries, even the related R&D to analyse the raw materials and to identify its economic/profit scope is happening outside its borders.

3. Outsourcing and offshoring strategies

This is a double-edged weapon that should be carefully used only when it is absolutely necessary. The business leaders and national leaders must consider all aspects before green lighting these strategies. Consideration of only the business profits due to low incurred costs may lead to a very short termed interim benefit which may prove to be harmful in long run (remember what missing rains, vanishing snows and drying springs can do to your country).

Consider that we do not have many industries like the IT industry, that is easily providing job opportunities, that builds brain capabilities like abstract thinking/modelling and architecting. Hence, we see the need for other considerations besides the profit related motivations.

4. **Large scale out-migration from a place** (Job opportunities in villages are less compared to cities)
Local economists/planners need to carefully observe data, identify opportunities to create the needed economic 'buzz' to stop the death of a village/town or a city. In this regard, innovative thinking like planning to be a hub in the transport sector or to be a place that hosts a solar farm etc., should be considered. Where we are unable to take advantage of the local skills and knowledge, we have to be innovative to see what kind of services are in need – now and later (can it be supported remotely?) and adopt intelligently. Needless to say, we need high quality leadership that are truly nationalistic.

5. **Change of public preferences** (fast foods and ready-to-cook foods are widely accepted nowadays)

6. **Raising of macro-economic factors** like inflation/cost-of-living, when people try to optimize and practice thriftiness.

7. **Any other elements that are visible to local/national leaders/economists.**

Similarly, employment opportunities will increase because of the below possible actions:

1. **Large scale in-migration** (This may affect the employment opportunities of the local population and may lead to social tensions. But temporary high population in places due to activities like tourism is a preferred happening).
When this happens, lots of people will need the same basic things and hence the labour level job counts tend to show an upward tick.
Local governments, if possible, with the help of SMEs and central support, should analyse these trends carefully in almost real-time basis and convert/direct them into positive outcomes. For this to happen, decisions have to be taken based on solid high-quality real time data. Thus, the initial growth in low quality jobs, can be used to generate the growth of next and subsequent level high quality jobs.

2. **Innovation and breakthroughs** – opening up new job

opportunities.

This is especially true if the local community has a high-quality education system in place like the Silicon Valley where a number of unicorn startups flourished. Even the perished startups provided high quality lessons to the general public and investors due to the analysis done on them by the local educational institutions.

3. **Allowing natural growth of population** in villages/towns/cities without affecting the quality of living.

If the quality of living is not in focus, this quick growth in population may lead to low quality sub-urbans that eventually become infected with crimes.

4. **Fall in the availability of certain skills/knowledge** that are in demand (assuming the quickest remedy chosen is offshoring/out-sourcing)

5. **Change of public preferences** (landline phones are out and Wifi is in)

6. **Raise of macro-economic factors like drop-in interest rates/cheap borrowing costs.**

7. **Any other elements that are visible to local/national leaders/economists.**

We can see how the forces of nature is playing all around and hence when we are stuck in a context like, job market or economy etc., it is easy for us to decide if we consider a naturally occurring analogy and draw helpful validation points to move forward.

In this article, the simple advice is – DO NOT take any decisions that dry out your sources of water!

Look at the options in the hand to grow job opportunities and to curb job losses. These are dynamic- remember water may dry or flow in abundance for many reasons other than mere geography. Some time, collaboration may lead to even better outcomes.

For catching rains - we grow trees and de-clog canals, seed the clouds, builds tanks and reservoirs etc., similarly, to catch new economic activities and related jobs., the local authorities should enable certain hygiene aspects related to business such as - easy and transparent tax regime, crime free neighbourhoods, ensuring top quality in schools, availability of recreation centres at affordable rates, fantastic transportation grid etc.,

Some examples of collaborations are as follows:
1. Sister city arrangements - to shift remote-working enabled jobs to

other city to help tide over tough conditions or to shift jobs of certain types in excess to other city while opening up for high valued new economy jobs.
2. Avoiding concentration of economic output of nations in certain metropolitan cities only. See what can be shifted outside the metropolitan cities without any major issues. Outsourcing within national boundaries is welcome!
3. If catchment and storing of rains are in different geographies - collaborate for the benefit of both places!
4. Data centres can be in one place and call centres, front offices, middle offices and back offices can be in other locations. Again, distribute for the benefit of all, rather than concentrate for a rich few!

Happiness as value should prevail over profit as money!

References:
https://www.cruxinvestor.com/posts/top-mining-countries-in-the-world-2024
https://www.iea.org/topics/critical-minerals

9 INTERPRETING NATURE TO IMPROVE AN ECONOMY

How to compare 2 complex yet similar systems to fill in the gaps of our knowledge and understanding?
I always liked to study similar systems in NATURE (divinely blessed) to solve any problems in the manually designed system that I am involved with. I sincerely believe such comparison helps and is a useful exercise in building knowledge.
If you compare 2 complex systems, each can benefit from the influence of the knowledge gained from the other system! This article is based on this simple fundamental premise.

Let us compare agriculture with common economic problems/issues.

The various types of crops are food crops (staple foods), feed crops (for livestock consumption), fibre crops (cotton, hemp etc., for making clothes/fibres), oil crops (for consumption or industrial use – corn, cottonseed), ornamental crops (for landscaping and aesthetics) and industrial crops (e.g. Rubber, tobacco)

> Set 1: Food/Feed/Fibre crops – supporting essential needs
> Set 2: Oil/Ornamental/Industrial crops – supporting non-essential functions or to provide comfort
> Since Set 1 is essential (life and living activities depends on this), national economies and global governing entities should land this safely before attempting to gain profits out of Set 2.

Similarly various economic units exist such as – Global Economy, Regional Economy, Country Economy, State/Province Economy, District/County

Economy and City Economy.

If we consider Country as a primary governing entity (since you need to implement policies satisfying the people of the nation), the below understanding helps.

>Set 1: Country Economy, State Economy and County/City Economy
>Set 2: Economy within Trade blocks
>Set 3: Global Economy, Regional Economy
>Set 1 above is most important before you focus on Set 3. Set 2 is relatively next in priority after considering Set 1.

For example, National leaders should support global corporations only if adequate benefits materialise in terms of persisting income/employment and advancement within its national boundaries or secondarily within the trade blocks that has symbiotic arrangement with the host nation. It cannot accept a global corporation if it carries a significant stability related risk that can possibly ruin the national economy (institutions with Systemic Risks).

Let us consider some of the major problems in Economy and compare it with its closest concepts in agriculture:

1. Employment and Unemployment in the Economy

There can be permanent or temporary workers in the agriculture. There can be workers in the preparation, production and distribution functions in the agriculture. While the permanent ones are the ones that are employed to monitor and cure the crops till harvesting, temporary workers are needed seasonally – while planting or while harvesting and distributing. The temporary workers should be used for storage/maintenance & distribution, animal husbandry, plant and equipment maintenance etc., till they revert to the seasonal agricultural assignments. Thus there will be more constancy in the labour demand. Predictability is easy.

Reckless automation/mechanizations should be avoided – These things build profits at scale for host organizations but snatch away employment opportunities. To some degree this issue can be best tackled by a co-operative model implemented for farms where there will be harmony between men and machines – men belong to constituent unit of the co-operative structure and machines belong to the co-operative structure itself and can be rented out with operators when needed. It is better to balance it with sound principles.

The same principles should be used for the labour management in a national or regional economies. .

Understand the labour market and implement those principles that provide stability to the various job functions. You do this while building the job profiles of the various essential job roles needed in the economy. If necessary, understand the job roles that are to be newly created, improved and obsoleted and develop necessary implementation plans including imparting job-related trainings at scale and thus improve employability of the nation's citizens. Also, focus on the product/produce flows (or input-work-output – chain of events) to build co-operative, sustainable networks of organizations/institutions that ensure some degree of stability and ensure predictability.

2. Interest Rates

This is an important monitory policy used to control money supply and borrowing costs. This operation should not alter the foundation layer of the economy agreed by experts as defined by employment rate, GDP and some securities promised by the constitution. So, the government should ensure discipline and some basic sanity check in foreign exchange reserves, foreign trades, exchange rates and balance of payments before trying to adjust this. The target objectives for interest rate manipulations should be a SMART goal (SMART goals are **S**pecific, **M**easurable, **A**chievable, **R**elevant, and **T**imebound) and not a moving target whose surrounding interpreted data is constantly mangled, not-useful and confusing. I vaguely remember, in high schools, we were taught partial differential equations to solve such complex systems with many significant parameters. So, we should use information technology to the right effect to identify the SMART goal and the necessary monitoring & controlling needed along with the recommendations on the corrective actions needed.

Simple – If the system is too complex and with lot of moving parts, don't try to correct it randomly – try to identify the 'ONE' or 'TWO' things that yields maximum results while we keep other things constant. This will need a lot of R&D before we act.

This can be compared to the laying of fertilizers on the land. Too much or too little can cause problem. The target strength – high or low can alter the effect. Continuous use may spoil the soil and possibly poison it. And there should be a natural way to cleanse it out before the next crop cycle since the fertilizer needed for the next crop may be different.

3. Inflation

'Inflation refers to the general increase in prices or the money-supply both of which can cause the purchasing power of a currency to decline'.

We can directly relate this to the glut in the production or in the stagnation of the produce. But, for better understanding of the comparison, we have to shift our focus to the consumers of the agricultural products too and not just the farm or the farmers.

In the first case, consider Excess money in the economy as Excess produce available to the public (similar to increase in money supply)

Customers are inundated with the same type of produce. This has the power to disrupt the farming community as the price of the goods drops. Excess money sometimes leads to substandard outcome like low-quality loans and mortgages.

Farming community manages this risk through farm insurance, commercial buy-back arrangements with food companies, and by developing good reliable storage and distribution facilities. Similarly excessive money in economy should be controlled by appropriately controlling interest rates, proper hedging of financial reserves and money market operations etc.,

In the second case, consider Price Increase as Low yield (increase in commodity prices)

Customers find the produce to be inadequate in quantity and hence the price jumps. Hence customers cannot buy other essential things. This has to be controlled by the farming community by practising appropriate due diligence in farming operations and processes and with continuous monitoring and control and with appropriate use of fertilizers and pesticides/insecticides. Similarly good financial discipline including discipline with our import/export situations and enforcement can save us from price increase. Remember – price increase can be beneficial for an organization but despite tax income it may not necessarily benefit the nation in long term. Thus, appropriate regulations should be in effect, possibly along with enforcements like MRP (Maximum Retail Pricing). If the economy is strong, other measures like temporary imports can be leveraged.

All, of the above will work only when we have strong data & data analysis skills/talents deployed over our monitoring, controlling and continuously improving system of governance.

References:
Crop | Definition, Types, & Facts | Britannica
Inflation | Definition, Theories, & Facts | Britannica Money

10 EVALUATION OF A NATIONAL ECONOMIC MODEL - AN ABSTRACT CONCEPT AND DESIGN

At the onset, I would like to emphasize that this is a very high level abstract conceptual idea involving the use of ML (Machine Learning) models to evaluate a giant entity like the national economy.

The field of AI/ML is now being used in almost all spheres of life. How best to use this technology when tackling a juggernaut like a national economy?

New ML models involving not millions, but billions of parameters are being created and deployed in production for various purposes. My mind vaguely recollects a recent data where it is suggested that on an average, a large global organization with a team of 300 data science associates (including analysts, engineers, scientists, SMEs) may evaluate about 1000-1200 models a year and only about probably 10-15 of them make it to the production.

I think , a ML model to evaluate a national economy may contain many sub-models and may need good integration logics with the encompassing model.

I am presenting below a very crude and raw-cut parameter/model list of a national economy.

STRANGER THAN FICTION

Abstact-ML-Model-For-Evaluating-a-EconomicSystem

Inputs	Controls	Outputs

• Forex Reserves
• Employment Rate
• Minimum Wages
• Various Economic Resources
   - Local Raw Materials
   - WIP
   - Finished Materials
   - Value of Goods-in-Stock
• Bank Loans
• Investments
• Imports
   - Finished Goods
   - CKD Kits
   - SKD Kits
   - Imported Raw Materials
   - Commodities, Food, Drinks & Beverages
• Some measure/sub-model of Innovation/R&D
• Some measure/sub-model of Investment Sentiment
• Demand outlook
   - Some measure/sub-model of Demands in Service sector
   - Some measure/sub-model of Demands in Manufacturing sector
   - Some measure/sub-model of Demands in Agricultural sector
   - Some measure/sub-model of Demands in Natural Resources Harnessing sector
• Supply outlook
   - Some measure/sub-model of Supplies in Service sector
   - Some measure/sub-model of Supplies in Manufacturing sector
   - Some measure/sub-model of Supplies in Agricultural sector
   - Some measure/sub-model of Supplies in Natural Resources Harnessing sector
• Some model of Weather Pattern Influence
• Some measure of Local and Geopolitical Risks
• Balance of Payment Parameters
• Interest Payment Parameters
• Taxation Parameters
• Some measure/sub-model of integration of national economy to regional and international economies
• ESG Risk data
• Insurance cost
• Cost of Quality
• Outsourcing/Offshoring appetite
• Power sector outlook data
	• MONETARY CONTROLS
	   X1 = Printing Money
	   X2 = Open Market Operations
	   X3 = Interest Rate Operations
	   X4 = Bank Mandatory Reserves
	
	• FISCAL CONTROLS
	   Y1 = Government Expenditures
	   Y2 = Taxation
	
	• OTHER CONTROLS
	   Z1=Government Policies
	   Z2=Member Trade block Policies
	   Z3=Regional/Global Influencers
	   Z4=National Sentiments/ Constitutional Guarantees
	   International sentiment on ease of doing business
		• Exports
		   - Finished Goods
		   - CKD Kits
		   - SKD Kits
		   - Imported Raw Materials
		   - Commodities, Food, Drinks & Beverages
		• Outcomes
		   - Manufacturing data
		   - Services data
		   - Agricultural data
		   - Natural Resources Harnessing data
		• Financial Data
		   - GDP
		   - GNP
		   - National Account Data
		   - Tax Inflow
		   - Forex Earned
		   - etc.,
		• Employment Data
		• Sector/Industry wise outcome data
		• Flow of Money Data
		   - Incoming
		   - Transit
		   - Outgoing
		• Productivity
		• Some model/measure of resiliency
		• Power use data
		• Resource use efficiency data
		• Resource use effectiveness data
		• Quality of life measure
		   - Health spend
		   - Shelter spend
		   - Food spend
		   - Recreation spend
		   - Education spend
		• ESG impact data

In the representation above, some may be parameters, some-may be sub-models and some others can be just critical Hyperparameters.

> *In machine learning a **hyperparameter** is a parameter that can be set in order to define any configurable part of a model's learning process. Hyperparameters can be classified as either model hyperparameters (such as the topology and size of a neural network) or algorithm hyperparameters (such as the learning rate and the batch size of an optimizer). These are named hyperparameters in contrast to parameters, which are characteristics that the model learns from the data.*

STRANGER THAN FICTION

I think, to build a gigantic ML model representing national economy the process may look something like how I have outlined below.

> 1. Set the mission, vision and milestones for the project/program and define the MVP and project success criteria - be reasonable at the pilot attempt.
> 2. Preferably use SAFe (Scaled Agile Framework) for the program.
> 3. Identify the needs and boundaries of the main program and the pilot projects.
> 4. Identify the first round of Project Directors, Program/Project Managers, Engineers, Analysts, SMEs, Data Scientists, Statisticians and Mathematicians needed to identify the early raw models and sub-models along with the pipeline design and program executing/operating parameters.
> 5. Create the Program structure consisting of project teams, governance team and program management team.
> 6. Create a repeatable project structure and process to be followed by each project team with defined goals with appropriate milestones and definitions of done for requirements.
> 7. Create program and project teams with assigned G&Os. (A ML model like the model for a national economy may need may different sub-models where each sub-models may contain hundreds if not thousands of parameters). If possible, start identifying the early hyperparameters for the encompassing model.
> 8. Conceptually design and test how the integration of various sub-models is going to be achieved procedurally, process-wise and technically. Start with a raw design and improve as you go.
> 9. Create the sample production pipeline for the ML model and test it.
> 10. All necessary technical infrastructure and software should be available for the team.
> 11. Technical processes related to meta-data repositories, data catalogue, data governance. data security and data obsoletion should be evolved
> 12. Each team targeting a sub-model should perfect the techniques on –
>   a. Data acquisition
>   b. Data Cleansing
>   c. Data Transformation
>   d. Feature Extraction
>   e. Feature Selection
>   f. Feature Iteration

13. The integrations of sub-models are expected to be hard-to-tackle-beasts and will need involvement of high-level SMEs.
14. Processes around model documentation, testing, cataloguing, retirement etc., should be established and should be integrated with the production pipeline.
15. Model testing includes, testing of sub-models, model-integration testing and testing of encompassing models. It also includes model evaluation and performance testing.
16. The deployment of the model may be designed to happen in 3 stages – pre-production, production and post-production. (Evaluate the suitable deployment mechanisms like the multi-service deployment, Blue-Green Deployment, Canary Deployment etc.,)
Next, how can we use data coming out of the model runs?

This is a model which is encapsulating an ultra-complex gigantic system. Hence the inputs can be complex – it may not be some point values but ranges with probabilities. Similarly, it is expected that the recommendations may present several scenarios with assumptions again each with a range and probability. We may need brainstorming by SMEs before we interpret the results and create action plans (SMART Goals).

We can be very innovative with respect to the arrangement of models and sub-models to the extent that, in a proposed 3-layered model consisting of base layer, integration layer and results layer, the last 2 layers - i.e the integration layer and results layer can be expected to dynamically evolve as the execution progresses!

If necessary, we can expect the execution to pause for analysis and critical inputs from SME after the execution of the base layer. Optionally a similar pause can be arranged post execution of the integration layer models for analysis and critical inputs. To tackle complexity, an elemental layer can also be considered before the base layer.

The various scenarios that is expected to be tested using this encompassing, configurable (at layer level and at model/sub-model levels in that layer), dynamic (at layer level and at model/sub-model levels in that layer), decoupled (across layer and in-between models in a layer) model are:

- Given a group of inputs and controls, what can be the values of a group of target output parameters
- Given a group of outputs and controls, what can be the values of a

group of target input parameters
- Given a group of inputs, expected output parameters and controls, what can be the values of a single target output parameter
- Given a group of outputs, expected input parameters and controls, what can be the values of a single target input parameter
- Given a group of outputs and inputs, what can be the optimal settings for a group of controls
- Given a group of outputs, inputs and some expected controls, what can be the optimal settings for a single target control parameter

The executive team should charter the program team with the action outline – may be to identify the optimal interest rate cut or to favourably increase the balance of payments etc., Please note that the launch of the production model for the first time may take more time but the subsequent changes can be done in a reasonable time frame. The model will also be expected to have a great deal of configurability and decoupling along with the ability for quick execution post changes. The team, then should identify the dynamic parts, quasi-static parts and static parts and work on the encompassing model system. It should have access to top-quality data.

The final output may be a report for the executing team consisting of –
- Range of results and probabilities
- Assumptions for each of the results
- Constraints expected for each of the results
- Confidence level and probability of success towards achieving the goal set for each result
- Information on Risks and Rewards
- Contingency measures if the risks materialize
- Time expected to be available to implement the measures
- Expiry time for each of the results before fresh exercises are needed again
- Information on any collateral damages

References:
https://www.udemy.com/course/deployment-of-machine-learning-models
Supervised Machine Learning: Regression and Classification | Coursera
Hyperparameter (machine learning) - Wikipedia
Feature Engineering - Overview, Process, Steps (corporatefinanceinstitute.com)
Scaled Agile Framework

11 MY POINT OF VIEW ON GNH (GROSS NATIONAL HAPPINESS) INDEX

I Recently there was a news about Bhutan which happens to be currently the only country that attaches more importance to Gross National Happiness (GNH) over GDP (Gross Domestic Product).

I am quoting from the reference below:

> *According to the Bhutanese government, the four pillars of GNH are:*
> 1. *Sustainable and equitable socio-economic development.*
> 2. *Environmental conservation.*
> 3. *preservation and promotion of culture; and*
> 4. *good governance.*
>
> *The nine domains of GNH are psychological well-being, health, time use, education, cultural diversity and resilience, good governance, community vitality, ecological diversity and resilience, and living standards.*
> ...
> *The Bhutan GNH Index is considered by progressive scholars to measure societal progress similarly to other models such as the OECD Better Life Index of 2011, and SPI Social Progress Index of 2013. One feature distinguishing Bhutan's GNH Index from the other models is that the other models are designed for secular governments and do not include religious behaviour measurement components.*

But I think, we can interlace at least some of the ideas that we have come across that are widely prevalent and also mentioned in my other blogs on economy.

What may be the factors that will promote the adoption of GNH?

- Promote a national culture and ideology that will give importance to overall happiness and well-being than over just financial success. This includes mutual respect, cooperation and co-development and other unselfish attitudes such as supporting (as necessary), sharing, caring, exhibiting benevolence and paying attention to greater goodness of the cause while in pursuit of excellence.
- Publish national policy on GNH considering all aspects impacting the overall well-being of the society. From the reference given below, we can understand that there may be multiple approaches that had been tried earlier. We must ensure the focus on continuous improvement aspects of such policies and implementations.
- Develop regulations, processes, standards and frameworks as applicable to implement GNH and to monitor, control and measure its progress.
- Adoption of an apt lower minimum wage, promoting wealth-distribution, affixing lower to higher income ratio, wage cap and wealth cap in the constitution will install some financial discipline that will go a long way to promote overall wellbeing of one and all. Also implement the Basic Minimum Income concept as appropriate because of the inevitability of money in the new age economy.
- Develop processes and policies that will help avoid the concentration of money and power which are the root causes of corruption. Widespread corruption is inherently evil and will spread vicious unhappiness with domino effect if unchecked.
- State of honesty and integrity of the Government can be mostly accepted if the money is converted into digital format that are protected by adequate biometrics and other relevant security measures. Needless to say, the importance of maintaining the audit trail of all income and outgoing funds to the required degree.
- Increase the factor of safety for handling economic resources of the country including the reserve currencies by
  o Spreading the control points around controlling, stocking, releasing and using aspects
  o Building genuine 4 or more eyes principle
  o Instil interlacing bureaucratic and judicial interjections at appropriate levels and process stages
  o Promoting publishing of financial reports at local and regional levels before publishing the national level financial reports that will

not be deviant from each other.
o   Publish conformance report on the source and application of funds for the strategic national projects and for those projects that take a huge financial toll on the national economy. This to ensure that the strategy, execution and results are all properly aligned even under long term engagement timelines.
- Leverage the role of NGOs as appropriately since the concept of GNH is a bit abstract and the government may need all hands on deck including for the spread of efforts and to collect reliable data (while the definition of happiness itself is a bit abstract, as a sane responsible individual we are expected to know the things that should be avoided and the ones that should be promoted).
- Remember – Charity begins at home and hence without solving large scale local issues such as issues relating to lack of shelter, food, clothing , jobs etc any large scale donations crossing the border should not be done in a mindless manner.

Reference:
- Gross National Happiness - Wikipedia

- Quoting from a spiritual ascetic of South India - Thayumanavar -
எல்லாரும் இன்புற்று இருக்க நினைப்பதுவே
அல்லாமல் வேறு ஒன்று அறியேன் பராபரமே
                              - தாயுமானவர்.

Meaning of the Prayer Song:
Oh Supreme! I do not know anything other than thinking that everyone should be blissful!

STRANGER THAN FICTION

PART D

SOME POLITICS FOR SPRITUALISTS

1 A CLASSIC CLASSIFICATION PROBLEM

A natural way of classifying a government of a country is by using a combination of its names of the political system(s), economic system(s) and social system(s) adopted in its charter such as its decree/constitution etc., Clearly a naming convention can help here to avoid confusion. Later we can see how to effectively leverage this name type to classify better.

For example, if I quickly look up the internet and try to see how the nature of governments are defined worldwide, I quickly arrive at a classic classification problem – there are a wide variety of definitions. Let us look at some of the definitions from the Wiki/world atlas and similar other sites:

USA - Federal, democratic republic
UK - Constitutional monarchy with a multiparty, parliamentary form of government
India - Sovereign Socialist Secular Democratic Republic with a Parliamentary form of government which is federal in structure.
China - One-party communist dictatorship
France - Republican State and a parliamentary democracy
Germany - Democratic and federal parliamentary republic
Singapore - Parliamentary representative democratic republic
KSA – An absolute monarchy and a theocracy
Malaysia - Constitutional elective monarchy with a parliamentary system

Some of the common issues with the current types of government are given below:

1. A country can be constitutionally democratic, but the people may not have power to change the government before the term is over, even if its performance is rated as worst. This can result in a situation where, for the

remaining term of the ruling period, the government is not of type democracy but of authoritarian type.

This gives us questions around the soundness of principles and processes on forming of alliances/associations, continuous performance evaluations, authoritative interjections, and onboarding & handoff processes.

2. The structure itself is problematic. It is not self-governing, self-auditing, self-healing, or self-learning; Nor does it have other self-optimizing governance structures that prevents accumulation of power, ensures wealth distribution, ensures optimal use of national resources etc., that leads to continuous development.

3. Besides the above-mentioned structural issues, other transactional issues like lack of transparency, honesty, integrity along with corruption, inefficiency, ineffectiveness, fascistic leanings of leaders, sidelining of meritocracy, nepotism etc., have rendered the type of the government— as questionable i.e., is what it claims to be the true type is not true in ground reality.

4. Lack of effective international intervention, usually by a world body like UN (e.g., external audit of the country entity by the UN), which needs a whole set of reforms to make it effective. The value system and related enforcement mechanisms of the world body is weaker than at least some of its constituent country level value systems. If this is the case, then UN can never play an effective policing part in its functioning.

5. Questions like the influence of economic and social systems on the nature of type of government is not understood correctly. For example, we cannot be sure if the lobbyists powered by business houses are subverting the interests of the people who voted in a democratic government? If this happen, have we failed in upholding the ethos of democracy? Similarly, if the social systems are having a skew (say a particular faction is strong and is able to enforce its will by its virtue of being a king maker), how do we ensure that common interests and the interests of the population prevails? Is the reigning order capable of ensuring integrity and fairness?

6. In any form of government, be it aristocracy, communism etc., and which is so enshrined in it's constitutional decree, if the well-being of its population is not upheld, is it OK for the world to turn a blind eye and to sweep the dust under the rug?

We saw earlier how a combination of political, economic, and social systems can identify the form of government. I will briefly dwell into the problems around the classification of social systems that if done properly can help us classify the type of government in a better way.

A proper web definition of a social system is as below:

A social system is a group of individuals or an institution that combines to create a functioning society with goals. (study.dot.com)

Different types of social systems are in vogue.
Let us consider the below aspects before we move on.

1.Classification based on size (from helpfulprofessor.dot.com)

a. Macro analysis (looks at broad categories and systems like countries, populations)
b. Meso analysis (studies communities and groups in a society)
c. Micro (observes patterns and data from small entities like families or individuals)

I am not sure how this will help us tag the type of government. Even if the political and economic systems shout out loud that they are set in a democratic form of government, the social systems may cry foul! Sometimes, we have to worry about the degree to which the democracy is impaired! If it happens, should it still carry the tag of being a 'democratic government'?

2. Classification based on belief, class, status etc., - again I am not sure how this will help us tag the type of government. But we know that these can impact the choice of the government.

3. We have to look at dynamic ways of classifying the social behaviour that vouches for the type of government that the country entity ascribes to.
Let us consider how an external entity like a UN body or a group like Transparency International may look at an entity like a country.
- Is it transparent, opaque, or translucent?
- How does it fare on social stability? What is the nature of issues that are proliferating? Are these issues indicative of a malfunctioning government? Is its type credible anymore?
- How transparent are its electoral process? How can the population gain control over a very wrong ruling government? What are the powers at play? Are the powers at play be classified as some factions, business houses, elites, proletariats, wealthy individuals, religious

groups etc.?

(Please note that none of the social systems mentioned above may be satisfactorily classified under any one popular social system classifications currently existing!)

So, we have to be adaptive in identifying the social systems that can alter the type of the government. Thus, we will have to look for social systems' classification that is generic enough yet help us evaluate the type of government.

I recommend using a social system that is a common denominator across the globe that is generic.

The classification can be based on:
1. Its transparency to international scrutiny (can be any type of scrutiny preferably well-structured and covering all grounds).
Possible States: Transparent, Opaque and Translucent
2. Its stability based on national issues.
Possible States: Highly Volatile, Volatile, Predictable, Calm
3. Will the issues identified affect the functioning of the government?
Possible States: Yes, No, Perhaps, NA
4. Degree of corruption in the functioning of the government:
Possible States: Very High, high, Medium, Low
5. A score (to be brainstormed) on wealth accumulation or wealth spread in the country.
6. Effect of factions (based on religion, class etc.,) – Again we need to determine a scoring model on this.

So, in the above points, I am not directly looking at the social system entities or its interactions– rather the meta information on these entities that can point to a malfunctioning government and thus affect its type claimed. We have to convert this whole evaluation around social systems and translate the result effect on to the acceptable definitions of the government types as published by
some central entities like the UN.

Thus, the result of the social system evaluations can be converted into the possible states as: Helpful, Neutral and Not helpful.

Based on this, an external audit of a central body like UN, should accept or decline the type of government as claimed by the constituent countries. We may be in for a surprise to see a corrupt communist government claiming to be a democratic country, or a semi-feudalistic government branding itself as democracy etc.,

Let us look at some of the combinations of the common types of governments in the different political systems, economic systems, and social systems.
This is just indicative and not a complete list.

S. No	Political Systems	Economic Systems	Social Systems – Meta Status
1	Anarchy	Capitalism	By Internal Audit: • Compliant • Deviatory
2	Aristocracy	Market Economy	By External Audit: • Helpful • Neutral • Not Helpful
3	Bureaucracy	Mercantilism	
4	Capitalism	Mutualism	
5	Confederation	Network Economy	
6	Communism	Participatory Economy	
7	Democracy • Direct • Representative or Republic • Constitutional • Monitory	Socialism	
8	Ergatocracy	Centrally Planned Economy	
9	Fascism • Dictatorship • Syndicalism • Authoritarian • Ultranationalist • Militarism	Command Economy	
10	Republican	Marxian Economy	

A country can claim to be adapting 1 or more of the political systems and can claim to be adapting 1 or more of the economic systems. The country's internal audit system can arrive at the meta status of the existing social systems.
A central body like UN can trigger an external audit on the politico-economic condition of a country after ascertaining the social system meta status and check the veracity of the claim on the type of the government on its constituent members.
Needless to say- certain types of governments like the fascism or variants of it should be inadmissible into UN.

2 DYNAMIC POLITICAL SYSTEMS

The following appears to be a standard reoccurrence world-wide - long standing corrupt political parties with a penchant for avarice and rooted in nepotism/cronyism and unholy alliances. How do you tackle such a menace and still deliver the values expected of a well-meant democratic system??

The answer, to me, seems to be around the concept of dynamic political systems. In this design, each citizen registered as a voter should be assigned to at least 3 to 5 or more social groups. These social systems or groupings (the same groups which is also defining some values for adoption) may or may not be legally registered. I expect these groupings to have at least some lower limit criteria on the count of memberships and about its origin and functioning. These groups may have the option to register under the rules stipulated by the constitution.

For those who do not choose to associate with any groupings, AI technologies can be deployed on a person's education, profession, gender, age, economic background etc., to assign him the default groupings. There should be an option for the person to accept the assignment or modify and accept. This should be made mandatory and should be enforced in some easy-to-use manner.

I consider these social groupings to become the foundation of the dynamic political systems. Thus, for me, a dynamic political system is a concept where the political parties are dynamically formed before the elections (may be 6 - 8 months before the election date). By election, here, I mean the main elections resulting in the formation of local and national governments. These groups are expected to announce their core vision, mission, and G&Os. Those groups, where there is a sync in the ideologies may form alliances. The sync can be based on complimenting principles or matching principles. Transparent negotiations can happen between the groups on forging alliances. At the end of this phase, the top 5/10 or any number of alliances (based on the number of members) should be published for public feedback. Finally, after the consideration of public feedback, the top three alliances should be allowed to form the political parties that will contest in the elections. Again, AI technologies can be used to publish expected popular alliances and aid in the formation of meaningful and strong alliances that root for the nationalist interests.

The announcement of political parties must happen probably about 6 months in advance to the elections. The process of electing the candidates from the dynamic political parties should be expected to be smooth and should be part of the alliance forming negotiations. Thus, the new political parties dynamically, , will have about 6 months for campaign before elections.

The entire process starting from alliance formation till declaring the leadership should be over in about a year roughly - 6 months for alliances to emerge and resulting in dynamic political parties and their candidatures and 6 months for campaigning before the election dates.

Issues affecting the nation as a whole should be subjected to 2 phase voting - one by the electoral vote by the elected representatives of the democratic system and followed by the popular voting by the citizens eligible for voting. By this, we will note if the elected representatives are principally aligned with the citizen's expectations or not. And, if they are difference, further course of action can be planned.

The whole process will be effective if the following controls are applied to the processes:

1. No elected representative is locked-in as elector for the entirety of the term. The alliance or the popular vote should have the right to recall them at any time based on events like allegations of corruption.
2. The public can provide feedback on the candidatures after the alliances are formed. This can be powered by AI resulting in useful suggestions.
3. The elected representatives should be expected to provide a publicly visible journal of their activities during their term.
4. Any alliance can be provided 2 chances to appear in the election of the local and central governments.

5. Any elected member can be provided 2 chances each to appear in the election of the local and central governments.
6. Strong background check on the candidate's education, professional performance etc, should be part of the due diligence process before the candidatures are announced.
7. If any alliances are failing, then alternate arbitrary mechanisms, legal recourses etc., can be considered. This process should also evaluate the idea of any alliance that joined the election fray to join the newly formed political parties to provide stability and continuation of the government. The reasons for the failed alliances should also be made public by the news outlets.

3 SOME STRATEGIES FOR A PRO-PEOPLE GOVERNMENT

Now based on the classification type of a government, we can derive pro-people strategies that may be well received.

First let us look at the classification type of a political system of a country:
The possible types include but not limited to Anarchy, Aristocracy, Bureaucracy, Capitalism, Confederation, Communism, Democracy, Fascism etc., We probably have seen various types of governments that functioned in the past under any of these declared types.

The best option, in my opinion is to adopt the democratic form of government.
Hence, the iron clad constitution should register in in its founding charter that the type of government adopted will be democratic. The general accepted principles of a democratically functioning government apply here that can be further elaborated in the founding charter. The founding charter should also register the basic rights of an individual and the basic rights of groups that matter. Other articles, laws and regulations can follow later in the written constitution.

Next let us consider the classification type of a economic system of a country that needs to be captured in the constitution. Here again the possible types include but are not limited to capitalism, market economy, mercantilism, mutualism, socialism, etc., Based on the outcomes that history has recorded in the post, we can adopt the socialism as the best candidate economic type for adoption. (Please refer to the referenced article whose link is given at the bottom)

The philosophy of a socialistic form of government states that this type of model is -
Internationalistic with idealized future based on redistribution of wealth to fund and support social programs.

The ownership aspect of a socialistic form of government is as below –
Individuals may own property and small businesses. State ownership of essential services (electricity, water, internet)

Next, let us focus on the word- federal. Dictionary meaning of the word 'Federal' means -
'having or relating to a system of government in which several states form a unity but remain independent in internal affairs.'

Here the idea is to give freedom to the federal states, through the iron-clad constitution, to decide for themselves on whether to continue/discontinue being a federal state on a certain cadence and if the need arises. Based on the context/time, the rejoining or discontinuing can be assumed to be a very dynamic repetitive affair. In this setting, special provisions can be considered in the constitution to consider having joint security, currency, labour & economic arrangements to continue, as-it-is, even if dissociation is approved by any concerned major stakeholder. This arrangement will have the power to serve as a safety-value in times of unacceptable political turmoil and pressure. This arrangement can open up new ways of resolving disputes that go way deep into the past. Optionally, this dissociation can be staged in several milestones, possibly starting with in-principal agreement and ending in formation of separate militaries. The re-joining can also be staged.

Let us focus the essential functions/services that needs to be supported by an IDEAL federal socialistic democratic government:

Government will recognize the need for a dynamic political system such as the one outlined below in the article 7 of the reference section.
- Government will create the necessary bodies of government such as the ones outlined in the articles 2,3 ,4, 5, & 6 given below in the reference section.
- **Healthcare Security:**
  Government will recognize the need for a national policy on this aspect and this will be used by the government to roll out a national

level healthcare plan. Health care is 100% supported for all living things in that country!
- Government will ensure that education is free 100% from elementary to doctoral pursuits.

- **Economic Security:**
  Government will declare a policy for UBI implementation and will adopt some form of UBI (Universal Basic Income) scheme.
- Government will apply cap on individual's wealth and the wealth of a company or group.
- Government will operate on a non-profit basis. Though it is expected to keep some form of strategic reserves, largely all profits coming out of the systems that it is operating will be deposited with the nation's central bank.
- Any outcomes based on significant decisions of the government should be shiftable to the target (larger) group(s) recognized in the constitution that can absorb the shock better than the individuals.
- **Housing Security:**
  Government must mention the need to have national policy to tackle housing crisis. This should be followed by a strong and sensible plan which should be appropriately directed by the national planning commission.
- **Food Security:**
  National policy on food security should be adopted by the incumbent government. It is advisable to have a significant percentage of all food needs (say 60-70%) to be home grown within the national borders.
- **Physical Security:**
  Physical security is defined under the following bodies of governance:
  1. National External Security – Provided by the Military
  2. National Internal Security – Provided by the Police. Here we have to be extra careful not to allow the accumulation of power that leads to corruption and related evils. Hence the jurisdictional mandate of a local police should be at the lowest possible levels – say at the level of a city or a town or a village etc., only (hiring mandates should be at this level – delegated appropriately). This should never be allowed to be a national level body since a corrupt national body with lots of constitution bestowed powers can itself become a national level threat. The higher-level security function can be adequately covered by politicians and bureaucrats with the able aid of Reserve Security Forces.

  Its function should also be limited to civil and criminal law enforcement.

The investigations should be separate from policing and it should ideally not have direct public interface.

3. National Industrial Security Force (NISF) – To provide protection and cover to the national level strategic assets.

4. National Strategic Reserve Security Forces – Can be in 2 parts with appropriate job rotation cadence. These 2 parts are:

> § NDRF – National Disaster Relief Force – base-camped in several strategic locations primarily aiming for disaster prevention, containing and for providing relief.
>
> § CRPF – Central Reserve Police Force – base-camped in several strategic locations aiming for riot control, crowd control, containing threats arising out of local militant groups etc.,

Preferably this group members should have a base salary along with a higher bonus when activated into actions.

5. Additionally, there can be a separate force to overlook prisoner transport, prison systems etc.,

6. Another security force can be created with adequate training facilities to protect constitutionally designated VIPs.

- As part of Physical Security and to ensure freedom and fairness, the constitution should separate the processes and personal responsible for policing, investigations, prosecution, punishment and re-integration post punishment term.
- Government should ensure that all tier -1 jobs should be salaried by the Government. Please refer to the article 8 in the reference section.
- Government should bankroll at least one major mass transport system for public benefit and should ensure its affordability. My recommendation will be to have a national railway system along with a subway system for the metropolitan cities. All the nodal stations may be supported with minimal feeder bus systems. Rest of the transport can be with the relevant business leaders and business houses.
- Government should ensure capping of personal wealth and company wealth with appropriate safeguards and supporting mechanism. (please refer to article 8 in the reference section).
- Government should declare the nationally important assets and should have declared an engagement/business model around them.

For example, for the **Power sector**, the below can be a possible strategy:

Power Generation – Part Government and Part Private
Power Transmission – Fully private owned and
Power Distribution – Part Government (for the economically under

privileged) and part private.

Some of the national strategic assets are:
Power generation, transmission, distribution centres and facilities, Military bases, Scientific Institutions, Space Centres, Critical Manufacturing Facilities, National Data Centres, Agricultural Procurement/Storage Centres, Railway Nodal hub-Stations, Airports, Transport Nodal hub-stations, Central Bank Offices etc., This should be under the protection of NISF as mentioned above.

References:
1. Socialism, Fascism, Capitalism, Communism Background.pdf (navy.mil)
2. Please refer to the chapter on administering the economy in novel ways – Part 1
3. Please refer to the chapter on administering the economy in novel ways – Part 2
4. Please refer to the chapter on administering the economy in novel ways – Part 3
5. Please refer to the chapter on the fictional iron clad constitution
6. Please refer to the chapter on more on the fictional iron clad constitution
7. Please refer to the chapter on the dynamic political systems
8. Please refer to the chapter on some suggested financial reforms

4 SOME MORE ON THE FICTIONAL IRON CLAD CONSTITUTION

I briefly wrote about a fictional iron-clad constitution in my blogs including in my blog on equality. I envisioned the iron-clad constitution as –

- Deriving from an international (ISO?) management framework and guidelines
- Consisting of meta-structures (for example on suggested departments/secretaries of the government) to which all countries can map their implementation of the iron-clad constitution. This is similar to the guidelines found in Basel guidelines given to financial institutions for mapping their business units by BIS (Ref: www.bis.org). This will help in normalizing the data sourced from various countries to run any global level programs.

Annex 2: Example mapping of business lines

Business Unit	Level 1	Level 2	Activity Groups
INVESTMENT BANKING	Corporate Finance	Corporate Finance	Mergers and Acquisitions, Underwriting, Privatisations, Securitisation, Research, Debt (Government, High Yield) Equity, Syndications, IPO, Secondary Private Placements
		Municipal/Government Finance	
		Merchant Banking	
		Advisory Services	
	Trading & Sales	Sales	Fixed Income, equity, foreign exchanges, commodities, credit, funding, own position securities, lending and repos, brokerage, debt, prime brokerage
		Market Making	
		Proprietary Positions	
		Treasury	
BANKING	Retail Banking	Retail Banking	Retail lending and deposits, banking services, trust and estates
		Private Banking[2]	Private lending and deposits, banking services, trust and estates, investment advice
		Card Services	Merchant/Commercial/Corporate cards, private labels and retail
	Commercial Banking	Commercial Banking	Project finance, real estate, export finance, trade finance, factoring, leasing, lends, guarantees, bills of exchange
	Payment and Settlement[3]	External Clients	Payments and collections, funds transfer, clearing and settlement
	Agency Services	Custody	Escrow, Depository Receipts, Securities lending (Customers) Corporate actions
		Corporate Agency	Issuer and paying agents
		Corporate Trust	
OTHERS	Asset Management	Discretionary Fund Management	Pooled, segregated, retail, institutional, closed, open, private equity
		Non-Discretionary Fund Management	Pooled, segregated, retail, institutional, closed, open
	Retail Brokerage	Retail Brokerage	Execution and full service

(Above image Ref: BIS)

- Consisting of global event types similar to the Basel event types which will be used to direct local, regional and global responses to such events with predefined SOPs.
- Consisting of 3 pillars of constitution – Elected Government represented by prime minister and his team, People's Voice represented through either a royal lineage or presidency and finally the voice of the Spiritual class represented by say association of mutt or head church etc.,
- The Elected Government headed by prime minister, People's Court headed by the royalty and the Spiritual Groups headed by spiritual head of the country - each will have its own democratic setup with iron-clad internal election process that will avoid nepotism, cronyism and patronage. This is figuratively represented by the below image each hand is a functioning level 1 department or secretary or office.

- Governance, Compliance and Audit checks will happen on each of the 'hand' in both modes – internal auditing and external auditing.
- Besides a central statistical organization (CSO) and an aligned educational institution specializing in statistics and data management should the different hands of the 3 pillars with top notch quality data to make well informed decisions and to analyse and infer any potential risks and issues underlying the country as a whole.
- Guidelines will be published by the framework (which undergoes plan-do-check-act – continuous improvement cycles) to specify the governing models involving the 3 pillars and how they can effectively checkmate each other from making costly anti-national mistakes. For example, each can annually audit the other 2.
- Each of the 3 pillars should track their own metrics which is setup and managed by the central statistical organisation of the country.
- Monitoring and control of the country's significant indicators should be independently done by the 3 bodies with their own models and also, they should track metrics that are specific to their own operations with the infrastructure and capabilities provided by the CSO. The metric status can be colour coded as - red (error), yellow (warning) and green (normal) based on the values of the metrics.

Some of the national metrics that can be tracked may be:
- Crime rate related.
- Crimes against women related.
- Happiness index related.
- Mental health of the population related.
- Occupation related.
- Salary related.

- o Diversity, Equity and Inclusion related.
- o Immigration related.
- o Value systems related.
- o Unemployment related.
- o Education related.
- o Health care related.
- o ESG related.
- o Transparency related.
- o Economic progression related.
- o Government Revenue and Spending related.
- o Sports related.
- o Spirituality related.

Based on the above metrics, the framework may suggest level 1 issues and remedies. But the host country should process this information and identify its own course of action(s) for each metric indicators that are either red or yellow. A preset list of issues/SOPs/remedies can be formulated against each indicator
and their status which may be reviewed periodically for relevance.

- Data sharing mechanism with any global bodies should be done after appropriate data scrubbing and by following the imposed meta-structures to help harmonize.
- The guidelines may supply best practices suggestions for up to 2-3 levels of the governance of the 3 pillars and their interactions.
- The framework should also leave some room for local/regional cultural variations in governance but should provide high level guidelines on integrating them.
- Elected government follows the mandate of the election office that comes with its own governance setup following the directives of the framework and extracting help from CSO.
- People's Court should have an easy mechanism to muster the opinion of the people with the help of the CSO – say by means of national surveys which is processed by the king's court.
- Spiritual groups should run their own interactions with people through their spiritual institutions and taking help from the CSO.

The CSO will be the data owner (strategic), data custodian (Governance related), data steward (SMEs) and data controllers (tracking the data lineage, data use, data transformations and data archival and data obsoletion).
The CSO should be expert in the best-in-class data management practices. (For example, in data classification of data as live data, current data and

archived data). It should also me mindful about continuous improvement and should also be open to change its significant operational parameters (like the time frame for classifying the data types) based on the change management principles.

PART E

SOME SOCIAL ASPECTS FOR SPRITUALISTS

1 WHY TEACHING AS A PROFESSION IS VITALLY IMPORTANT

In any given country or a local community there is always a need for quality teachers. When the rest are gone for conducting their profession, it is the teachers who teach the children in their formative years and in the years preceding their entry into the productive workforce. What I meant by teaching is just not a reference to the act of imparting of knowledge related to basic subjects to the children, but more importantly it is about teaching the young ones how to live their life in a wholesome manner. The teachers, especially the ones who teach the young kids, have to go to extraordinary lengths to prepare for their teaching hours with the young children. The teachers in general should be aware that , children for all walks of societies and back ground may attend their school and that such children's guidance from the parents. especially the underprivileged parents, may be sup-optimal or non-existent. The teachers, hence, should realize the real expectations of their job function responsibilities and should take all the relevant measures to enable them to fill the void in the children's life.

If this is done properly, we can expect the children to become ideal citizens later and they also can be expected to become ideal parents and grandparents in life much later.

Constantly engaging the minds of the children is a tough job when we know that they cannot express their point of view in clear communications. Making it worse are other factors in the children's life such as bullying, abuse, threat, coercion etc., that have severe consequences. A teacher, in addition to engaging the children in the classrooms and counselling sessions, should also talk to their parents, and possibly should understand the community that the children are growing up and should also have keen sense to know what the children need, to properly blossom to their next stage of learning and living.

Since the children have different potentials and backgrounds, the teachers should be aware that their most valuable resource, their time, should be spent with the right kids, using the right time span and in the right way. The teachers, thus, besides mastery over their subject areas. should have deep spiritual knowledge, knowledge about their culture/tradition/sacraments etc., to reinforce their faith in good behaviours and in taking pride of their culture and traditions and also in believing in the prevailing righteousness of the universe .The idea of birth & death, meditation and mental well-being, importance of faith/prayers, knowledge about soul-astral body-gross body composition, education on prevalent value systems, the stories, historical records of good winning over evil etc., should also be part of the greater educational syllabus till they graduate out of their school or college. I would say that this imparting of life lessons should continue probably till at least the first year in the university.

Since the teachers need to sacrifice their whole life not only in grooming the children in the right way to make them into ideal citizens, but also to invest their time in learning all the things that are outside their core subject areas, and which are vital to the interests of the children, they need to be recognized well by the local community and their country for their contribution in shaping the future of the country itself by properly educating the children. The least we can do is recognize that this is a tier-1 super-important job and thus the society should increase their remuneration to dispel their mundane immediate worries (including financial) , so that they can use their peaceful, intelligent mind and their valuable time with the children for their betterment.

2 TOP 10 EVILS OF TODAY'S WORLD

I, often times, see the top 10 lists in different contexts – in software products in a particular category, top 10 vulnerabilities, top 10 militaries, top 10 economies etc., Coming to the context of spirituality, I tried to see the current top 10 evils that has manifested in this world that needs immediate attention. Perhaps, we can take a look at the top 10 good things that needs mention in a latter chapter.

1.   No Gender Parity
I have tried to explain why I think gender=parity is must at -my other chapter on equality.
Please refer to the current status on equality at –UNICEF-Gender Equality-Current Status.

Even among the most developed countries, there is gender inequality in below common situations:
- Governance groups and Boards
- Senior Management
- Political Leadership
- Policy/Influencer Groups
- Judiciary
- Civic Administration
- Military Leaderships

- Fashion
- Cinema/Arts/Music
- Etc.,

I have mentioned about the need for an interlocking iron-clad constitutional framework that will enable nations to implement a sound, democratic/inclusive constitution. Ideally, at the best, gender parity should be enforced through this proposed constitutional framework. Any tier-1 jobs (as explained in Chapter on Varnashrama dharma), be it in government or in private domain should adopt this policy by enforcing 50+- 5 % reservation for women.

Recently, one large democratic country announced 33% reservation for women in its central and state electoral seats. I think women should not accept anything lower than 50+-5% reservation. The +-5% play is just a suggestion to enable some sense of practicality, which means sometimes we can expect 55% women or 55% men in a given category of jobs.

2. No Wealth-Distribution

Again, I have mentioned earlier about inequal income distribution that is widely prevalent in the world in my *chapter*.

I think one of the core functions of an iron-clad constitution must be to ensure wealth distribution. Programs like capping income ratios, Universal Basic Income etc., should be implemented in a sound manner to ensure wealth distribution and to reduce income inequalities.

3. Rampant Consumerism

I happen to check this website – www.watercalculator.org - water used in everyday products - The Hidden Water in Everyday Products - Water Footprint Calculator (watercalculator.org).

I faithfully reproduce a table (Table 1) given in that site below:

Table 1. Water Footprint of Common Consumer Items.

Item	Water Footprint
Car	13,737–21,926 gallons *(52,000–83,000 liters)*
Leather Shoes	2,113 gallons *(8,000 liters)*
Smartphone (mobile)	3,190 gallons *(12,760 liters)*
Jeans (cotton)	2,866 gallons *(10,850 liters)*
Bed Sheet (cotton)	2,576 gallons *(9,750 liters)*
T-shirt (cotton)	659 gallons *(2,720 liters)*
Paper (1 piece; A4)	1.3 gallons *(5.1 liters)*

TABLE: Data compiled, converted and produced by Water Footprint Calculator. Sources: Berger et al; Water Footprint Network, "Water footprints of nations"; Friends of the Earth/Tracost; WFN, "The water footprint of cotton consumption"; WFN, "The water footprint of wood for lumber, pulp, paper, fuel and firewood"

Beside the individual consumerism habits, I think there is consumerism bias where we see per-capita consumption of almost most essential things are high in the advanced countries.

Please refer to the links below:

1. Charts - Our World in Data (search for different consumption patterns)
2. The World's Largest Consumer Markets in 2030 (visualcapitalist.com) – This is even more shocking – Japan with a population of 122 million is in 7th place. Nigeria with 218 million is not figuring in top 20. In fact, no African countries are among the top 20 despite having 1.28 billion people.

It is very clear, that by careful observation and analysis of data, we can conclude that the major consumers are the developed and developing countries. And add to this the fact that populations are not considered too high in the developed countries and consumerism is more in developing countries only because of their high population. (China, India, Indonesia, Brazil etc.,). In case of a country like Nigeria, despite having high population, it is not being considered a lucrative consumer market! Looks like the economic resources of this world has its own mind to flow only in the rich lands!

4. Crime/Corruption

Because of the above 3 issues, – crime and corruption are on the raise. Crime/Corruption is high in poor neighbourhoods/countries and Corruption is high in the rich neighbourhoods and wealthy countries! Even crimes in poor neighbourhood pales in comparison if you would understand what a resourceful rich nation can do to a poor country with rich natural resources! (read the book – *Kleptopia by Tom Burgis*)

5. Undesirable Power Concentrations

Another major evil manifested in most countries is this – the concentration of power to undesirable levels. Again, the cure for this malady is the adaptation of an iron-clad constitution that is guaranteed to prevent power concentrations at any levels of the governance in any positions.

There should be more than one fail safe mechanisms to address this issue of power concentration (which is also a major cause for cronyism, nepotism, and corruption) in the new iron-clad constitution. Please refer to my other article on Dynamic Political Systems.

The writers of the new iron-clad constitution should become the Devil's advocate and make sure to outline various methods/arrangements to diffuse power concentrations in various workings of the government and they should also outline how common man can use various means to question/correct misuse of power coming out of power concentrations.

We have to note that some organizational power concentrations can derive from political power concentrations, and they too can play a detrimental role in the national development. Some basic guidelines should be issued to private organizations on this regard.

6. Lack of All Inclusive Growth Plans

Most of our economic development plans are oriented towards the wellbeing of humans only!! But it does not mean that we are excelling in the wellbeing of humans! When are we going to expand this human centric growth plans to all-inclusive growth plans?

Economic activities like, large scale fish trawling (that too in breeding season), whale poaching, excessive meat consumption, ocean explorations, Arctic/Antarctic explorations, wiping of pristine habitations for mining activities etc., are being ignored or the control measures are ineffective.

When are we going to be responsible humans who are mindful about the fact that this world is a shared space with other species?

7. Unsustainable Economic Outcomes

Depletion of natural resources is a major issue. Are we sure that we are doing the right thing in our actions, that we are converting the natural resources from its natural state into a commercial state at this pace and scale?

Can we be able to set aside the immediate human benefits and ponder - Are we using the natural resources for its intended purpose? The oil reserves, for example, took millions of years to form, and we have depleted a huge stock of it in the last 80 years just to move things and goods to various places!! Should we be a bit careful about what is left? Maybe we can drive its use towards the pharmaceutical industries or to some function that is sustainable, recyclable while supporting a large set of world population.

8. Insensitiveness to Other's Sufferings

Recalling different news from the above points over a morning coffee and not feeling even a wee bit of recoil for the impacts is a different level of mental insensitivity that can even be termed as mental leprosy!!

I sometimes think that large scale stocking of money piles, arising out of insensitivity towards the poor is a classic sign of a new mental malady and that affliction should be assigned a new name as such.

Humans should organise themselves better under various groups and banners including government and private sectors groups to energise a mass movement perhaps under the ambit of an organization like UN and cultivate and address this insensitivity affecting billions of lives on this planet.

9. Loss of Faith

Despite having numerous temples, churches, monasteries etc., we do realise the above 8 afflictions and more as a thinking human. Why aren't our spiritual mentors not able to correct this situation despite having immense visibility? Looks like we are losing our faith in having and being grounded in good virtues and in believing in being a responsible and decent citizen of the universe.

Please refer to the other chapters on 'good and evil' and 'value systems'.

10. Failure of responsible Societal Groups

Please refer to my chapters on what I mean by groups in my earlier chapter on the formative years of a group.

We are working most intensely- only as a nuclear-single unit- family. We are not well integrated as one or many groups. Our constitutions, while acknowledging the rights of the individual is completely ignoring group interests!!

Significant societal groups ignore all the above problems at ease! It is high time we re-learn what it means to be a responsible citizen of this earth and the universe!!

3 VALUE EDUCATION AT SCHOOLS AND UNIVERSITIES

In my earlier chapter articles, I wrote about value systems and formative years of a human.

I pondered upon the kind of value educations that can be imparted at our schools and universities. Timing is critical. We cannot break the bubble earlier or later. Besides, some value educations (e.g. sex education) has to be delivered keeping in mind the maturity of the audiences – adolescent teens at schools and as young adults in universities. Hence it is safe to break that up into several lessons that are well timed.

As a teen, around their 5th or 6th grade, moral value systems can be taught. In the place where I come from, these moral lessons were presented through ancient Tamil literary works like "Thiru Kural" and "Aathichoodi". There are many such worldly wise literature from the Tamil Sangam period (Please refer - Sangam literature - Wikipedia) that can be used to impart moral lessons to the adolescent teens and young adults (yes ! for university students too). The other parts of the world can similarly explore their traditional literary works that can be used to deliver moral lessons. Again, new content can also be created by the experts to meet the demands of the changing times.

Important moral/value lessons can be from the local and local cultural aspects that are related to

1· Nation's constitution/law & order
2· Local religious bodies not violating any other general moral principles and constitutional rights/laws.

3. Local culture and traditions related understandings
4. Sensible use of time – Dos and Don'ts
5. Mental and Physical well-being.
6. Nurturing relationships and managing one's ego.
7. Career options/path discussion.
8. Meditation and focus.
9. Academic counselling to identify and align students with interests, passion and skills at high school and at A-levels (secondary levels).
10. Education about exploring family history, local history besides nation's history and world history
11 Understanding local economy – what powers us
12. Integrating self with community and volunteering.

At the right age, when it is time to bring the adolescent teens out of the bubble, sex education should be imparted. This should be basic, and I leave it to the experts in this field to deep dive and construct the syllabus.

At the intermediary stage of the University/Collage, the advanced lessons related to sex education can be imparted. Again, I leave it to the experts in this field to deep dive and construct the syllabus.

When the time is ripe when the young adults of the universities are ready to enter workforce, additional value education related to the below can be imparted:
1. Corporate social responsibility
2. Corporate communication nuances
3. Corporate culture and its importance
4. Workplace ethics
5. Pointers on keeping one relevant in his field of choice.
6. Decision science
7. Common Productivity techniques
8. Handling the proverbial mid-life crisis
9. Basic Financial planning
10. Important global initiatives such as the ones related to climate change, UN SDG 2030, ESG etc.,
11. Forces shaping the current times.
12. Diversity, Equity and Inclusion (DEI).

Thus, a very sophisticated supplementary value education system is much needed in our times along with the curriculum/syllabus driven primary education programs.
life.

4 THE 3-DEGRESS OF ATTRACTIONS

In any healthy living society, for the purpose of procreation, a strong male-female, tendency of mutual attraction is fundamentally essential. I am a straight guy and No – I am not against any LGBTQ groups. I understand that it is a status blessed by nature in some of the humans.

I am just looking at the falling rate of population in some geographies (e.g. Japan) which have a rich legacy of accomplishing great things as individuals and as various groups with a strong concern.

Let us look at the various degrees of attraction that are needed in a healthy society.

1. A healthy mutual and decent attraction that exists/happens between opposite sexes (a male and a female) preferably in the same age groups.
This, not just leads to, styling oneself better to attract the opposite sex members! This state is fundamental for the occurrence of the other 2 degrees of attraction, mentioned below. If the problem of not observing gender-parity is resolved in all parts of the world in a truly genuine and honest/integral way, the next 2 degrees of attraction are easily achieved by humans in any modern societal setup.

2. A naturally occurring intense love that blossoms between a like-minded male and female that may lead to marriage and childbirth. Some groups in the world also have the concept of arranged marriages.

3. A naturally occurring powerful sexual attraction/lust that exists between a matured male and female, sometimes intended to lead to

marriage/childbirth.

The above 3 attractions should exist in a naturally blessed state in any healthy society to halt the decline in population.

What could be the many reasons that hamper the above 3 attractions leading to reduction in population? I could think of a few reasons given below:

1. Economic hardships leading to acute stress to life and living. Hence, I strongly urge the governments to adopt the concept of basic minimum income scheme which can also lead to additional benefits like reduction of exploitation of the vulnerable population and the various crimes that occur against women and children in particular.
Somebody said that – "How do we know that this Earth is not a heaven and that we are in the act of spoiling it already !!". And if this is true, in heaven, it is expected that people take care of each other as individuals and as members of the same group to live a perennially happy life while in pursuit of human excellence. Hence the grumble against a proposed blessed scheme like basic minimum income should be done away with quite quickly to become a progressive state.

2. In some parts of the world and in some secret societies, initiation ceremonies like the gay/lesbian initiation ceremonies apparently exist which if it happens on a scale, can wipe out the very fundamental degree of attraction mentioned in point-1 above from the communities around. , – i.e the naturally healthy mutual attraction that exists/happens between a male and a female member of the society - If this fundamental degree of attraction is impaired, the other 2 degrees of attraction becomes difficult to realize.
If we consider the nature blessed male-female attraction/love/lust as a vibrant, breathtaking beautiful painting, the above-mentioned ceremonies and its effects are like a opaque/translucent/transparent (I cannot help relating this to the new gender identity and sexual orientation terms) dust that is settling on the painting. Nevertheless, the dust obstructs the beauty of the painting and creates artificial impairment. At some point in his/her life, that person may wipe away the dust intentionally or accidentally (even subconsciously) and the beauty of the painting cannot be ignored any longer! When that happens, the pain felt inside by the person may be profound. If this phenomenon is not understood properly the whole thing may convert into a state of suffering, dejection and delusion.
Besides, if I may extrapolate the situation and speculate a fictitious scenario, where there are more such above mentioned conversion programs for males

than for females, the situation in the society becomes untenable - there will be more males who are gays and more females who will be heterosexual and hence, naturally blessed act of procreation itself may be impaired, not to mention about the loss of intimacy and trust between couples!

If such practices like the initiation mentioned above is practiced at scale, additional ill-effects can also manifest. For example, a male person who has the natural preference to be with a female, undergoes such a conversion practice (without his liking) , then his interest in a female may get diminished. Since naturally blessed preference is organic and powerful than the imposed preference, his interest in a female may get re-kindled at a later stage in life, leading to late marriages and late child births! Other ill effects that can happen include divorces, forced marriages and certain moral issues (like insensitivity, cheating, exploitation etc.,).

Sometimes, if things are not going well, even enrolling in same-sex institutions especially at a life-stage when the forces of nature are at the strongest can cause similar problems.

3. Our tendency to become more digital leading to the be-numbing of our sensitivities leading to havoc in individual lives and among the various groups.

4. Our tendency to adopt to fast paced life that causes us to move away from organic way of living.

Any group/society in any parts of world have to understand the 3 degrees of attractions with a matured mindset and build appropriate value systems in their country/local communities that will lead to harmonious way of living with a sustainable strength of population with a healthy male-female ratio.

If the above 3 degrees of attractions are maintained in a healthy manner in any country/group with appropriate value systems in place, then other synthetic problems like conceiving a child majorly by IVF and not by conjugal relationships can be avoided and in-fact policies may be considered for implementation

- that makes IVF potentially less attractive and
- for promoting natural way of conception/birthing.

5 IMPORTANCE OF GOTRA AND KULA SYSTEMS

Mankind faces a peculiar problem since a long time. It is about how inbreeding can be stopped. Why should inbreeding be stopped?
Rather than me trying to explain, I urge you to please refer to the below links:
https://en.wikipedia.org/wiki/Inbreeding
What are the effects of inbreeding? | BBC Earth
Inbreeding depression (berkeley.edu)

To avoid inbreeding in a population, the concept of Gotra was conceived in ancient India. But before that let us be clear in some of the terms that we use in this context. While I was at it, I could see a lots of variations of the interpretations of these words. I decided to settle for the definitions found in English dictionary and Wikipedia. I tailored this chapter based on the understanding that I derived from these sites for these specific words. I have also added some other references.

Hindu Terms:
1. Gotra (Clan):
A Hindu clan tracing its paternal lineage from a common ancestor, usually a saint or sage. This is akin to the word clan. (Collins definition)

2. Kula (Lineage):

STRANGER THAN FICTION

The word kula is used in Asian traditions to indicate any type of family or grouping, whether philosophically or figuratively. Kula is related to Kulachara, "tradition, duty, or practice of a group or family" (glorian definition)

3. Inam (Tamil word) (Race or Tribe):
This word has several different meanings including tribe and race.

Similar English Terms:
1. Clan (Gotra):
Ref: https://en.wikipedia.org/wiki/Clan

A clan is a group of people united by actual or perceived kinship and descent. Even if lineage details are unknown, a clan may claim descent from a founding member or apical ancestor who serves as a symbol of the clan's unity. Clans, in indigenous societies, were not endogamous: **their members could not marry one another.**

2. Lineage or Family (Kula):
Ref: https://en.wikipedia.org/wiki/Lineage_(anthropology)

In anthropology, a lineage is a unilineal descent group that traces its ancestry to a demonstrably shared ancestor, known as the apical ancestor. Lineages are formed through relationships traced either exclusively through the maternal line (matrilineage), paternal line (patrilineage), or some combination of both (ambilineal). The cultural significance of matrilineal or patrilineal descent varies greatly, shaping social structures, inheritance patterns, and even rituals across societies.
Hence, **it seems members of the same lineage cannot marry one another.**

3. Tribe (Inam):
Ref: https://en.wikipedia.org/wiki/Tribe

Tribes are therefore considered to be a political unit formed from an organisation of families (including clans and lineages) based on social or ideological solidarity. Membership of a tribe may be understood as being based on factors such as kinship ("clan"), ethnicity ("race"), language, dwelling place, political group, religious beliefs, oral tradition and/or cultural practices.
Hence, it seems members of the same tribe can marry one another but should avoid the same clan and lineage.

Now that our terms are aligned, let us focus on the 2 words that I want to focus in this chapter – i.e Clan and Lineage directly related to the words Gotra and Kula.

STRANGER THAN FICTION

Y chromosomes are responsible for an embryo to become a male offspring. X chromosome is present in both males and females whereas Y chromosomes are present only in males. Hence gotra is attached to the male lineage. Hence, when a female is married, her gotra changes to that of her husband.

Since inbreeding leads to defects in gene pool and possibly consistent inbreeding may lead to extinction of the species itself. Hence any culture should have a system like Gotra to avoid inbreeding.

Gotra — it seems starts with a significant ancestor whose lineage can be tracked. The society is expected to organize by Gotra besides lineage (kula). It is possible that, in some parts of the world, the gotra and kula knowledge has vanished leading to unintended inbreeding and its related ill effects.

The good part is it is still possible to identify and organize the society by Gotra and Kula by looking at the family history, ancestral clans, religious affiliations, roots, places of habitation, occupation of the lineage etc., and set up a strong social system consisting of Clan (Gotra) and lineage (Kula)that can prevent inbreeding. Other records like historical records, birth records, church records etc., can also be considered in this effort.

I found lot of thoughtful information on Gotra from the sites given in the reference section and hence I request the readers to get familiar with those content too. By avoiding marriages within a same clan and lineage, in breeding can be avoided. Everyone is expected to know their Gotra and Kula and should be informed about it through the elders in the family/clan as a tradition. Besides that, some other traditions can also be set - for example, a Christian family may also record the Gotra and Kula of a new-born with the church while performing religious ceremonies like baptism. Also, while registering an interest to marry the Gotra/Kula details of both the bride and groom should be verified by the church.

References:
Hindus Gotra System: Scientific Meaning of Gotra in the Vedas (indiadivine.org)
Hindu Gotra Lists and Surnames: A Comprehensive Guide - 99Pandit
Gotra | History, Origin & Significance | Britannica
Gotra - Wikipedia

6 SOME ESG THOUGHTS VALID IN CURRENT TIMES

I was walking through the city for my morning walk and was observing the loading/unloading of cartons from the semis in front of various shops at the city centre. If this is the buzz of activities in a relatively small town, It stuck me like a thunder, when I understood what it means to feel the integrated buzz of activities on a global scale.

No wonder, the global packaging industry is a mammoth on its own right! https://www.mordorintelligence.com/industry-reports/sustainable-packaging-market
The below italicized extract is from the above link:

> *The Sustainable Packaging Market size is estimated at USD 292.71 billion in 2024, and is expected to reach USD 423.56 billion by 2029, growing at a CAGR of 7.67% during the forecast period (2024-2029). Sustainable packaging is the creation and use of packaging that improves sustainability.*

I found a decent definition of environmental sustainability at Environmental Sustainability: What Is It & Why It Matters | Perch Energy

> ***Environmental sustainability is the practice of interacting with the planet responsibly to maintain an ecological balance and conserve natural resources. It involves preserving natural resources so that future generations can enjoy the benefits they bring.*** *Sustainability is about saving ourselves and ensuring that our species can survive and prosper long into the future.*

Before the rampant consumerism results in the belting by mother earth, we should get serious about sustainability and more importantly on recycling resources. I thought about 3 of the niche areas where recycling should be promoted in an aggressive way. There may be many other areas that needs a mention. But I am listing 3 of the many that is close to my heart:

1. **DEEP - CONTAINERIZATION**:
We should take the container revolution to the next stage – deep containerization where only standard sized pallets on a global scale are used for packing goods and products. This should be enforced by regulations applied on a global scale. Special permission should be mandated to deviate from this standard packaging sizes coupled with some environmental tax. Every truck that unloads packaged products should also load the used packaging and bring it to the recycling facility.

There is a large-scale trend among consumers to adopt sustainable packaging which his adequately captured in the below report:
https://www.prnewswire.com/news-releases/new-data-reveals-consumers-increasingly-choose-products-in-sustainable-packaging-globally-despite-rising-prices-301804273.html

Not only that, smart AI technologies can ALSO be deployed during the loading of goods inside the truck. When we input the 'package design IDs' along with the number of such boxes into the truck's computer, the truck floor should be lit up with stack plan showing the contours of the boxes guiding the loader to pack in the most efficient manner. This will also result in increased sustainability.

2. **ADDRESSING THE SPACE-DEBRIS PROBLEM**

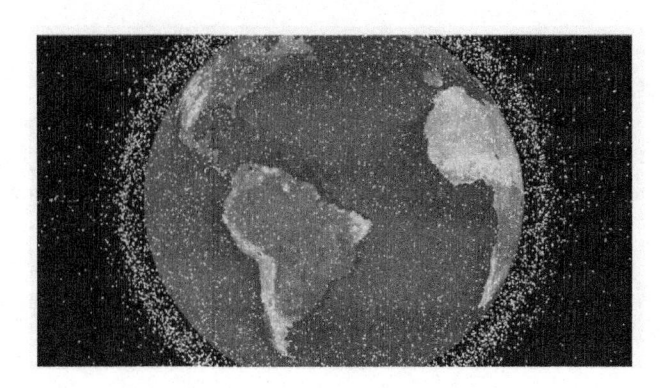

Next is on what we throw up in the sky that results in space debris! I found a decent report covering this topic of 'Sustainability in Space' – Publication_Final_English_June2021.pdf (unoosa.org) and at NASA's Space Sustainability Strategy - NASA

We have to sink into the fact that what we throw up is not going to come back to us if we stick to our old ways of working. We are talking about special materials used in costly technologies that go into our satellite building routines. Please look at the above image showing the tracked space debris – it seems to me that we are administering an unwanted and cruel acupuncture therapy on mother earth!

Our earth is limited in its capacity to give us resources – but our capacity to use and deplete is limitless. Without sustainability we may eventually be looking at a grotesque earth gouged out all over by our recklessness!

Thus, we should aim to build only recyclable satellites and similar other space systems!

3. **ON PRE-OWNED DRESS MATERIALS**

I am glad to see how dress materials are being used in a sustainable way in certain countries like UK. Organizations like British Hearth Foundation, Cancer Research UK etc., re-sell dress materials pre-owned by people and there seems to be good market for the pre-owned dress materials. These organizations also give wonderful volunteering opportunities with rich meaningful outcomes to the local community.

Besides the profits are pressed into noble causes!

I think public should extend their large-scale support to such organizations. I am glad that not just dresses, but books, furniture and other household goods are also getting similar attention.

I hope I can write more on other sustainable concepts and business models in future blog posts.

PART F

END NOTES

STRANGER THAN FICTION

This book may come under the genre of 'Spirituality' or 'Meta-Physics'. As a spiritualist you not only have to explore what it means to be a spiritualist, but also know about education, economy, politics and social systems that have a large wielding power over a nation's population.

I am not trying to be a Guru and present 'soothing statements to alleviate pain' to the general public. The contents of this book, as far as I am concerned, are possible truths about the ways of the working of the universe as I understand it as a concerned common man. I know that there may be differences of opinion and that is intended – since I think, when it comes to spirituality, each person is for himself! Hence, I am happy if for some people, my contents become a steppingstone and for some others it becomes an abstract map and so on and so forth. There are countless other Gurus who have spent a lifetime pursuing the mystery of life and are quite well-versed to 'guide' people out of their distress and who have written many well-known books and commentaries.

For more colorful rendering of diagrams in this book, please refer to my site at www.mayoan.com.

ABOUT THE AUTHOR

I (VIJAYABHASKAR NATARAJAN with pen name as 'MAYOAN') am a newbie writer. I am an engineering graduate, an MBA grad and a seasoned IT expert with over 2 decades of experience.

I am an avid seeker of truth and constantly in the endeavor to gather spiritual knowledge and intelligence. Given the current state of chaos and confusion existing in the world, I convinced myself that the best way forward to get clarity and purpose in life is to be in the knowledge seeking endeavor myself. I believe that religion is inspired by culture and spirituality is inspired by the universal truths or 'Ways of Working of the Universe'. I consider myself to be more of a spiritualist and omnist than a religionist.

I have been writing about these possible truths on my website – mayoan.com under the topic – 'Spirituality'.

I chose my knowledge sources randomly but with utmost care since I believe that whatever time you spend on the source of knowledge (books, podcasts, videos etc.,) in the quest should be worthy of the quest with little or no time wasted on frivolity. These sources are a range of spiritual texts from India like the Upanishads, commentaries. Puranas etc.,

Printed in Great Britain
by Amazon